"THE EYE THAT NEVER SLEEPS"

"THE EYE THAT NEVER SLEEPS"

A History of the
PINKERTON
National Detective Agency

——◆•••◆——

FRANK MORN

INDIANA UNIVERSITY PRESS · BLOOMINGTON

To Megan and Cassie

Manufactured in the United States of America

Library of Congress Cataloging in Publication Data

Morn, Frank, 1937–
"The eye that never sleeps."

Bibliography: p.
Includes index.
1. Pinkerton's National Detective Agency.   2. Police,
Private—United States—History.   3. Watchmen.   I. Title.
HV8087.M67   338.7'61363289'0973   81–47776
ISBN 0–253–32086–0   AACR2
1 2 3 4 5 86 85 84 83 82

CONTENTS

Preface: Themes and Issues

Private businesses frequently become centers of public controversy. Few, however, have touched American nerve endings as much as the private detective. Historic dichotomies developed early around the private detective that exist to this day in various guises. Americans have viewed their private detectives, and sometimes their public detectives too, with a mixture of fear and fascination. Their presence was explained and debated in negative and positive ways so often throughout the nineteenth and twentieth centuries that a popular compromise occurred. In a fit of ideological and intellectual exhaustion the occupation was simply shelved and relegated to a "necessary-evil" category until occasional outrages forced public debate, investigation, and censure anew. The pioneer detective agency, which forms the focus of this book and the focus of much of the controversy, was established by Allan Pinkerton in the 1850s and directed by his sons Robert and William during the late-nineteenth and early-twentieth centuries. Although Pinkerton's is America's largest private police force, the substance of this book is the story of this business until the 1930s, when directions in the agency's history shifted sufficiently to warrant a terminal point in the narrative. It is hoped that this is more than a history of one detective agency or for that matter the private detective business in America generally. Attempts are made toward that end, to be sure, but the Pinkerton agency also served as a weathervane in the social history of the United States. Implicit here are themes, issues, and attitudes that transcend a mere trace-and-chase treatment of famous law enforcers and criminals.

One element of this history that has been neglected by previous writers is the relationship between the private and public police and also the relationship between those police industries and America's larger concepts of proper policing. In the formative days, clustering around the mid-nineteenth century, decisions were made as to who could exercise the lion's share of legitimate force in society. The result was a commitment to the official police, carefully balanced with respect for unofficial policing. Today, even though there are more private than public policemen in America, the public police are the legitimate police mechanism. This division of labor and responsibility seems obvious now, but it was not always so. In fact, the last half of the nineteenth century was characterized by Hamlet-like attitudes over the proper place of public policing in America. The private detective agency highlights this indecision by providing an attractive alternative to expanded governmental power.

After the 1920s, Pinkerton policy emphasized protective rather than detective services. That is not to say both functions had not been intertwined before—in fact the official Pinkerton philosophy proclaimed them to be the same. Still, in terms of police technique and emphasis, they were different. Limited development of city, state, and national police forces kept most crime fighting in private hands during the nineteenth century. Historic fears of standing armies and governmental spying stalled the rise of the public police until urban disorderliness in the 1840s and 1850s stimulated the modern police movement across the country. But these centralized, patrol-oriented, tax-supported police departments quickly became patronage pools for city bosses. At the same time redress from rural, national, and international crime problems remained largely in the hands of private citizens. Historically, people protected their own property. Governmental responsibility for such activity slowly expanded to forestall feud. Businesses within the city became more vulnerable as department stores, transit lines, hotels, and sporting facilities increased faster than the capability of public police to protect them. In rural areas the ineptitude of country sheriffs and town marshalls, as well as the splashy exploits of bandits, perplexed the law-and-order minded citizen. In such cases the private police supplemented the public police in the city and frequently monopolized rural policing.

Advances in crime control and the rigors of crime fighting depend upon the nature and outrage of the victim. Businessmen in need of protection and detection, yet fearful of powerful police development within city government, formulated their own means of warring on crime in the nineteenth century. To such business elites the profit motive was sufficient stimulus for efficiency. Faith in private enterprise over public enterprise meant that private police were logical counterparts to public police. Indeed, one thesis of this book is that in the beginning of the modern public police movement Pinkerton's was an alternative to the police for those fearful of expanding governmental power. In the nineteenth century the private police agency filled the gap left by inadequate public police activity and police jurisdiction. Although the private detective's portfolio always contained such services as spying on workers and gathering evidence for divorce cases, the private agency—with its corps of detectives and army of patrolmen—clearly resembled an urban police department. In fact, some Pinkerton officials liked to boast that their Protective Patrol appeared on Chicago streets in uniforms five years before the city public police were uniformed.[1] The Pinkerton family and Pinkerton management, therefore, thought of themselves as heading a respectable police profession and were in the forefront of reform in police administration, philosophy, and technique. Certainly, then, Pinkerton history is part of police history, and the interplay between private and public policing in America is an important part of the story.

That interplay, in spite of some tensions, lasted throughout the nineteenth and early-twentieth century because a concerted parcelling out of work functions occurred. Private detective agencies provided detectives, and, if large enough, supplied watchmen. Public police specialized in patrol, and detective work, as a specialized activity, was minimal. Policing outside city limits was scant, and private detective firms quickly provided such services. By the turn of the century, however, readjustments occurred. City police and the new federal police mechanisms offered more detective services. By the 1920s most private detective agencies were becoming private police agencies. By the 1930s Pinkerton's had begun to subordinate their detective activities. Some detection was offered, and undercover investigators still reported on dishonest employees. But these nineteenth century emphases changed as the protection of property became most important. This did not happen overnight, and one of the purposes of this book is to show that glacial drift from a detection to protection speciality.

On the other hand, there were some areas in which the private detective agency enjoyed a natural monopoly simply because fears of a police state haunted America. Programs to check the honesty of employees, apprehend railroad bandits and bank thieves, and thwart organized labor were responses of businessmen to threats against property. The chief reason for the Pinkerton detective agency's formation was surveillance of employees who stole or might steal from employers. The primary investigative technique was spying. In a curious twist, those who feared spying by public officials created a system of spying by private agents. It pointed to a new problem, which would become clearer later in the century: the invasion of privacy. Unlike the public police, these detectives were private agents for private parties. That is not to say government did not hire Pinkerton detectives, because it did. But it did mean that either as private agents for business or government they did not have much public accountability. It is significant that of the many historic metaphors of the "Robber Baron" era, one was that Pinkerton's was a throwback to a medieval special interest army. In short, they were the "knights of capitalism." To the more critical they were "hired hooligans." Some of the general suspicion of police power was turned against the private detective because he was too free and unregulated, an attribute that accounted for so many of the practical successes in the first place. That, plus the growing threat to privacy gave all detectives, including Pinkerton's, a negative image. Feelings of betrayal, suspicion, and untrustworthiness were implicit in reasons for Pinkerton work. They also came to symbolize both the widening gap and the friction point between diverging social classes and social values in American culture. Increasingly, Americans could read Victor Hugo's *Les Miserables* and agree "that society inexorably keeps at bay two classes of men—those who attack it, and those who guard it." It was not long before a consciously contrived public image became as much a preoccupation of the Pinkerton family as fighting crime and protecting private property.

Another issue in this history is the creation and persistency of a private detective mystique. Today the sobriquet "private eye" suggests a picture of a gun-carrying Sam Spade or Mike Hammer who nonchalantly and roughly fights crime, seduces women, and befuddles police. This picture is largely a fiction created by twentieth century writers such as Dashiell Hammett, himself a onetime Pinkerton operative. Rather, most modern private detective agencies are security services that emphasize the guarding of property. But the glamor, adventure, and mystery of criminal investigation—certainly a more dominant activity in the nineteenth century detective agency

—overshadow the security activities of the twentieth century. The myths persist. The detectives themselves contributed to the illusion, especially in the formative years of their businesses. Allan Pinkerton was one of many private detectives who saturated a large audience with his escapades in articles, books, and newspapers. For advertisement purposes, private detectives became very public, tapping a growing public fascination for adventure, mystery, and rational problem solving. But there is a double edge to publicity. The wisdom of notoriety for a business whose main value is the secret or discrete handling of sensitive jobs is questionable. Consequently a dual distortion quickly occurred. The enemies of the private detective overly emphasized the disreputable aspects of the detective world. Simultaneously the detectives themselves and the friends of the detectives selectively publicized the glamorous and less controversial cases. On both accounts the real picture was blurred. Since they were pioneers in private detective work, the Pinkertons received abundant treatment by novelists and journalists. The Pinkerton motto, "The Eye That Never Sleeps," caught public attention and was shortened to "The Eye" in both criminal and popular cant. The phrase evolved into a common noun for the entire profession, and frequently other detectives were casually referred by a journalistic shorthand as "Pinkerton men." In a very real way the Pinkerton agency became the early guardian of the occupation's reputation.

Pinkerton's ongoing quest for respectability was only partially connected to shifting public tolerances for detectives and detection in America. As the agency matured and became the leader in its field, its self-contrived image changed. Semifictional adventure stories were abandoned and soon the agency and its work were portrayed as methodical, stable, and conservative. There was some truth to the conventional wisdom of the day that detectives tended toward criminality because of exposure to the criminal classes. Actually this contagion theory had another side that was never articulated. At mid- and upper-management levels, at least, Pinkerton's became a carbon copy of their clients, the business community. According to nineteenth century business standards, how was one to manage employees whose job compelled them to associate with and frequently emulate criminals? A tidy business house was most difficult when subordinates, in the name of their own brand of bureaucratic efficiency, leaned toward criminal skills and techniques while management leaned toward business skills and techniques. As will be shown later, William Pinkerton and Robert Pinkerton, during the long second generation of leadership, personified these two tendencies at managerial levels. On the level of the operative, a term most frequently applied to on-the-line detectives, the reality of work experience and the public perception of the occupational character coincided, and a long-lasting impression of the entire profession was formed. All too often other private detective agencies, in a scramble to find a place in the field, undermined the Pinkerton quest for respectability and acceptance in the business world. Almost from the beginning Allan Pinkerton drew careful distinctions between his type of business and the more disreputable detectives. This process of defining what constituted proper private detective work lasted well into the twentieth century and became every bit as important as warring on criminals. It seems that Pinkerton's, and those satellite agencies that spun off the mother business, felt compelled to convince the public, their own personnel, and competing agencies of the respectability of private detection. They were creating and sustaining their own version and constantly trying to correct the picture created by others. Perhaps, too, it was because so many of their deeds were interpreted as villainous that Pinkerton's sought so hard to appear as heroes.

Acknowledgments

The preparation of this book has incurred many debts to colleagues. Neil Harris, Arthur Mann, and John Cawelti at the University of Chicago were very helpful at the early stages of this work. Richard Wade and Mark Haller provided useful insights as well.

The Regenstein Library at the University of Chicago, and the manuscript staffs at the Chicago Historical Society and the Library of Congress made my labors less laborious. A summer at Pinkerton's Incorporated Archives was very important. George F. O'Neill graciously tolerated my academic intrusions in the corporate work environment.

Thanks go to Susan Carter–Call, Linda Padera, Irene Rojas, Mary Scesnewicz, and Mary Pallen for various typings of the manuscript. The Center for Research in Law and Justice at the University of Illinois Chicago Circle was generous in providing its facilities to expedite my work.

Ultimate responsibility for the factual and interpretative content of this book, however, remains mine.

INTRODUCTION

Thief-takers and Thief-makers

IT WAS MAY 24th, 1725, when they hung Jonathan Wild from Tyburn Tree. He was still drugged and nauseous after an unsuccessful suicide attempt in jail. The sensational trial, which found him guilty of falsely assuming public authority, heading a syndicate of thieves, and smuggling stolen goods was nothing compared to the public execution. The recorders of the *Newgate Calendar,* a gossipy publication dedicated to the last actions and words of the condemned, were astonished at the thousands who attended the spectacle.

> It is not easy to express with what roughness he was treated by the mob, not only as he went to the tree but even when he was at it. Instead of those signs of pity which they generally show when common criminals are going to execution, they reviled and cursed him, and peltered him with dirt and stones continually.[1]

Jonathan Wild, notorious thief-taker of London was to die. Londoners could love a thief, but not a thief-taker turned thief. Daniel Defoe, who probably attended Wild's execution and reported it for the *Applebee's Journal,* wrote

> On Monday, about the usual Time, *Jonathan Wild* was executed at Tyburn. Never was there seen so prodigious a Concourse of People before, not even upon the most popular Occassion of that Nature. The famous Jack Sheppard had a tolerable Number to attend his Exit; but no more to be compared to the present, than a Regiment to an Army, and, which is very remarkable, in all that innumerable Crowd, there was not one

Pitying Eye to be seen, nor one Compassionate Word to be heard; but on the contrary, whenever he came, there was nothing but Hollering and Huzzas, as if it had been upon a Triumph.[2]

The crowd was not only venting its particular anger at Wild, but also demonstrating its concern over a new profession. As early as 1597, an angry condemned convict, Lucke Hutton, referred to a thief-taker as "the black dog of Newgate." Of course it would push credibility to expect a doomed thief to appreciate a thief-taker. Apparently the beginnings of this occupation were as clouded as the activities of the practitioners and little was known of these criminal chasers until a piece of legislation stimulated their growth in 1692. By the end of the seventeenth century the highwayman had become a significant menace to ruling elites. Not only did these criminals ply the king's highways, areas that for over four hundred years had been under royal jurisdiction, but they began to enter the folklore and balladry as heroic assaulters upon authority. The Highwayman Act of 1692 offered a £ 40 reward to those who captured and prosecuted highway bandits.

This public policy of offering reward money was a significant innovation. On one hand it represented an unclipped thread of ancient crime fighting policy in England. In Medieval England citizen participation in police work—whether it was in forming a *posse comitatus,* responding to hue and cry, or taking part in a local night watch—was seen as both a natural civic duty and a way to forestall the expansion of the "king's peace," a name given to governmental peace keeping. The Highwayman Act also represented one contemporary adjustment to a rising capitalistic society in which volunteer citizen participation had diminished. Busy middle-class folks increasingly searched for substitutes for their active participation in the criminal justice process. Already the intricacies of law had created a legal profession. Movements to abolish public executions, ancient rituals that allowed community participation in the punishment process, would soon be under way. But one of the earliest inconveniences was crime fighting, and already by the seventeenth and eighteenth centuries a subclass of professional ne'er-do-wells monopolized the ancient constable night watch. Rather than forming or reforming policing, citizen participation was to be stimulated. Such financial incentives as offered by the Highwayman Act were defended by those leery of governmental expansions and by such notable Utilitarian reformers as Jeremy Bentham and Edwin Chadwick. On the other hand, "blood money," as it was increasingly called, made the apprehension of thieves a profitable business, and early in the eighteenth century a new entrepreneur arose to exploit the crime problem. In the process these new entrepreneurs evoked new fears toward detective work. The most notorious, of course, was Jonathan Wild, the "Thief-Taker General."[3]

Wild, who had been born at Wolverhampton, Staffordshire, around 1683, had deserted his wife and migrated to London. He settled with a streetwalker and moved freely in the underworld. After a while his knowledge of London low life proved valuable, and he served a short apprenticeship with city marshal Charles Hitchen as thief-taker. In 1718 Wild proclaimed himself "Thief-Catcher General of Great Britain and Ireland" and began to carry a silver staff as symbol of his position. He opened an office near the Old Bailey and began seeking out stolen property for a reward.

Ever since 1691, when antipawn shop legislation drove the fence underground, thieves had to find new ways of disposing stolen goods. Wild maintained a semblance of respectability by making upwards of 120 legitimate arrests, but his main activity consisted of returning stolen property to the victims for a fee, which was shared with the thief. In short, he became a go-between, a negotiator between victim and victimizer, obtaining fees from both. Not only were the victims duped, but the criminals themselves were controlled and forced into crude syndicates with Wild at the top.

Besides being a thieving "thief-taker," Wild represented another trend that would recur in both England and America much later. That is the fragile relationship between criminals and criminal chasers as heroic rogues or villians. Indeed, rogues were often sympathetic figures, such as the famous housebreaker Jack Sheppard. Wild repeatedly arrested Sheppard, who escaped some five times before the robber's execution at Tyburn Tree. In the process Sheppard captured the public imagination as outlaw hero and Wild suffered in comparison.

Wild's mentor and main competitor, Charles Hitchin, in a jealous rage, labeled Wild a thief in a 1718 pamphlet, *A True Discovery of the Conduct of Receiveiers and Thief-Takers, In and About the City of London.* One result of the squabble was that Sir William Thompson sponsored a bill in 1718 making it a felony to receive rewards under the pretense of restoring goods. This "Jonathan Wild Act," as it was referred to after its passage, was only a temporary setback for the enterprising thief-taker. He responded by creating an elaborate shipping system and disposed of the stolen property in Holland, a practice that did not end until his final exposure in 1725. During the investigations Wild's career was laid bare, and it was discovered that the thief-taker actually headed a kind of corporation of thieves. Outrage engulfed any sympathy and Wild was ignominiously executed at Tyburn.

Wild's ghost continued to haunt England and the entire thief-taking profession. Shortly after the thief-taker's death, Daniel Defoe published *A True and Genuine Account of the Life and Actions of Jonathan Wild,* in which the thief-taker's character and methods of directing a criminal syndicate were highlighted. DeFoe drew a distinction between the rogue—a criminal who, because of adventurous exploits, tapped public sympathy—and the scoundrel. Wild, according to DeFoe and writers for the next several years, was a villain. In 1743 Henry Fielding, future magistrate at Bow Street, also wrote *The Life of Mr. Jonathan Wild the Great,* a satirical semihistorical novel using the career of thief-taker to poke particular jibes at the political leadership of Robert Walpole. In a subsequent addition, however, Fielding became more concerned with using Wild as the personification of knavery. In the twenty years after Wild's execution, the public, in its ongoing romance of the low life, became infatuated with the dead thief-taker. Thus the image of the detective working in close cooperation with the criminal was fully developed by mid-eighteenth century. It was soon obvious, too, that thief-takers stimulated crime by becoming *agents provocateur.*

On July 29, 1754, James Salmon was robbed on the highway near Deptford, England. The next day the robbers were captured by the thief-taker Stephen Macdaniel, who collected the reward. Joseph Cox, a local constable, investigated the case and discovered that both the victim of the robbery and the thief-taker were in league to get the "blood money." Two young thieves, it seems, had been pressured and encouraged into the crime by a third accomplice so that they might be caught by the thief-taker. Cox arrested the entire gang in 1754 for this crude form of entrapment and exposed the practice in *A Faithful Narrative of the Most Wicked and Inhuman Transactions of that Bloody-Minded Gang of Thief-Takers, alias Thief-Makers.*[4] The entire profession was at low ebb in the mid-eighteenth century. When John Fielding, the half-brother of Henry Fielding, planned to reform the system he correctly understood that since the thieftakers are extremely obnoxious to the common people, perhaps it might not be altogether politic to point them out to the mob; and the less they are known, the better able they will always be to execute the purpose of their institution.[5]

Fielding understood the problems and potentials of the private thief-takers, and he sought to set them within the realm of public control and management. What he did not understand, however, was that public fears went much deeper to the very roots of the occupation. Perhaps it was the very tools of successful detection that were the real center of concern.

The Fielding brothers—Henry and John—were responsible for an intellectual and administrative shift in eighteenth-century English crime detection. Five years before he took up residence at Bow Street as justice of peace of Westminster in 1748, Henry Fielding had written of the thief-taking scandals in *Jonathan Wild the Great.* While a magistrate of Bow Street between 1749 and 1754, Henry Fielding wrote five tracts on public order and crime issues and founded *The Covent Garden Journal,* a periodical dedicated to showing how effective or ineffective existing laws were in eradicating crime. In addition, every issue of the *Journal* gave summaries and comments on the cases he tried at Bow Street Court.[6] Both he and his half-brother, John Fielding, who held the magistry from Henry's death in 1754 until 1786, attempted to offset the thief-takers by creating a small force of constables called Bow Street Runners. At that time constables were private citizens drafted to serve one year in the various courts as public servants. The Fieldings sought to maintain permanency by paying a small retainer fee and promising a portion of the reward money if the constables remained runners. By 1750 there were eight constable-detectives working out of Bow Street, but they were confined to the city limits. John Fielding, however, extended a patrol service to the approaches of the city, and by 1797 the runners numbered sixty-eight. In 1805 an official Horse Patrol was organized at Bow Street to care for the rural areas on the outskirts of London. The Bow Street Runners were successful, and by 1792 seven other public offices followed their example and established similar constabularies.

These corps of thief-takers were a departure from the past, and John Fielding drew a distinction between the official and unofficial thief-takers in *The Rise and Establishment of the Real Thief-Takers.* The system of night watchmen created by King Charles II in the late seventeenth century—The Charlies, as they were called—and the runners bracketed a century of predominantly private policing. Although limited in jurisdiction and only intermittently scattered over the London landscape, the Bow Street Runners were under official direction. Apparently judicial control was less threatening to the citizenry than executive supervision. As officers of the court, the runners grew in prestige and power, depending upon the leadership of the various magistrates and the tolerance of the public.

For nearly a century the Bow Street Runners provided an alternative to the disreputable private thief-takers. But in order to stay informed about criminal cases, runners had to frequent tavern hangouts of thieves. Local citizenry were soon enraged. Public outcry plus concern over the corrupting influence of the reward system led to a parliamentary investigation in 1828. Bribery and criminal collusion were discovered and the runners were censured. The next year Robert Peel's new police would appear on the scene. One critic, Charles Dickens, saw the bifocal imagery of the runners and wrote in the 1830s:

> We are not by any means devout believers in the old Bow Street Police. To say the truth, we think there was a vast amount of humbug about those worthies. Apart from many of them being men of very indifferent character, and far too much in the habit of consulting with thieves and the like, they never lost a public occassion of jobbing and trading in mystery and making the most of themselves. Continually puffed, besides, by incompetent magistrates, anxious to conceal their own deficiencies, and hand-in-glove with the penny-a-liners of that time, they became a sort of superstition. Although as a preventive police they were utterly inefficient, and as a detective police were very loose and uncertain in their operations, they remain with some people, a superstition to the present day.[7]

Vocations die hard, and the runners, after the parliamentary investigations and the arrival of the Peelers, became a private detective organization, a business that lasted until 1856.[8]

Although some magistrates experimented with the Fieldings' ideas, London by and large remained policed by a constable-night watch system in spite of three parliamentary investigations of crime and policing in 1750, 1770, and 1772 that determined the inadequacy of the police. Further, as the repetitive use of thief-takers, runners, constables, and night watch attest, even the word "police" was slow in reaching respectability in the English language. John Fielding advanced the word's use, but since it was believed to have been invented in France and represented the Continental spy state, considerable aversion and prejudice hampered its coming into lexical fashion until the late eighteenth century. No serious reform of the police was advocated. Instead the policy was to encourage law-abiding citizen participation in criminal justice with rewards and to discourage law-breaking citizens with severe punishments. Parliament even failed to act after the famous Gordon Riots of 1780 proved the incompetence of the police as an order maintenance mechanism. The government's only flirtation with police reform, the London and Westminister Police Bill, failed passage in 1785. Consequently, a number of self-help organizations sprang up because, as Romilly wrote later, "it had become necessary for every man to trust himself for his security."[9] The Honourable Artillery Company and the London Military Foot Association were only two of several voluntary associations for defense that punctuated the English commitment to unofficial policing.

Another example of lay-policing would strike a responsive chord later in nineteenth-century America. An "evangelical police" system developed to watchdog the lower classes with spies and informants and to enforce the Puritan notion of propriety. Early in the eighteenth century several Societies for the Reformation of Manners appeared, and by the end of the century numerous moral societies existed. The most prominent, the Society for the Suppression of Vice and Encouragement of Religion, was founded in 1801 and borrowed from Edmund Burke a phrase that acted as its motto and at the same time summed up the prevailing attitude of law-and-order citizens: "When bad men combine, the good must associate."[10]

The most formalized example of citizen association is government, and as crime and disorder worsened one could expect concern for better policing to increase. Using the base periods of 1811–1818 and 1821–1828, the population of London increased 19 percent while crime increased 55 percent. London had been the scene of riots almost every year between 1815 and 1828.[11] In that same period, in response to growing citizen concern in London, there were no fewer than eight parliamentary investigations of policing in the metropolis. Intellectual models, formulated in the late eighteenth and early nineteenth centuries, were aired once again. Both Patrick Colquhoun and Jeremy Bentham had argued for a centralized preventative police force. Control of such a police would move, they had argued, from private or judicial personnel, as had been true in the past, to the executive ministries of government. Some resistance persisted. A parliamentary committee in 1818, for example, feared such a police "would make every servant of every house a spy on the actions of his master, and all classes of society spies on each other." Another committee, this time in 1822, felt it was "difficult to reconcile an effective system of police with that perfect freedom of action and exemption from interferences which are the great privileges and blessings of society in this country."[12] John Stuart Mill captured the essence later: "In England there has always been more liberty, but worse organization, while in other countries there is better organization, but less liberty."[13] This safety in inefficiency had to be overcome. Crime and street disorder, apparently, were not enough to overcome latent fears of a police state. As would be true in other times and other places, police reform also needed the presence of a strong political leader to both reflect and direct societal concerns.

Robert Peel, a man of middle-class origin himself, had seen the necessity of a strong policing mechanism while Secretary of Ireland from 1812 to 1818. After he became Home Secretary and during the days of struggle for the new police, Peel wrote the Duke of Wellington that one purpose of the police was "to teach people that liberty does not consist of having your house robbed by organized gangs of thieves, and in leaving the principal streets of London in the nightly possession of drunken women and vagabonds."[14] Peel finessed the police bill through Parliament in 1829, and England's modern police was created.

It was Charles Rowan and Richard Mayne, the first two police commissioners, however, who created the new police model. They set the policies and practices that fleshed out the organization and gave it direction. The typical Englishman equated the police state with spies and soldiers. Peel and his commissioners understood and compensated for this bias. They had to parry public fears of "Peel's bloody gang" and create acceptable images of the bobbie. The police were quickly uniformed to waylay fears of spies. It would be over ten years before a plain-clothes detective component was added. For those concerned over militarism, the police were dressed in blue civilian-cut suits of tails-and-trousers with the word "police" inconspicuously on brass buttons. They also wore a top hat, in keeping with current middle-class styles. Professionalism meant detachment, restraint, and impersonality. Officers were recruited from outside the city, and, in hopes of safeguarding them from the temptations of politics, they were denied the vote. Order was to be maintained with a minimum of provocation and violence. Force was downplayed and weapon carrying was discouraged. The truncheon would not be a visible part of the bobbies' attire until 1863. By that time mob disturbances, especially during the Chartist riots of the 1830s and 1840s, proved the value of the new police and the word "bobbie," which had first been a term of derision, became one of guarded respect. Also, by the 1830s a counter-model existed across the channel from which to draw comparisons. The police state of France represented all that was good and bad in a supremely efficient police system.[15]

Another source of popular notions about detective police work came from eighteenth- and nineteenth-century France. The Paris police was founded by Louis XIV in 1667. This example of the Continental model of policing was a spin-off of the military. All of the early personnel, techniques, and disciplines came from the king's army. Lieutenant-General Nicolas La Reynie and his successor, the Marquis d'Argenson, introduced a standard of order, regularity, and cleanliness into the city life that was admired throughout the Continent. Restrictions on the wearing of weapons by citizens, extensive military-like police patrols, and the introduction of street lighting made Paris one of the safest cities in Europe. The police also customarily supplied the king with detailed information on the conduct of private persons, and the *mouchard,* or spy, became an important part of detection in the Paris police. The police accumulated dossiers on private persons whose only crime was that of attracting the attention of the authorities. Claude Saint-Simon was convinced that Argenson "had so imposed order on the innumerable Parisian multitude that there was not a single inhabitant whose conduct and habits he did not know from day to day." Then the *lettre de cachet,* a blank warrant signed by the monarch, allowed indiscriminate arrests in Paris of all malcontents. Such imposed orderliness was one cause of the French Revolution, and the lieutenancy-general of Police of Paris ended with the storming of the Bastille.[16]

There were attempts to democratize the police by the revolutionaries, but soon the old lieutenant-general office was restored under a new name: Prefect of Police of Paris. The chaos of the revolution and the imperial designs of Napoleon Bonaparte indicated the need for a strong police force. A national police, the

Ministry of the General Police of the Republic, was created in 1796 to transcend the Paris police. Established to provide for the tranquility of the republic, to police the prisons, and to suppress vagabondage, the national police became a political tool in the hands of Joseph Fouché. This apostate priest, responsible for so much violence and bloodshed during the Reign of Terror, became minister of police in 1799. He spent little energy on the ordinary business of policing, a task he left to the Prefect of Police of Paris. Instead, Fouché reintroduced the prerevolutionary practice of opening all mail. The press was strictly controlled, as Fouché reduced the seventy-three political journals of January 1800 to eleven by the following May. Indiscriminate arrests and imprisonments without trial became as common under the empire as under the ancient regime. While Napoleon conquered Europe, Fouché conquered France. After the conquests, however, Napoleon feared the power of the minister of police, and Fouché was dismissed. Even though Fouché's ministry was abolished in 1818, his innovations remained throughout the nineteenth century and served as a model for other totalitarian governments. Even France resurrected Fouché's ideas and methods when Louis Napoleon reestablished the empire and a police state between 1851 and 1860.[17] Significant dates, daresay, for the development of American policing. Indeed, American fears of a police state and of the detective as spy were rooted in the work of Argenson and Fouché.[18] But in this strange dual-imaged world, people at the same time could fear Fouché's administration but be fascinated by the techniques of a Vidocq.

The police spy Eugene François Vidocq was the greatest single sleuth in France. Born in Arras in 1775, Vidocq spent the first thirty-five years of his life as a gypsy, military deserter, and thief. To avoid arrest he became a master of disguises, and when captured, he created a legend with his successful escapes. In 1810 Vidocq negotiated his way into the Paris police and became the famous *Chef de la Sûreté,* a position he held until 1827 when he retired to write his *Memoirs.* In 1828 his autobiography was translated into English, and the following year a popular stage play by Douglas William Jerrod, *Vidocq, the French Police Spy,* appeared. Vidocq formed a private detective agency in 1831, and his popularity was so great that large audiences came to his special exhibition of criminal relics and disguises when he visited London in 1845.[19]

By mid-century the themes that grew out of French history in the

eighteenth and early nineteenth centuries had crossed the Channel.
Based upon the English experience, detectives were suspected of
being criminal brokers and *agents provocateur,* thoroughly cor-
rupted by a reward system. Many admired the operational efficiency
of the French system but feared the price to be too high for such an
orderly society. After a series of grisly murders in 1811, for example,
one English commentator noted that

> They have an admirable police at Paris, but they pay for it dear enough.
> I had rather half a dozen people's throats should be cut in Ratcliffe
> Highway every three or four years than be subject to domiciliary visits,
> spies, and all the rest of Fouché's contrivances.[20]

At best Vidocq's life proved that it takes a thief to catch a thief.

With the exception of Vidocq, private detectives never assumed
a prominent place in French policing. Spying was already part of the
official apparatus of Continental-style police systems. Any kind of
private police work was quickly relegated to divorce activity. In
England the creation of the London Metropolitan Police was due to
mob violence, growing crime rates, and the bankruptcy of the private thief-taker profession. In a twist of historical continuity, America entered an era of dependnce upon private detectives as England
shifted in the opposite direction. Private enquiry offices opened in
England especially after the Matrimonial Causes Act of 1857 created
the modern divorce court. Even though there were prominent British private detectives (firms like Jefferson and Jarrett, Besson and
Hemming, Stephen Comer, and Harry Benson) in the mid-
nineteenth century, they were never as important or controversial
as their American counterparts.[21]

By the mid-nineteenth century, most large American cities had
abandoned the old colonial models of law enforcement for the modern police department. Prior to that time citizens in general were
responsible for the prevention and detection of crime. At night,
when all respectable people retired, the streets were patroled by
watchmen. During the daytime everyone was supposed to be on the
watch for crime, and only a small number of constables existed who
specialized in crime detection, a practice that often amounted to
returning stolen property for a fee.[22] America, however, was changing faster than American attitudes. Between 1820 and 1860 the
urban population grew 79 percent, and much of the old homogeneity
was lost as large numbers of immigrants arrived from Europe. In the

first half of the nineteenth century, Boston expanded from 38,000 to 212,000, and Philadelphia increased from 75,000 to 450,000. New York and its suburbs experienced an elevenfold expansion in the same period. The midwestern cities of St. Louis, Cincinnati, and Chicago grew even faster.[23]

But the establishment of the London Metropolitan Police system in 1829—with its uniformed patrolmen, centralized leadership, and disciplined regimen—found few admirers in America. With a mixture of Anglophobia and a Jacksonian distrust of big government, old institutions persisted into the second third of the nineteenth century. As late as 1839, New York had eight hundred watchmen and one hundred constables to meet the expanding needs of the city.[24] But weaknesses were evident as many night-watchmen held full-time jobs during the day and slept on duty at night. Constables were thought to be closely connected with the criminal class through the stool pigeon system. Both daytime and nighttime policemen stayed away from the newly developing criminal districts such as "Five Points" in New York, the "Swamp" in New Orleans, the "Hill" in Boston, and the "Sands" in Chicago. Then in the 1830s and 1840s a series of nativist and antiabolitionist riots occurred in New York, Boston, Philadelphia, and Cincinnati that proved the inadequacies of the existing police apparatus.[25] New York responded in 1844 by creating a new police roughly patterned after the London Metropolitan Police. Cincinnati and New Orleans followed in 1852, Boston and Philadelphia in 1854, Chicago in 1855, and Baltimore in 1857.[26]

A constant theme throughout the rest of the century was the public distrust of the urban police departments, especially the detective bureaus.[27] Fearful of taking a giant step toward an effective police, Americans instead haltingly transferred earlier inadequacies to a different level. Politics dictated the future of the policeman, and he enjoyed only limited tenure.[28] He had to work in the political ward of his residence, which often caused him to sacrifice professional detachment. Large numbers of unfit men were recruited, giving most departments high rates of absenteeism, and there was no formal training in the New York police office until 1853. The poor distribution of men was further hampered by the lack of communication between the patrolman and precinct headquarters. Furthermore, the patroling of public streets did not always guarantee the protection of private property, especially as large commercial houses, hotels, and transportation and entertainment facilities developed. Already in the early 1850s, residents of the upper part of New York—Union Square, Madison Square, and Gramercy Park— paid $6.00 each a year for private police to guard homes from burglary. The absence of a river police forced New York shipowners and merchants to hire their own watchmen at the wharves.[29] Since the number of policemen seemed inadequate, one prominent New Yorker, George Templeton Strong, advocated in 1852 that a society be created to supplement the police by employing agents to prosecute violence and corruption.[30]

The police detective fared even worse. In the 1840s the constable-detective was believed to be closely linked with the criminal classes as a "go-between."[31] Boston's six-year flirtation with a vigorous detective bureau under city marshal Francis Tukey came to an end in 1851 when he was fired by city politicians fearful of the growing spy system and jealous of the growing power of one of their subordinates.[32] Enough misgivings existed toward the arts of detection that when the new police departments were created in the 1850s, the emphasis focussed upon preventative rather than detective services. Of course, crime detection did go on, but it was not a specialized function as under the old constable system. The modern patrolman during the formative years of police history also performed detective duties. At first, the entire police force was filled with plain-clothes men. Uniform-wearing connotated both militarism and livery, images to be avoided in democratic America. But by 1853, eight years after its creation, the New York police became costumed. The police officers themselves stubbornly resisted but cogent arguments carried the day. Some had charged that the years of plain-clothed patrolmen allowed cowardice and criminal collusion to go unnoticed.[33] Uniformed policemen, the argument went, would more effectively deter street criminals. More important, in terms of the antispy attitudes forming in America, the policemen, by being more visible, would be deterred from spying. Other cities were equally delinquent in addressing the uniform questions. Boston's police were not uniformed until 1858, Philadelphia's in 1860, and Chicago's in 1861. The New York police did not have an official detective bureau until 1857, thirteen years after the department was organized. Philadelphia's police established detectives in 1859, interestingly enough, a year before they were uniformed. Chicago followed in 1861.[34]

The rise of the professional police had some unintended consequences: the work load of the entire criminal justice system increased, arrest rates swelled, the dockets of the criminal courts expanded, and the prisons became more crowded. As a response, throughout the states, criminal codes were rethought, and the penitentiary ceased to be a place for penance and became one of custody.[35] Public attitudes were predictable. New criminal classes originating among ethnic youth were identified, and the fear of crime increased. At the same time the economic tempo of America was picking up, and most merchants and professional people were more interested in quick recovery of stolen goods than in lengthy prosecution proceedings. Consequently, several retired constables established private police agencies to protect property, restore stolen goods for a commission, and, whenever possible, circumvent the official criminal justice system.[36] These early detective agencies filled a useful function for urban society, but also they perpetuated the image that there was little difference between the criminal and the detective. It is against this intellectual and institutional backdrop that Allan Pinkerton formed his police business in mid-nineteenth-century Chicago.

PART ONE

THE FORMATIVE YEARS

ALLAN PINKERTON:
THE DETECTIVE
AS ENTREPRENEUR

CHAPTER 1

Chicago Genesis: *Two Models of Private Detective Agencies, 1855–1860*

IT WAS NOVEMBER 1855, and the Chicago courtroom was uncommonly crowded with sympathetic spectators. Oscar Caldwell, the defendant, was a popular conductor for the Burlington Railroad, and, though it would be some fourteen years before unionization of the railroad conductors, numerous friends viewed the proceedings as an opening battle between management and labor. A fund raised by fellow workers permitted Caldwell to hire some of the finest attorneys in Chicago. But the evidence was compelling. Before coming to the Burlington Company in 1853, Caldwell had been a ticket agent for the Michigan Central. The same job was available at the Burlington, but, instead, Caldwell chose to take a $300 pay cut and become a conductor, a suspicious decision in light of his later confession to having "lived too fast." Perhaps the choice was prompted by a sense of adventure. In those early days of railroad development the conductor's job was a somewhat footloose vocation. Very early, management became suspicious of the young unmarried men working the lines who had few traditional elements of stability. If crime grew as temptation grew, it was believed, then employee dishonesty might increase as business expanded and trains traveled further from managerial control. Furthermore, workers who felt exploited or unappreciated might take unauthorized compensations and privileges. Stolen ticket receipts were found on Caldwell and, inspite of claims of honest mistakes and task short-cuts due to the rush of work, the court found him guilty of theft and sentenced him to one year in prison.[1]

Besides the personal attractiveness of young Caldwell and the implicit split and mutual distrust between management and labor, there were other reasons for the importance of the Caldwell trial in Illinois. Employee dishonesty was increasing to such an extent that a new body of law was formulating around the concept of embezzlement. Historically, a necessary ingredient of theft or larceny was proof of trespass. But what of goods or monies obtained legally, say receiving legitimate fees by a clerk or agent, that were not turned over to the proprietor or owner? By the end of the eighteenth century, England had recognized the problem of theft by "trusted servants" who, in effect, did not trespass according to common law. A new kind of theft, embezzlement, was invented by governing elites to plug the loopholes in the law.[2] America did not have a servant class, but it did have numerous clerks and agents, those most readily suspected of embezzlement. In a piece-meal fashion statutes were passed to control theft by employees. As early as 1827, Illinois had considered embezzlement crimes by public officials, clerks, and apprentices. It was not until 1859, however, before a statute formally convered embezzlement of ticket receipts by conductors, though the Caldwell case did establish a judicial precedent. Even the official report of the trial published in 1855 used the term embezzlement to designate Caldwell's crime. In short, his crime was defined as embezzlement by the courts, and four years later the legislature made it statutory.

Caldwell's trial was almost Kafkaesque; he was guilty of a crime, but no one was sure where that crime fit into the existing criminal law. One thing for certain was that the success of this particular conviction was due to reliable eye-witness accounts of his wrongdoing. By the mid-1850s a few businessmen saw the need for greater control over their employees; their solution was to sponsor a private detective system. In February 1855, Allan Pinkerton, after consulting with six midwestern railroads, created such an agency in Chicago. Pinkerton's business would be both an anchor to the past (private initiative and manpower being used to confront a particular problem instead of relying on governmental power) and a new business concept (the hiring of an outside business on a retainer basis to confront that particular problem). It was due to the work of Allan Pinkerton that Caldwell was convicted.

Phrenologist O. S. Fowler examined Allan Pinkerton in 1865 and described the detective as earnest, enthusiastic, excitable, hard working, and combative. Fowler then advised Pinkerton to go west because "Chicago was not fast enough" for a man of his talents. Pinkerton agreed, and even rejoiced, over the character analysis, but did not take the advice.[3] Chicago, it seemed, was fast enough, and already at mid-nineteenth century the city was a symbol of America's urban explosion. From a wilderness village in 1830, it grew to 80,000 in 1855. The following year a southern tourist, James Sterling, visited the Midwest and described Chicago as a city in revolution because "growth is much too slow a word for the transformation of a hamlet of log huts into a western New York, in the space of a few years."[4] In such a place Pinkerton settled in the early 1850s.

Allan Pinkerton was born on August 25, 1819, in Glasgow, Scotland. His father, William, was a policeman who received invaliding wounds during a street riot in 1829, and young Allan had to care for the family as an apprentice cooper. Disillusioned with the political and economic oppressions in Scotland, American freedoms appeared especially attractive. "In my native country I was free in name, but a slave in fact. I toiled in and out of season, and my labor went to sustain the Government," he recalled years later.[5] Such working-class frustrations found expression for him in the Chartist crusades.

Chartism was an English social movement of the 1830s and 1840s. Mass meetings and demonstrations were held throughout Great Britain at which fiery orators like Feargus O'Connor inspired young workers like Allan Pinkerton to sign large petitions asking for the broadening of enfranchisement to the lower classes. Basically, there were six points of Chartism: broader manhood suffrage, secret ballot, abolition of property qualifications for members of Parliament, equal electoral districts, annual Parliament meetings, and payment to members of Parliament. Seditious language occasionally caused confrontations with the military, especially in 1840 and 1841 when the loose movement gelled with the establishment of the National Charter Association. The upwards of 40,000 Chartists seemed sinister. Troops were in London and Manchester, but enough unrest existed in Scotland, where young Allan Pinkerton had become a minor spokesman for the movement, that military intervention would occur in 1848. Enough government persecution, however, hounded Allan Pinkerton's efforts earlier so that he and his new bride fled to the United States in 1842.

Well over one hundred Chartists, attracted by American freedoms and tolerance, came to America in the 1830s and 1840s. Expansion and liberalizing of suffrage plus disestablishment of church and state were especially appealing. After 1840, however, political pressures and police harassments accounted for numerous emigrations. James T. Payne, John Rees, John Stevens, William Thornton, Mark Thompson, Benjamin Worswick, and Richard Mellor were just a few who had to leave England in a hurry. Most settled in New York and Boston, but at least nine went to Chicago. Matthew Mark Trumbull was impressed with the Chartist-like constitutions of Indiana, Illinois, Michigan, and Wisconsin, and emigrated in 1846. After the Civil War, in which he became a general, Trumbull moved to Chicago and became a successful lawyer. He remained true to his liberal beginnings, and after the Haymarket Affair of 1886, Trumbull began publishing the *Open Court,* a radical pro-labor magazine. He would become an enemy to Pinkertonism, and under the pseudonym of "Wheelbarrow" he wrote scathing attacks in his *Articles and Discussions on the Labor Question.* [6]

The Pinkertons arrived in Canada poverty stricken after a shipwreck destroyed most of their possessions. A friend from Scotland, the printer Robert Fergus, invited them to Chicago, and Allan found work as a cooper for Lill's Brewery. Pinkerton wanted his own business, though, and in 1843 he headed for a small Scottish settlement, Dundee, forty miles northeast of Chicago. Already the Allisons, Crichtons, Dempsters, McAllisters, McCulluchs, and McQueens were lending a nostalgic Scottish flavor to the midwestern village. [7] Pinkerton felt the town could support a cooperage, especially if additional business came from Chicago meat packers and Milwaukee brewers. He built a cabin near a commercial bridge that spanned the Fox River and soon employed eight apprentices. [8] He then settled down to raise a family and became a successful businessman in rural Illinois. Within three years the same social awareness, reforming zeal, and economic opportunism that brought him into the Chartist movement in Scotland disrupted his quiet life in Dundee. This time, however, it was due to crimes against the state rather than the crimes of the state.

For some time business throughout the rural regions of the Midwest had been haphazard because of "wild cat" bank currency. Laws protecting and regulating the national currency did not extend to the increasing number of state and independent bank notes. Problems of the unreliability of specie were compounded by numerous counterfeiters passing spurious money on the few existing credible banks. Itinerant rogues traveled the countryside selling bundles of fake money to those who wanted to turn a fast profit. That they had a ready market for their "green goods" testifies to the touch of larceny present in many village folk. Counterfeit money did not directly affect Pinkerton's cooperage, but it harmed those upon whom he depended for business. He had a vested interest in the smooth working of the community, and it was no surprise when Pinkerton accidentally discovered a counterfeiter's camp in 1847 that he returned with the county sheriff to make the arrest. Two Dundee merchants, H. E. Hunt and I. C. Bosworth, irritated over official inefficiency and impressed with Pinkerton's discovery of a rural counterfeiter gang, asked the cooper to help in ending the menace. At first Pinkerton was reluctant to enter such a "wil-o'-the-wisp piece of business," but police traditions were in his family, and he agreed to watch for counterfeiters on a part-time basis.[9]

Allan Pinkerton's methods were as bold and rustic as the criminals he sought. For example, when a stranger named John Craig arrived in Dundee, the amateur detective made his acquaintance, asked to buy some counterfeit money, and then made the arrest. The simple case electrified the region, and Pinkerton later recalled that:

The country being new, and great sensations scarce, the affair was in everybody's mouth, and I suddenly found myself called upon, from every quarter, to undertake matters requiring the detective skill, until I was soon actually forced to relinquish the honorable though not over-profitable occupation of a cooper, for that of a professional detective.[10]

Soon after Craig's capture, the Kane County sheriff, Luther Dearborn, appointed Pinkerton a deputy, and he continued to search out counterfeiters at the same time he managed his cooperage.

Another force drew Pinkerton away from the pastoral life of Dundee. Dundee was divided into two sections by the Fox River: East Dundee inhabited by German families, and West Dundee where the older immigrants from New England resided. The more conservative elements of the village resented the liberal religious and political ideas of the newly arrived Scottish families. The issue of slavery split the community. Pinkerton was active on the underground railroad in the late 1840s and helped many runaway slaves escape to Canada. Such activities made Pinkerton controversial, a role he would play throughout his life. When he ran as a candidate on the Liberty party ticket for the state's constitutional convention in 1848, Pinkerton was branded a drunkard by his own minister and forced out of the Dundee Baptist Church. In the election he ran last in a field of nine candidates as the antiabolitionist forces in Dundee prevailed.[11]

As antiabolitionism stiffened in Dundee, it eased in Chicago. The Democratic party had lost its hold in 1848, and the Whigs elected James H. Woodworth as mayor of Chicago. That same year Woodworth presided over an immense antislavery meeting at the City Saloon where Cook County residents demanded the cessation of the extension of slavery. Two years later, with the passage of the Fugitive Slave Act, Chicago became a clearing house for runaway slaves. This was at a time when, in the rural areas such as Dundee, some enterprising young men were forming businesses to hunt fugitive slaves for a reward.[12] An urban-rural split over this issue was occurring in Illinois. When Pinkerton finally moved to Chicago he quickly became prominent in abolitionist circles. In 1857 he was one of a delegation called to investigate a suspected slave catcher passing through town. Then in March 1859 he helped John Brown and a party of slaves escape to Canada. Later that same day Pinkerton addressed the Cook County Bar Association and raised $400 for Brown.[13] By 1860 Pinkerton was well established in abolitionist circles in Chicago.

But abolitionism was only one reason for Pinkerton's affinity for Chicago. By the early 1850s he was becoming well known outside Dundee. As a deputy in Kane County, Pinkerton's work against counterfeiters brought him to the attention of the federal government. A characteristic trend of federal policing in the first half of the nineteenth century was to hire private persons for police work as occasion arose. This was true also in the post office department. The Treasury Department had had a mandate to investigate and police counterfeiting since the founding of the nation, but it did not create a detective force to carry out that mandate until after the Civil War. Thus Pinkerton was hired in 1851 and 1853 to investigate counterfeiting in Illinois. In the first case he was based in Chicago; in 1853 he made an arrest across the state in Galena.[14] In 1852 Cook County Sheriff William Church asked Pinkerton to rescue two kidnapped Michigan girls who had passed through Chicago heading westward. Pinkerton found them in Rockford, Illinois, where he shot one of the seducers.[15] Increasingly, these experiences drew Pinkerton away from pastorial Dundee and destroyed most provincial notions he might have had toward police work. It was obvious that effective law enforcement could not be confined within any boundaries. Finally, after returning the kidnapped girls to Michigan, Pinkerton became a deputy sheriff in Cook County, a position he kept under Church and Cyrus Bradley. At least one criminal resented the meteoric use of Pinkerton in local crime fighting circles. In September 1853, the young deputy sheriff was shot as he was walking home from the sheriff's office. The wound was not serious, but newspapers were appalled and one called for lynch law.[16] But even during this period, 1853 and 1854, Pinkerton accepted jobs outside his official poistion. Then in 1855, shortly after he opened his private agency for the railroads, he also became a special agent for the post office. Not only geographical but occupational borders were fluid in these formative years of policing.

As special agent for the Chicago post office, Pinkerton had three responsibilities. He was to stop the increasing number of mail robberies, keep Washington informed about the operations of the local offices, and check on the honesty of the workers. These latter duties introduced Pinkerton to techniques that formed a central part of his future detective operations—spying upon employees.[17]

Perry Denniston and Theodore Denniston were related to the Chicago postmaster and obtained jobs as "pilers"—workers who arranged letters so that distributing clerks could see the addresses easily. The Dennistons, therefore, handled large amounts of mail and could easily recognize thick envelopes containing money. Several complaints of unreceived mail reached Pinkerton in March 1855, and he sent a decoy letter through the mails to check on postal employees. An arrest was made after Pinkerton caught Perry Denniston stealing the letter, and the detective was proclaimed a "terror to evil doers" by local newspapers. Four months later Theodore Denniston was taken into custody after Pinkerton broke into his apartment and found $4,000 pasted to the backs of wall pictures. A friendly press declared it "the most important arrest in the annals of post office depredations ever brought to light in this country. . . . As a detective police officer Mr. Pinkerton has no superior, and we doubt if he has any equals in this country."[18]

Postal employees were not the only suspects in postal theft. In April 1855, W. S. Buck, owner of a large lottery business, was aroused by the Denniston revelations and blamed the post office for the loss of several expected letters. Once again Pinkerton planted a decoy letter but this time everyone was cleared, and suspicion settled upon the member of Buck's firm who picked up the mail at the post office. The arrest and confession of John F. Gould quickly followed.[19] Other incidents of breaking and entering the post office occurred, but these two cases best illustrate the type of work Pinkerton was doing. They were symptoms of a nation growing fast, where the size of many institutions and businesses simply outstripped the informal means of control—a condition which, more than any other, brought Pinkerton's private detective agency into existence.

American businesses changed in the 1840s and 1850s, a process that thoroughly modernized principles of management. Old styles of administration were no longer appropriate as regional and national markets opened. The pioneer in these developments was the railroad. Innovations by the railroads in the 1850s affected most business for the next fifty years. Adam Smith's notions of business units helpless to invisible market forces gave way as new management techniques and personnel became more assertive in directing and manipulating the market. A new professional managerial class developed that needed a constant flow of information for the efficient operation of these new businesses. Modern accountancy, as well as administration, grew out of this development. So did the private police. Pinkerton would be the invisible eye for these professional managers, whom their historian has called the "visible hand."[20]

American railroads displayed the dual problems of rapid growth and this country's cherished conceptions of "home rule" in law enforcement. In the spring of 1851, Illinois had ninety-eight miles of track; five years later there were 2,086.[21] The Galena and Chicago Union first opened the upper Mississippi region to Chicago trade. The Michigan Southern and Northern Indiana connected Chicago to the Atlantic coast in February 1852. In May of the same year, trade with Detroit was made available by the Michigan Central. Thirteen railroads laced Illinois in 1854 when one booster crowed that "the influence of railroads upon the progress of our State.... is without a parallel in the history of the world."[22]

This railroad expansion quickly exposed the weaknesses of police work in a country enamored with federalism. Once the train left the city it lost all the protections of urban society until it reached its destination. If valuable cargoes and passengers were waylaid on the road, the railroad company had little redress from the official police. Since a state police was nonexistent and the federal government took no responsibility for railroad protection, the miles of track, bridges, water towers, and terminals depended upon weak county law authorities. As the railroads fanned out over the state in the 1850s concern increased over the protection of railroad property. Occasionally, rowdies burned terminals.[23] More frequently, irate farmers, ex-employees, or young hooligans derailed trains.[24] Of even greater concern was the lack of control over the growing number of employees. As the Illinois Central quickly expanded southward in 1856, one official warned that soon his company would "overlap all calculation and override all management."[25] Driven by such anxieties, six midwestern railroads gave Pinkerton $10,000 on February 1, 1855, and the North West Police Agency was created.[26]

Allan Pinkerton first worked for the railroads in 1854 when he apprehended a railroad wrecker for the Southern Michigan line.[27] As a special agent for the railroads, he arrested the station manager of Oak Ridge, Illinois, for pilfering a Galena Railroad freight car in March 1855.[28] Most of his attention, however, was devoted to checking on the honesty of railroad employees. The passenger conductor, having the greatest authority and greatest freedom on the train, was especially suspect. Conductors could sleep on the job or socialize with passengers at the expense of official duties. In a growing commercial society, the theft of time and delinquency of duty was almost as bad as the theft of property. They could also allow friends free rides, or, worse yet, pocket money they collected for tickets. Although most passenger tickets were purchased from terminal agents, a significant amount of business was transacted along the route where passenger buildings were unavailable. In 1857, for example, Illinois Central conductors sold $147,856 worth of tickets, and in 1858, $103,790.[29] In such cases a passenger boarded the train and paid the fee to the conductor, who turned it over to the company later. In subsequent years a large portion of Pinkerton's business was spying on railroad conductors to ensure or "test" their honesty. It all started in 1855 with the Caldwell case. Once a stalwart for the laboring classes in Scotland, the ex-chartist reformer now appeared to be the workers' greatest enemy. Pinkerton operatives were called "vipers," "spies," "scoundrels," "jailbirds," and "thieves set to catch a thief," sobriquets that would be used over and over again during the next seventy-five years. Railroad management and Pinkerton, on the other hand, saw the Caldwell case and the entire "testing" program, a name given to the spying, as essential to establish control over employees. Benjamin Johnson, an executive for Burlington, thought the Caldwell trial therapeutic. With additional examples, he felt, the "railroads would begin to have some control over their agents."[30] That was Pinkerton's job: establishing control in a fast-growing industry that could not rely upon the official city police.

The need of business, especially railroad business, to control workers and instill a new industrial discipline, in part, explains the rise of Pinkerton's detective agency in the 1850s. The weaknesses of law enforcement outside the city also placed responsibility of policing in private hands for much of the nineteenth century. In the absences of adequate state and federal police mechanisms, Pinkerton flouished. Meanwhile, in the city the competition between the public and private sector and within the private sector itself was greater, and private detectives assumed slightly different roles and reputations.

By 1860 most major cities in the United States possessed modern police departments. Reforms of the previous decade and a half had eliminated the constable-nightwatch system and established centralized police departments. Initially these reforms were accomplished at the expense of the old constable-detective services, and the first private detective emerged when these retired constables continued to retrieve stolen property for a fee. Gil Hays, for example, was a New York City constable who opened an "independent police" office in June 1845 because of the rise of the new city police. Similar situations happened in St. Louis, Baltimore, Philadelphia, and Chicago.[31] A few of these new businesses also supplied watchmen and were anachronistic reminders of police organization before the reform. As police departments increased in size and competency, these constable-detectives either concentrated on noncriminal work or became aggressively competitive with the urban police. Less than half a dozen of these private detective police agencies existed in the United States when the competitive relationship between the public police and the private police was highlighted in Chicago during the late 1850s.

Attempts to reform the Chicago police in 1851 had failed, and the constable-night watch system survived to mid-decade. Nativism spread throughout America, and, in Chicago, dissatisfaction over the Irish domination of the police peaked in 1855 when Levi D. Boone was elected mayor on the Know-Nothing ticket. Espousing anti-Catholicism and antiforeignism, Boone dismissed members of the constable-night watch who were of foreign birth. He then tried, unsuccessfully, to create a uniformed police much like that found in London and New York. The city council balked. Then he precipitated the Lager riots of April 22, 1855, by closing Chicago's ethnic saloons. Shortly thereafter, this time with the acquiescence of the mob-shy city council, Boone dismissed the entire constable-night watch and created the "new police," composed fully of native-born Americans. Boone had been mayor for one month.

The new police not only reflected some new civic concerns but also inadvertently stimulated the development of urban private detective agencies. Under the old system there were twelve daytime constables and thirty-nine night watchmen in Chicago. The new system expanded the number of police to eighty and broke down the old distinctions between constabulary and night watch. Three shifts were created. The night watch had twenty-six officers, a decrease of thirteen from the old system. The daytime and twilight periods, each with twenty-six officers, had absolute gains. Historically, the period of concern for criminality centered around the night hours, but Boone and Chicagoans were increasingly aware of the need for daytime crowd and crime control. Chicago's police placed greater emphasis upon daytime policing, and, since there was a commitment to the patrolmen, policing was to be preventive in nature. There was no detective component in the police until 1861; every patrolman was also a detective. Furthermore, from the beginning it was clear that Boone's "know-nothing police" under the right political circumstances might do nothing. They were political puppets in the hands of the mayor, a characterization that held for several years. For example, when Senator Stephen Douglas came to town to defend his anti-Know Nothing views, Boone's police were conspiciously absent during the subsequent mobbing.[32]

Boone's chief of police was former Cook County Sheriff Cyrus Bradley, with whom Pinkerton had served as deputy in 1854. After Boone left office in 1856, Bradley was retired by the new mayor.[33] Politically active since his arrival in Chicago in 1837, Bradley planned to establish an agency like Pinkerton's but specializing in city work. The time for such a move seemed auspicious in March 1857 when John Wentworth was elected the city's first Republican mayor in one of those disorderly elections that proved the inadequacy of the city police. The previous month state Representative John V. Eustace of Lee County introduced "An Act to Suppress Police Agencies of a Private Nature," in an attempt to protect the embryonic modern police from competition. The legislation proposed to make all contracts for the detection and capture of thieves or the recovery of stolen property illegal. There was some justification for Eustace's concern. In the previous two years some old constable-detectives, now in private business, had been planting counterfeit money and burglary tools on unsuspecting strangers so as to make an arrest. Pinkerton had opposed the bill and filed an affidavit of protest. In sympathy with Pinkerton, a downstate newspaper felt that "a vigilant police agency [was] a greater terror to evil doers than all the municipal officers of a whole state. Villains never harbor in the vicinity of a vigilant detective."[34] Although the bill was reported out of committee favorably, no vote was taken and it died.[35] Apparently, there remained considerable ambiguity over the growing juxtaposition of public and private police. Bradley, sensitive to the urban needs of further detection and nighttime protection, established the Chicago Detecting and Collecting Police Agency in March 1857. His partners were Batholomew Yates, Chris Noyes, and Isaac Williams.

Within the month Mayor Wentworth felt the competition of Bradley's firms and editorialized in his newspaper

> our police system has been gradually falling into disrepute; and it is a lamentable fact that whilst our citizens are heavily taxed to support a large police force, a highly respectable private police is doing a lucrative business. Our citizens have ceased to look to the public police for protection, for the detection of culprits, or the recovery of stolen property.[36]

Wentworth was as ambitious as Bradley. To reverse the trends toward the private policeman, Wentworth tried to demonstrate the aggressiveness of the city police. For example, on April 20, 1857, the mayor personally led an attack on a thieves' district north of the Chicago River called "The Sands." The area was leveled with the mistaken expectation that the criminals would leave town. Instead, burglaries increased to such an extent that Wentworth was forced to issue proclamations offering rewards to those helping convict criminals. Chicago criminals were too numerous for the existing police to contend with, he conceded, and neighborhood groups were advised to employ special police for nighttime protection. Bradley's business increased and so did the public outcry. Wentworth ordered a midnight curfew and in a comedy of coincidence the first arrested were three of Bradley's detectives who were guarding some commerical establishments.[37]

Thereafter the issue of private and public police competition heated. In June, after asking "What Shall be Done?" about the prevalence of burglary in the city, the *Chicago Tribune* proposed a public meeting to raise funds to hire Pinkerton's and Bradley's forces. Within a week, the editor believed, burglary and pocket-picking would cease in Chicago.[38] Wentworth responded by placing the blame for the criminal "crisis in our city" on the shoulders of Bradley.

> We are pained to state that we have come to the conclusion that the present condition of our city with reference to robberies, burglaries, etc., is owing to the contest going on all over the Union between the Independent Police and the Public Police.

> It is the aim of the Independent to make rogue catching a profession as much as the practice of law, of medicine or of preaching the Gospel. In order to do this, the Independents all over the Union are conspiring to prove that a Public police is entirely inadequate to public protection, and they *help the proof* as far as they dare.[39]

Because "a private police cannot live where an efficient public police exists," Wentworth saw a national conspiracy of private detectives sending criminals from major city to major city in an attempt to make the public police look bad.[40]

Although Mayor Wentworth's attacks were widely recognized as politically inspired, Pinkerton publicly disassociated himself with the Bradley-type detective and declared that at no time had his agency been in competition with the public police. "On the contrary," he wrote in 1857, "we always hold ourselves ready and willing to assist and cooperate with them in every way when the public interest could be served, and, in more than one instance, volunteered our services and rendered them assistance."[41] By the fall of 1858, however, Pinkerton recognized that the weakness of the public police had placed private policing in a profitable position. G. T. Moore created his Merchant's Police in 1858 and charged customers fifty cents a week for protection. "We take small beats, so that we are able to visit the alleys and streets four or five times an hour, and once each hour we try each subscriber's door," Moore proclaimed.[42] It was at this time that Pinkerton's Protective Police Patrol was formed to compete with the independents, as the growing number of private police were called, and with the public police.

The Pinkerton Protective Police Patrol, a small body of uniformed watchmen, contracted with several businesses to offer night protection. In its first year of operation, 751 instances were reported where bank, office, or store doors were either open or insecurely fastened. Four hundred and forty cases of improper employee conduct were discovered as spying continued to be a mainstay of Pinkerton services. A friendlier mayor, John C. Haines, had been elected, and the patrol was given the power to arrest. In 1858, fifty-three persons were seized by Pinkerton patrolmen for a variety of crimes ranging from disorderly conduct to larceny. In fact, Mayor Haines relied on the Pinkertons to supplement the official police, and he paid the agency $700 in 1858 to watch for pickpockets on public occasions. Part of that money was a consulting fee, as Pinkerton advised the mayor on the possible reorganization of the city police.[43]

This, of course, raised the issue of police powers possessed by private detective agencies. Common law dictated that citizens could detain or arrest an offender if the criminal act was committed in their plain view. Other kinds of arrest, based on what we call today "probable cause," were reserved for the police or those officially deputized. The Pinkerton detective had no greater arrest power than ordinary citizens.[44] Detectives, therefore, simply spied out criminality so as to become complainants and courtroom witnesses. Watchmen, on the other hand, encountered suspicious street people and circumstantial situations. They did not necessarily see criminal activities in progress, and, therefore, they needed arrest powers similar to the police. This introduced an entirely new level of business complexity into Pinkerton's enterprise. Close working relationships with city officials became crucial. Consequently, the patrolman aspects of Pinkerton's force remained localized to Chicago. It would be several decades before the watchmen corps would be tried in other cities. The detective branch, much freer from such legal restraints, spread more rapidly and was more aloof from local politics.

By 1860 the detective agencies of Cyrus Bradley and Allan Pinkerton more closely resembled a modern police department than the Chicago police force itself. This was true in other cities as well. As early as 1846, for example, St. Louis newspapers recommended one private detective agency because it resembled New York City's new municipal police.[45] Pinkerton published an annual report of arrests and duties in the newspaper in these early formative years, just as the public police did. Of course, this was good business advertisement, but also it reflected a degree of public accountability. By 1861 such reports disappeared from the papers. The public police gave abbreviated reports and presented completed statements in pamphlet form to the city council. Private detectives, by the 1860s, were viewed differently by the public and by the private detectives themselves.

Even before Wentworth's first term expired, some of his political enemies acknowledged the potential abuses inherent in the private police system and declared "the only legitimate or proper detectives to be those created and sustained by the law."[46] Pinkerton also was concerned about dishonest detectives and perhaps about business competition, and he encouraged a thorough investigation of Bradley's firm as early as 1857.[47] The investigations were never carried out, and during the next few years, the private detective profession's reputation suffered. One blatant example occurred in 1860, when Michael Kirby, an arsonist with a long list of crimes to his credit, was arrested by one of Bradley's detectives for burning down the city lumber yard. When the detective, Michael Finucane, appeared in court as a witness, it was learned that he had encouraged the crime to gain the reward. Finucane had been a first lieutenant in the Chicago police when Bradley was chief and was either moonlighting or shifting his occupation from public to private policeman. The case was thrown out of court, and Wentworth, now serving his second term as mayor, attacked the entire private detective profession. "The more that is learned of this system the more truly infamous must it appear to every man who has a heart and a conscience," he wrote in his newspaper, the *Daily Democrat.* Pinkerton also saw the dangers of the Bradley model, and for the rest of his life he tried to maintain a counter-model against those detectives "who care less for personal integrity and the honor of their profession than for quick gains."[48]

Wentworth's concern about the private police was justified, but many felt that he was an inadequate alternative. Consequently, the private detective, especially Bradley, became involved in politics. During his two administrations, Wentworth was involved with the most trivial details of police work; he was his own police chief. Even the leather badges his men wore for identification were his invention. On more than one occasion he led forays similar to that which destroyed the Sands. But, beginning in 1857, Chicago was hit hard by an economic depression, which filled the streets with idle men whose presence increased the threat and fear of crime. At the same time, Wentworth was forced to reduce the number of his policemen from eighty to fifty, leaving some areas of the city unprotected. Dissatisfaction over the mayor's administration of the police grew, and, in 1861, the state government placed the administration of the city police in the hands of a three-man commission appointed by the governor.[49]

New York City set the example in 1857. Fighting for control of the police, Governor John King's metropolitan force confronted Mayor Fernando Wood's municipal force in several show-down situations for over two months until the state supreme court passed on the constitutionality of the state control plan. The city police, in short, became central in the issue of "home-rule," and rural-urban rivalries in state politics. Others would move toward state control too. Baltimore (1860), St. Louis (1861), Kansas City (1862), Detroit (1865), and Cleveland (1866) were just a few. In Chicago the commission was made up of Wentworth's political enemies. When it was rumored that Bradley would be in charge of the new police, the enraged mayor warned that "the whole private detective system is wrong and it is wrong to place the public police in the hands of any one of the private detective firms."[50] As Wentworth feared, Bradley was named the superintendent of police, and the night before the new system was to go into effect, the mayor dismissed the entire police force leaving the city defenseless for several hours. For most, this eccentric act verified the wisdom of taking the police out of the mayor's hands.

A professional hierarchy was established in the new police, and direct administrative control was assigned to a general superintendent. In this case, the ex-sheriff of Cook County, the ex-chief of police under Levi Boone, and the ex-private detective, Cyrus Bradley, became superintendent. Sixteen hundred new applicants were screened. An official uniform was designed, and hair and beard styles dictated. In an attempt to patch up their public image a new motto was stitched on the police flag and frequently paraded on the streets of the city: "At Danger's Call We'll Promptly Fly, and Bravely Do or Bravely Die," it promised. Then, appropriately enough, Bradley established Chicago's first police detective bureau. After two years, Bradley became secretary of the police board until he accepted a position with the federal secret service during the Civil War. He died in 1865.

Need for a new industrial or commercial discipline gave rise to the Pinkerton-type detective in the 1850s; increasing numbers of employees had to be controlled in new ways. At the same time, the public police and the Bradley-type of detective arose in response to the need of a new urban discipline; increasing numbers of new city dwellers had to be controlled. The Pinkerton and Bradley models would coexist into modern times. At first the differences were fluid and vague. Pinkerton did seek city business by creating the Protective Police Patrol, but that was purely a Chicago-based operation, and it was not until Pinkerton's death that the patrol was expanded to other offices and became important in strike work. Pinkerton, in this entrepreneur stage, was more detective than protective oriented. He was responding to the threat of regional crime and the absence of a regional police. His commitments were narrow in terms of clientele, but broad in terms of geography, the exact opposite of public policing at the time. Most of Pinkerton's activity was outside the city limits, and it is significant that his early business was named the North West Police Agency. In those early days, his business covered the area that had once been the Old Northwest Territory. Equally significant, the main representative of the constable-detective model was Bradley's Chicago Detecting and Collecting Agency. Bradley did solicit railroad contracts, but involvement in the politics of Chicago quelled further development. Other aspiring detectives soon followed their example, and by the end of the century, Illinois was regarded as the "state of detectives."[51]

With the exception of some grumblings in the railroad conductor circles, Pinkerton emerged a hero at decade's end. Because of his political activities, Bradley had more enemies, but his reforms of the city police were heralded. Private detectives were more romantic than sinister, and Wentworth's fears would not find widespread appeal until after the Civil War. Businessmen, and others with a conservative ideological orientation, gladly paid for extra police protection. The Boones and Wentworths proved that the social and economic elites did not control the police anyway. Besides, the public police had to handle "democratic crimes," those that hit all regardless of class or color. Private detectives, whether in protecting or detecting, specialized for the well-to-do. They became symbolic reminders of the shortcomings of the public police and the lack of total acceptance of them by large segments of Chicago society.

As his activities in the abolition movement indicate, Pinkerton was not afraid of political involvement. But he did try to remain aloof from most of the Wentworth-Bradley squabbles. Wentworth's attack on the private detective system was aimed at Bradley and the urban private detective. Occasionally, Pinkerton, reacting to the possibility of ricochet, defended his own agency. But he did not earn the emnity of Wentworth, an old comrade in the abolitionist fights, until after the appearance of the Protective Police Patrol in 1858, and even then it was muted. Pinkerton did learn a lesson from the Wentworth-Bradley conflict. If the public police continued to be political, the capriciousness of a single mayor or governor needed to be avoided. Perhaps expansion, the creating of a broad business base, was necessary for economic and political security. By 1860 Pinkerton headed a midwestern regional police force of growing repute. The Civil War acted as a springboard and Pinkerton was able to create his National Detective Agency. He became America's national and even international policeman. Ironically, one of the unintended consequences was greater involvement in politics.

CHAPTER 2

Lessons of War:
Regionalism to Nationalism

AMERICA'S EXPRESS SYSTEM underwent rapid growth in the 1850s that paralleled the growth of railroads. As railroad mileage increased, the express and fast-freight businesses went from local to national enterprises. Express cars on railroad trains became important features. One excited booster, an editor of the *Express Messenger,* credited the express business for annihilating the country's "magnificient distances."[1] William F. Harnden started America's first express company in 1839. Before that time, most packages were carried by stagecoach drivers, railroad conductors, friends of the sender, or sometimes perfect strangers going to the desired destination. Harnden, a conductor and ticket agent for the Boston and Worcester Railroad, noticed the large number of packages carried by passengers and offered to take parcels and newspapers in his valise to various train stations. At first his activities were confined to New England. In the early 1840s the European market opened, and Harnden specialized in overseas traffic in conjunction with the Cunard Steamship Lines.[2]

A competing express line had been established in 1840 by Alvin Adams and P. B. Burke. For five years they, too, were restricted to New England, but obtained several customers when Harnden concentrated on the European market. The California gold rush also enriched the transporting opportunities of Adams, and he began assimilating many of the smaller Eastern lines.[3] Henry Wells left Harnden in 1850 and joined Livington, Fargo, and Butterfield to establish the American Express. Within a year their business expanded from New York to Milwaukee, St. Louis, Cincinnati, and Buffalo. In 1852 a division called Wells, Fargo Company was created to operate cross-country.[4] Several other lines developed in the 1850s. In 1855 the National Express was founded by J. A. Pullen. The Eastern Express was established in 1857 and the Central Express Company in 1858. In 1854 the United States Express, organized by D. N. Barney, connected the "most remote settlements in the western country." An office was opened in Chicago, and in 1855 a broker shipped three and one-half million dollars from the city by express.[5]

Responsible for transporting goods and money across the country, the express industry suffered because of inadequate police protection. Problems of thievery and dishonest employees were much the same as with the railroads, but because of the amount of money involved, the crimes were more dramatic. In November 1843, the Pullen Company had a trunk stolen, and another company was robbed in Rochester, New York, in 1845.[6] In September 1855, the American Express was robbed of a large gold supply outside Dubuque, Iowa. The real boxes of gold were taken and lead-filled ones substituted. After several months of futile investigation, the company agent hired a detective named Captain Best to find the thieves. Two friends of a company agent were arrested, but the stolen gold was never recovered.[7]

New York City was the business hub of the express system, and Allan Pinkerton remained relatively unaware of the growing potential of the new industry until the Adams robbery in 1858. The Adams Company had just undergone a period of rapid expansion with eight new offices opening throughout South Carolina, Georgia, Tennessee, and Alabama. It was from the Montgomery, Alabama, office that $40,000 was stolen. Vice President Edward S. Samford was a friend and associate of many railroad managers in the Midwest and had heard of the Chicago detective. Pinkerton was called upon to gather evidence against one suspect, office manager Nathan Maroney. Within two years Maroney was convicted and all but $400 of the money was recovered.[8]

The Maroney case was a turning point for Pinkerton. Once again growing concern over embezzlement was highlighted. Business leaders were becoming increasingly occupied with the possible dimensions of the relatively new crime. Pinkerton received widespread publicity and made many new contacts outside the Midwest, especially in the express industry. Railroad and express companies became the major source of business for the North West Police Agency. The business name now would be changed to Pinkerton's National Detective Agency, a declaration of independence from the geographical confines of the Midwest. Furthermore, in this case Pinkerton's detective technique became a model for future investigations. Shadows—trailing and spying on suspects—had been used before, but now the undercover agent emerged as the most important detective device. Pinkerton thought that criminals could not keep secrets but instead had to have confidants. Exploiting this weakness, he planted operatives with the suspect or among the suspect's acquaintances to gain confidences and confessions. Then the secret agent would appear in court as a witness for the prosecution and insure the conviction. In the Maroney case, operative John White shared a cell with the suspect while a female operative, Kate Warne, struck up an intimate friendship with Mrs. Maroney. White convinced Maroney that his wife was unfaithful and that with well-placed bribes he could be freed. Maroney consented and disclosed the whereabouts of the stolen money. He was convicted in June 1860.[9]

The Adams Company was overjoyed and Pinkerton was put on retainer for future robbery cases. (Pinkerton retold the story fifteen years later in one of his earliest writing endeavors, *The Expressman and the Detective*.) Although the Maroney thefts occurred in the Montgomery, Alabama, express office, by the 1860s much of the express industry was becoming attached to the railroad system. Express cars were now commonly a part of the trains, and Pinkerton's detective services, even without the impetus of the Maroney case, would have naturally extended to the express system in time. The Maroney case, however, did act as a catalyst. Robberies came rapidly. In 1860 and 1863 the company was robbed of $20,000 and $85,000 respectively. Although Pinkerton was busy organizing an intelligence system for the Union army, his agency pursued and apprehended the robbers. In January 1866, Adams' was looted again, this time for $600,000, and Pinkerton recovered all but $15,000 from a gang headed by a railroad brakeman. In 1867 the Harrenden Express Company was robbed of $25,000 in Baltimore, and in 1869 the express car on the Hudson River Railroad was attacked by "Piano" Charley Ballard with the cooperation of the express messenger.

In the late 1860s and throughout the 1870s railroad bandits increased the railroad-express companies' need for policing the western country. At first, however, it was mainly a concern on the eastern seaboard. As the menace from robbers increased, the Adams Company encouraged Pinkerton to open offices in New York City.[10] Henry Sanford, general superintendent of Adams, told Bangs that "he desired a thorough espionage kept upon his employees so that he could know what they were doing and to then be enabled to make corrections." The press of business had kept Sanford from personally keeping an eye on them, it was reported.[11] These early years of business development with the railroad and express companies, however, was interrupted by the Civil War, a war that greatly determined Pinkerton's future.

Ralph Waldo Emerson spoke for most war-weary generations when he said in 1864 that "the cannon will not suffer any other sound to be heard for miles and for years around it. Our chronology has lost all old distinctions in one date,—Before the war, and since."[12] For those involved in the Civil War, it was impossible to muffle the sound of that cannon. Firmly committed to abolitionism, Pinkerton was eager to see slavery stamped out. Youthful radical zeal still ran high. Later it would settle into conservative contentment as he and old abolitionist cronies periodically met to celebrate one of America's few really successful radical movements.[13] His detective experience and acquaintances with Abraham Lincoln, George McClellan, and other political figures gained through the railroads, made him a likely choice for heading a government spy service. After all, his detective service for the railroads was nothing less than a spy system. The war also broadened his detective experience and allowed him to formalize the administration of a spy business. It provided romantic adventure as well, something an imaginative detective-entrepreneur could put to good advantage in creating a public image. Finally, the unsettled conditions after Appomattox placed a greater demand upon law enforcement. Many detective agencies arose after the war, but Pinkerton had the advantage of experience, publicity, and ambition.

Shortly after Maroney's conviction, Lincoln was elected president of the United States. South Carolina seceded on December 20, 1860. Six Southern states soon followed, and Lincoln was left a divided country to govern. Tensions on the eve of the war were dramatically evident in Baltimore. Maryland was strategically important because of its proximity to the nation's capital. Most of the state was against disunion, and Gov. Thomas Hicks tried to stall the secessionist forces. Both the mayor and chief of police of Baltimore, on the other hand, advocated the Confederate cause. One of the few remaining links between Washington and the North was the Pennsylvania, Wilmington and Baltimore Railroad. Railroad president Samuel Morse Felton feared hostile Marylanders would show their contempt for the Union by destroying railroad property.[14] In January 1861, Felton was advised by a close friend, Colonel Bingham of the Adams Express Company, to hire Pinkerton to watch for railroad vandalism. These new leaders of the express and railroad industries had no police or surveillance systems, as yet, within their company structure. There was, however, considerable contact and willingness to share with others this new idea of managerial control: the Pinkerton police. In February 1861 the Chicago detective moved to Philadelphia with five operatives.[15]

This was Pinkerton's first railroad contract outside the Midwest, and his bill for services indicated something of the economic opportunity in private detective work. Pinkerton charged $10.00 per day for his individual services and $6.00 a day for each of his five operatives.[16] This at a time when the Chicago city marshal was making $1,500 per year. Even when Pinkerton paid the individual operative one-third of the $6.00 fee, the employee could make more in a year than a first lieutenant of the Chicago police. Of course, such remuneration depended on the constant flow of business, and in hard times the operative turnover was high. This competitive advantage continued in Chicago until 1867 when the patrolman's minimum salary was raised to $800 per year as compared to the average Pinkerton operative's salary of $728.[17] For the twenty-eight days in February, Pinkerton's bill amounted to $1,120, but he later reduced it to $509.00 because of expenses he felt should not be charged to the railroad.

That portion of the bill not charged to Felton was for work done in protecting president-elect Lincoln. Pinkerton placed a number of operatives in key places in Baltimore to discover potential train wreckers. He assumed the identity of John H. Hutchinson, a stockbroker, and went into Maryland also. Aware of the hostile feelings in the city, Pinkerton was not surprised when a letter came from William Stearns, master machinist of Felton's railroad, disclosing a plot to kill Lincoln in Baltimore. Operatives Timothy Webster and Joseph Howard infiltrated some secessionist societies and confirmed Stearn's fears that a Baltimore barber named Captain Fernandina was behind a conspiracy to cause a street riot when the president-elect arrived, commit the murder during the confusion, and then speed away to the South.[18]

Lincoln already had left Springfield, Illinois, and was traveling to Washington by way of Pennsylvania when the plot was discovered. He was to stop in Philadelphia on Washington's birthday to raise a flag over Independence Hall, then move on to Harrisburg and deliver a speech at the state capitol. Pinkerton rushed to Philadelphia to warn Lincoln, but the president-elect did not believe the story.[19] The two men were not strangers. Lincoln had been an attorney for the Illinois Central from 1853 to 1859, and his work brought him into occasional contact with Pinkerton's detective activities. An assassination attempt, however, seemed implausible. Nothing like that had been done since the unsuccessful attempt on Andrew Jackson, and Lincoln suspected that Pinkerton tended towards exaggeration. The day after his meeting with Pinkerton corroborative evidence came from another source.

The month before, New York Gov. William Seward, future secretary of state in Lincoln's cabinet, had sent New York detectives, headed by John A. Kennedy and George Walling, to Washington. (Kennedy was superintendent of the New York City police and Walling was head of the detective division.) They were to prepare the security for the inaugural and check the city for treasonous plots. There was no federal mechanism, outside of the military, to do such tasks. Washington was cleared, but Kennedy felt that Baltimore was dangerously hostile to the president-elect. Governor Seward and Gen. Winfield Scott agreed, and Kennedy's findings were sent to Lincoln. The two independent stories from Pinkerton and Kennedy converted Lincoln to the possiblility of a murder plot.[20] Obviously, the intrigue played on Lincoln's mind and guarded references to assassination appeared in his Independence Hall speech the next day.[21]

It was decided that Lincoln would finish his visit to Harrisburg and then leave secretly at night instead of on the scheduled day. Pinkerton disguised the president as an old lady, placed special agents along the route, cut the telegraph wires, and allowed no other trains to travel on the line until Lincoln's safe arrival. The party reached Baltimore at 3:00 A.M. and moved surreptitiously through the streets to meet the Washington train at another terminal. When Lincoln arrived safely in the nation's capitol that morning Pinkerton resumed working for Felton.[22]

The South immediately branded the assassination scheme as absurd, and resented the "Black Republican spies" that infiltrated their section.[23] Opinion was divided in the North, as the *New York Daily Tribune* disbelieved the stories about a plot, and the *New York Times* thought them genuine.[24] The *Chicago Tribune* gave Pinkerton full credit for uncovering a real conspiracy,[25] but John Wentworth's *Chicago Democrat* touched upon what would become an enduring theme and denounced this attempt to get publicity. "How much longer will the people of this country be the dupe of these private detectives?" Wentworth asked. "If a man is dependent upon his profession for a living, as these detectives are, they must have cases; and how are they to have cases unless they get them up? There was no conspiracy at all, save in the brain of the Chicago detective."[26] Pinkerton angrily responded and accosted Mayor Wentworth on the streets of Chicago. The two old friends fought and had to be separated forcibly as the tensions between public officials and private detectives were reaffirmed.[27]

Whether a plan to kill Lincoln really existed or not is difficult to determine. No arrests were ever made, but no real crime was committed. A congressional study in January 1861 claimed that no secret organizations hostile to the United States government existed near Washington,[28] but there was angry talk circulating in the barrooms and taverns of Baltimore. Indeed, Baltimore was a tinderbox as demonstrated on April 19, 1861, when a troop of Massachusetts soldiers was attacked while marching through town. Four soldiers and nine citizens were killed in that violence. In addition, as illogical and bizarre as the scheme seemed, it was as workable as the one created by John Wilkes Booth four years later. In fact, Pinkerton, pondering that awesome tragedy, thought that the Baltimore plot was a better plan than the one successfully carried out by Booth.[29]

If Pinkerton had a lively imagination, the outbreak of the war momentarily interrupted his exploiting the Baltimore incident. Lincoln had been president little over a month when the Charleston, South Carolina, cannons opened fire on Fort Sumter. Hellish as it was, the war provided tremendous opportunities for detective work. Agents had to be sent behind enemy lines for information, and Confederate spies had to be exposed. There was fraud and corruption at home as wartime needs stimulated the growth of industry. Contractors flooded Washington, hoping to supply the army with the tools of war. The result was haste, carelessness, and criminal collusion. For example, the War Department purchased 790 guns in 1861 that had been condemned years before the war started. Brooks Brothers supplied 12,000 shoddy uniforms, many of which had no pockets, that deteriorated faster than the Union army at Bull Run. A St. Louis contractor received $151,000 for the construction of fortifications that actually were built by the army. In 1861 a board of survey found only 76 out of 411 cavalry horses sent from St. Louis fit for service.[30] Many undoubtedly found their way into mess kitchens.

There was also the problem of the bounty jumper. At the beginning of the war soldiers were recruited in a burst of patriotism at mass meetings. As the war lengthened, however, enthusiasm shortened and incentives were used to stimulate enlistment. In May 1861, the War Department offered $100 to all three-year volunteers, and by the end of the war the government had expended $300,223,500 to induce enlistment. Hundreds of soldiers joined, collected the $100 bounty, deserted, and then reenlisted somewhere else for another bounty.[31] One patriot confessed he left the army thirty-two times to collect additional bounties. Provost Marshall Gen. James Barraet Fry, director of the Civil War drafts, felt the bounty system was the chief cause of the 268,000 desertions during the war.[32] In short, the government needed a police system to cope with the problems of war.

The federal government had no central police service in 1861, and Gen. Winfield Scott lamented that there were insufficient funds to even hire detectives. City police chiefs were asked to help apprehend bounty jumpers, and different cabinet officials hired their own detectives to investigate fraud. Intelligence gathering, however, was left to the commanders of the individual military departments, and Gen. George McClellan led the way by using his close friend Allan Pinkerton.[33]

McClellan had received an excellent education at the University of Pennsylvania and West Point. He served in the Mexican War and then taught at the Military Academy until 1853 when he headed an exploration party to the Pacific Northwest. In 1855 he went to Europe as an observer of the Crimean War, and was impressed with the military intelligence organizations he saw there. When he returned to the United States he left the army to serve as engineer and vice president of the Illinois Central Railroad where a deep friendship between him and Pinkerton developed. In September 1860, he became president of the Ohio and Mississippi Railroad until Governor Dennison asked him to lead the Ohio state volunteers in April 1861.[34]

In that same month Pinkerton wrote to President Lincoln offering to uncover traitors and deliver secret dispatches. N. B. Judd, a close friend to both Lincoln and Pinkerton, felt that Pinkerton would be invaluable to a president who was "surrounded ... by traitors."[35] But before Lincoln could act, McClellan called his old friend to form a military secret service, and Pinkerton moved his headquarters to Cincinnati in May 1861.[36] McClellan had some minor successes in the West Virginia area and was called to Washington on July 22 to relieve Gen. Irvin McDowell after the fiasco at Bull Run. McClellan, at first, headed the division of the Potomac and then in November took General Scott's place as general-in-chief. Pinkerton remained in Cincinnati because his men were spread throughout Kentucky, but McClellan asked the detective to be ready to move on short notice in case his services were needed in the East.[37] In August 1861, Pinkerton moved his operations to Washington and commanded the secret service until McClellan was relieved in November 1862.

Pinkerton had two wartime duties to perform: investigating suspicious people within the Union territory and gathering information from behind Confederate lines. Both endeavors, he believed, required the strictest secrecy, and he even changed his name to E. J. Allen because Pinkerton was "so well known that it had grown to be a sort of synonym for detective."[38]

On the homefront Pinkerton operatives uncovered a Chicago firm swindling the government on a beef contract.[39] They discovered large quantities of government goods being smuggled out of Washington for sale to private parties.[40] In July 1861, Pinkerton notified Lincoln that two southern agents, Butler King and William L. Yancey, were traveling through the North. King and Yancey were part of a Confederate delegation, including Pierre A. Rost and A. Dudley Mann, who were trying to get diplomatic recognition from England. Pinkerton suggested that the two Confederates be apprehended and held as hostages, but Lincoln, feeling the arrests would win English sympathies, refused.[41] A Washington doctor, named Lee, was investigated and reported to be a southern sympathizer.[42] Probably one of the more spectacular cases was that of Rose Greenhow.

Assistant Secretary of War Thomas A. Scott, future president of the Pennsylvania Railroad, assigned Pinkerton to spy on Rose

Greenhow in August 1861. She was a wealthy widow suspected of intriguing for the South, and Pinkerton caught her soliciting secret information from a Union army officer on August 23. She was arrested and imprisoned for ten months in her own home—now dubbed "Fort Greenhow"—along with several "ladies of fashion" suspected of southern sympathies. Later she was sent to the South where she wrote about her experiences and concluded that the federal government had made rapid strides towards despotism. Pinkerton's detective services figured prominently in that conclusion.[43]

The Greenhow case also pointed to the growing problems between Pinkerton and Lincoln. When Greenhow was exiled rather than hanged, Pinkerton grew disillusioned with the leniency of the administration. Likewise, Lincoln was increasingly embarrassed by the detective's techniques. For example, when Pinkerton followed the officer who passed information to Greenhow, he was arrested himself for suspicious conduct and had to use influence to get released. More important, Pinkerton was thoroughly loyal to McClellan, and his feelings for Lincoln were in direct proportion to the president's confidence in the general. Pinkerton frequently spied on the administration and fed gossipy political news to his general.[44] Consequently, many were anxious for Pinkerton to leave Washington and take the field when McClellan's army was ready for battle.

Determining enemy troop strength was a difficult task that was magnified by Pinkerton's lack of military experience. From Cincinnati and Washington Pinkerton sent his operatives throughout the South in search of information. To secrecy was added the use of disguises and the playing of roles, a technique already begun with the various employee testing programs in the late 1850s. Carrie Lawton and John Scobell, a black operative, lived in Richmond as a southern lady and groom and revealed evidence of large troop movements. After several months they were discovered and made a dramatic midnight flight to Union lines. Pinkerton occasionally assumed the role of a southerner and traveled in Kentucky and Tennessee. Operative Price Lewis acted the part of an English lord until he was captured and purchased his freedom by exposing the Pinkerton system in the South. The most famous Pinkerton spy, Timothy Webster, posed as a secessionist from Baltimore and won the confidence of several Confederate leaders before he was exposed by Price Lewis, arrested in Richmond, and hanged as a spy.[45]

Unfortunately, the operative was only one source of information.

Runaway slaves, rebel deserters, and refugees were also quizzed, and Pinkerton uncritically trusted all information he received. In November 1861 the detective reported that 126,000 enemy soldiers were in Virginia, and concern for the safety of Washington precluded any aggressive campaign.[46] In April 1862, McClellan began his peninsular campaign to take Richmond. The Confererate capital was defended by about 85,000 men, but Pinkerton estimated that number at 180,000.[47] On May 3 McClellan believed that between 100,000 and 120,000 enemy faced him, when there were actually 60,000. In June, Pinkerton estimated enemy strength at 200.000 when it was really but half that.[48] In short, Pinkerton consistently — overestimated enemy numbers and contributed significantly to McClellan's inherent "slows."[49] Many of McClellan's staff grew critical of Pinkerton's work, and one officer, Jacob Dolson Cox, remembered in 1900 that his contempt for all spies and detectives dated from the Civil War.[50] After Antietam, in September 1862, McClellan was relieved of his command. Pinkerton felt McClellan was treated unjustly by conniving politicians, and he resigned the Secret Service — in protest.

The war was a profitable enterprise for Pinkerton, as he earned $38,567 from the government between September 1861 and November 1862.[51] Additional monies were made in 1863–1864 when the federal government employed the Pinkerton agency to work in New Orleans. Numerous civil suits were being brought against the United States government as a result of the military occupation of Louisiana. These civil claims needed to be investigated by Pinkerton. Later, in a confessional letter to one of his sons, Pinkerton admitted that before the war he was poor and sick, but after McClellan put him in charge of the Secret Service, he "ammassed considerable money, which was all invested in property of one kind or the other in Chicago."[52] He also gained administrative experience in establishing spying and information gathering services. But by operating under a *nom de plume,* Pinkerton forfeited some valuable publicity, and many people did not equate E. J. Allen with Allan Pinkerton. After Lincoln's assassination, Pinkerton lamented to his good friend, Samuel Morse Felton, that

L. C. Baker head of the Secret Service has been appointed Brig. General for losing the life of Abraham Lincoln, while I have not even received so much as the merest acknowledgement for saving his life.[53]

After the war, Pinkerton was a private businessman with two new offices in New York and Philadelphia. He had been a member of the government police system for about two years and had considerable exposure to the elite network of business leaders who became military leaders, and military leaders who became postwar business leaders. In both cases, his fortunes moved along due to acquaintanceship with these interlocking elite systems. The historic development seemed natural: a prewar spy entrepeneur became a wartime spy pioneer then a postwar domestic spy administrator as the testing of employee honesty on a national basis became increasingly important.

Employee theft expanded with the railroad and express industry in the 1860s and provided private detectives with a major source of revenue. Line crews pilfered equipment and maintenance men took bribes to purchase higher priced goods. But it was the conductor who remained suspect when it came to stealing thousands of dollars in systematic thievery.[54] In the summer of 1863, while Pinkerton was in the military, George Bangs supervised the agency's domestic activities by running eighty-two tests on the Philadelphia and Reading Railroad. It was reported that many conductors pocketed fares from tickets they sold on the trains and never recorded the transactions. Others failed to cancel tickets purchased by passengers at terminals and gave them to an outside party to resell. Only $1,690 of the $2,476 (under 50 percent) collected by conductors during the testing period was given to the company. Due to Bang's investigations, one conductor, Frederick P. Hill, went to prison for a year, and several others quickly resigned their positions. Three years later, in 1866, a similar test on the same railroad revealed that there was only a 6 percent loss due to conductor stealing.[55] In 1867, the Philadelphia and Erie Railroad, suspicious of the "expensive habits of some of the conductors," arranged for a Pinkerton test, and one conductor, John Van Daniker, was charged with embezzlement. He was acquitted.[56]

In the beginning, for educational and promotional purposes, Pinkerton published the results of these tests and distributed them to the entire railroad establishment. Other lines continued to be victimized, and in 1870, the Pinkerton agency reported that one railroad lost 56 percent of its passengers revenue from conductor dishonesty, while three others lost over 40 percent.[57] The need for Pinkerton spotters seemed obvious, and by 1871 the entire six man detective force in the Chicago office was testing railroad employees.

This was true also of the six Pinkerton operatives in Philadelphia and the ten in New York.[58] By 1870, with the exception of the Protective Patrol in Chicago, Pinkerton's agency was solely concerned with spying upon employees. In the 1870s the purpose of the testing program shifted slightly. The true test, determining the honesty and dishonesty of employees, diminished as workers became alert to the spotter, a derisive term applied to the operative. But the test remained important to managers, less for capturing criminals than deterring criminal activity. The possibility of a test was as threatening as its reality. The test and the Pinkerton man remained part of a program of managerial control.[59]

An increasing number of private detectives appeared as competition. New York City, for example, had three "independent" policemen in 1855; fifteen years later there were nineteen men, besides ten Pinkerton operatives, all claiming detection as their profession.[60] When Bangs opened the New York office, he found William H. Scott, an ex-Pinkerton operative, had already established a small business for protecting the local express companies.[61] In Chicago several agencies along the Cyrus Bradley pattern opened. There was even some concern over the large fees these competing agencies charged.[62] William S. Beaubein organized the Citizen's Preventive Police in September 1861. John Hamblen's Merchant Police and Cornelius O'Callaghan's Private Protective Police were established by the end of the decade. But these agencies, like those in New York City, provided a minimal detective service.[63] Only one agency, William Turtle's misnamed Chicago Police and Insurance Bureau, resembled Pinkerton's business in geographical scope. As police chief, Turtle had been influenced by Pinkerton and often called upon the private detective to aid the city police. He established his agency in 1866 and won national fame for breaking up several insurance fraud conspiracies. It became "one of the largest and most powerful organizations of the kind in the world."[64]

As competition increased, Pinkerton needed favorable publicity. The publication of Benson J. Lossing's popular history of the Civil War in 1866 provided something of a springboard. In Lossing's book, a letter from Lincoln crediting Pinkerton for escorting the president to Washington during the Baltimore assassination plot was printed.[65] Immediately, John A. Kennedy, superintendent of the New York Metropolitan Police, wrote Lossing and complained that Pinkerton was glorified at Kennedy's expense. Kennedy and Walling wanted a share of glory for their part in the Baltimore plot revelations. Kennedy's letter was published in the *New York Times,* and Pinkerton was angered that the New York policeman tried "to steal the honors which belong to others and do not apply to himself."[66] The Chicago detective felt that publicity-hungry persons tampered and falsified history for their own purposes, and he proposed to publish his own account of the Baltimore plot. After soliciting letters from friends and those connected with Lincoln's secret arrival in Washington, Pinkerton compiled, in 1866, *The History and Evidence of the Passage of Abraham Lincoln From Harrisburg, Pa., to Washington, D.C., on the 22nd and 23rd of February, 1861.* This started a writing career that encompassed fifteen volumes in fifteen years. From then on, the public relation aspects of his profession took on more of Pinkerton's energies. Successfully defending himself on the Baltimore assassination matter, gave Pinkerton confidence

> The year 1868 has been marked by a determined fight against us: at the close of that year that fight still continues, but I tremble not before it. I feel no power on earth is able to crush me; no power in heaven or hell can influence me when I know I am right. I think it cannot be long ere our enemies flee—that they are vanquished; it cannot be long if we preserve in the right and they are continually in the wrong. . . . All we have to do is to manage our own affairs with discretion, with honor, and integrity and we must and shall win.[67]

He also became a bitter enemy of Kennedy.[68]

Tension between Pinkerton and the New York police predated the publication of *History and Evidence.* It began in November 1865 with the opening of the New York office of the Pinkerton National Detective Agency, which offered an alternative to those dissatisfied with public police services at a time when the New York police were being severely tried by the postwar conditions. It seemed as if the stage was set for a replay of the Bradley-Wentworth fracas, but this time in New York City. Contemporaries felt that a crime wave would surely follow the end of the conflict. The demoralizing influences of the war seemed clear, as the army camp was considered a schoolground of corruption. Country boys away from home for the first time had been easy victims, as well as sometimes eager students, of the criminally inclined. Swearing, drinking, prostitution, gambling, and stealing had been rampant, with comrades being victimized as readily as the enemy. One Wisconsin soldier wrote that

stealing is the most common practice in the army.... It will be a great wonder, indeed if the army does not turn out hundreds of men perfectly irresponsible and thievish, not to speak of uncontrollable licentiousness, who before the war were not bad men.[69]

New Yorkers readily agreed with the Wisconsin soldier as crime increased in 1864. Large numbers of people had become accustomed to the trappings, technologies, and skills of war. Sometimes, it seemed, selfish ends could be achieved more easily by violent means. One concerned newspaper editor felt that

our columns day after day, show that we are either getting a terrible influx of population from among the dangerous classes of other communities, or that we are breeding among ourselves a criminal population unprecedented, as to its number and daring in the annals of the city.[70]

Robbery became a science as elaborate tools were purchased from London criminals, and a battle between safe-makers and safe-breakers occurred. Crowded conditions in the city, especially on the street cars, provided a rich harvest for the estimated army of 3,000 professional pickpockets. In fact, the frequency of pickpocket activity prompted the *New York Times* in 1866 to publish several articles warning the public of the techniques of the criminals, and in August the police put eighty policemen on temporary duty as plainclothesmen to mingle in the crowds.[71]

There were twenty regular police detectives in New York by 1869, though the number occasionally tripled when particular criminal threats forced the temporary assignment of patrolmen to plainclothes duty. Many New Yorkers, especially those controlling the newspapers, considered the city detective system as obnoxious as the criminals. Regular uniformed police were judged more beneficial because "the very secrecy with which the detective officer works forms a defense against any shortcomings of his own." Besides visibility, the patrolman still basked in praise for his peace-keeping duty during the draft riots of 1863. Inefficiency was one shortcoming; statistics proved that 20 percent of all murders in New York between 1859 and 1869 went unsolved. During the robbery craze of 1866, the detectives, having recovered only small amounts of the booty, were suspected as being in league with the thieves. As in the past, the reward system was condemned, and the operations of the detective police "revealed something very closely resembling the compounding of a felony."[72]

Concern for crime inspired a new literature at this time, one that described the low life of the city. Mathew Hale Smith's *Sunshine and Shadow in New York* and Edward Winslow Martin's *Secrets of the Great City* appeared in 1868. James D. McCabb's *Lights and Shadows of New York Life* was published four years later. The purpose was to alert respectable citizens to the crime problem, but, more suggestive, was an obvious sense of wonder over the contradictions growing in the postwar city. The most perceptive observer of these contradictions was Edward Crapsey, a police reporter for *Galaxy Magazine,* whose musings would be compiled into a book, *The Nether Side of New York,* in 1872. Crapsey, reflecting on the postwar period, felt there never had been "a time in the history of any people when public morality had sunk so low as during those disgraceful years in the imperial city." New York police detectives were too well known by the underworld and only acted as "go-betweens" for thieves and victims. After discussing the question why thieves prosper, Crapsey concluded that the first step to be taken was eradication of the existing detective system.[73]

Boss William Tweed, certainly one reason for Crapsey's disgust over New York political corruption, blamed the condition of the police and crime problems on the concept of state control. Tweed, espousing home-rule arguments, sought to restore police jurisdiction, which had been lost during the Fernando Wood era, to city politics. Many more simply blamed superintendent John "King" Kennedy for the inadequacies of law enforcement.

George H. Bangs, the New York superintendent of Pinkerton's, hoped to use the situation to replace Kennedy with Pinkerton. Bangs sent Pinkerton a copy of the metropolitan police manual and assured him that holding a public police office would not interfere with the private police business.[74] Pinkerton did not discourage Bangs. Throughout the winter and spring of 1869, Bangs solicited political support from local express and railroad leaders, made overtures to the *New York Sun* for friendly publicity, and waited for the right moments to "show up Kennedy whenever such could be done."[75] New York police inspector Dilks told Crapsey that to most New York reporters "the object was to write Kennedy down, and write Pinkerton up with the view of a change."[76] But it all seemed too political. Tweed's Democrats won both houses of the state legislature and replaced the metropolitan with a municipal system in 1870. After more than a decade, New York gained complete control of its police force once more. Police leadership was fragmented under the Tweed ring with captains autocratically ruling their precinct kingdoms. This kind of police decentralization characterized much of the nineteenth century. There was no place for a strong police superintendent or chief.[77] Pinkerton's managerial style simply would not fit. Then in the early 1870s the Tweed ring crumbled into scandalous rubble.

Pinkerton, remembering General McClellan as a victim of politicians, wanted to avoid all encounters that restricted his independence. Bangs expressed official agency philosophy on the matter in 1869 to one of Pinkerton's sons. "While it is desirable that we should keep our relations with them [the city police] as pleasant as possible, and that we should retain the control which we have had, yet in doing so we should not renounce any of our General Principles."[78] One of those principles was that the agency was an "individual and private enterprise" free from governmental authority and restraint. The McClellan-Lincoln tensions coupled with the Bradley-Wentworth battles of five years earlier suggested that politics and police did not mix. Tweed's New York police proved the point.

Influenced by Pinkerton's exposure to military and business leaders, the agency's administrative philosophy crystalized in the immediate postwar period. In 1875 Bangs was asked by a reporter if the standards of control and honesty espoused by the Pinkerton agency could be applicable to the public police. Bangs, the number two man in the agency, felt the principles of honesty were always desirable, but that it was "doubtful if a vast machine, subject to the perturbations of politics, [could] ever be made to act with the same accuracy that is obtainable in a narrower sphere where one intelligence and one will make themselves felt arbitrarily in every department."[79]

With the insight gained from the Civil War experience, Pinkerton officials felt that a strong field general free from politics was the answer to the weak, politically dominated city police systems. Again, in 1875, Pinkerton justified his style of detective work with military rhetoric.

The individual detective of former days has passed away, or, if he exists, has become corrupt. In order to capture the perpetrators of crime in this immense country, peopled by every nationality on the globe, it has become necessary to establish large agencies, conducted with the most perfect system. In tracing criminals, the manager of an agency, like the general of an army, lays out the plans and selects the men to carry them out; sometimes, in important matters, going to the field of operations to direct in person, but generally giving his instructions from the main office, where he has hundreds of cases to look after at a time.[80]

After the war, Pinkerton thought of himself as a general at the head of an army warring on crime. By the 1870s the business correspondence was increasingly sprinkled with cryptograms. Operatives' anonymity was maintained by using their initials; particularly sensitive letters were completely in code.[81] Pinkerton had transferred his wartime skills to his peacetime business. Such coded letters may have originated during the war, but they were also a response to the especially sensitive work he was doing—spying on employees.

By the end of the 1860s, Pinkerton's fortunes were tied to the railroad and express industry. The young Chartist and abolitionist radical had become a fifty-year-old businessman. In the late 1870s he would find new causes to follow and proclaim, but the postwar years was the time for detective business growth and administration. A cerebral stroke laid him low in 1869, but that did not stop Pinkerton for long. In 1870, he wrote Salmon Chase, who had just suffered from a stroke, that "I was considered almost incurable. I had lost my speech and power was. . . . gone. Now, I can speak very well but have got to be slow and cautious. I walk every day eight, ten, and twelve miles."[82] Demand for his services had increased in the immediate postwar period and business flourished. His public task was chasing criminals, but his private and more important function was checking and regulating employee honesty. He was a managerial tool to control railroad and express employees. As his business grew it was obvious that, like any good field general, he had to control his own employees—the Pinkerton men.

CHAPTER 3

Pinkerton and the Pinkerton Men:
The Detective as Administrator

THE IMMEDIATE FLUSH of postwar prosperity encouraged Pinkerton to open two new offices; one in New York started business in November 1865 and another in Philadelpha did so in May 1866. By 1870 he supervised over twenty detectives and some sixty watchmen. The vagaries of business expansion and the growth of his own business as well as that of his clients became a main preoccupation for a decade after the Civil War. Tied so closely to the business elites, he had easily adopted similar world views and life styles. Now, like other business leaders, he became concerned with similar problems of internal management. Police personnel were called officers (connoting "official") or patrolmen (referring to work function). Pinkerton's detectives, on the other hand, were named operatives. That word was used frequently in nineteenth century industry. An operative was someone who operated a machine in a factory. Skill was required, but, nontheless, the person was merely a cog in a process, a process that transcended the individual. By naming his men operatives and himself the "principal," Pinkerton declared his affiliation to the business world and made statements on his own administrative philosophy.

After his death the agency experienced another spurt of growth, but the period between 1865 and 1875 was a time for consolidating gains and confronting problems of management due to the first phase of growth. By now Pinkerton's reputation as America's most notable detective was firm, but, in reality, he was becoming a manager of detectives. Rapid economic growth prompted a need that in turn stimulated and sustained Pinkerton's growth. His own employees, who had sensitive jobs that frequently took them beyond Pinkerton's direct control, now needed close supervision.

The public police were taking a different course. City police systems in the late 1860s and early 1870s were establishing patterns of decentralization. Power dispersed to mid-level administrators in their precincts or districts. Captains and lieutenants became satraps, and patrolmen wielded uncommonly powerful discretion. Police chiefs were less powerful than their subordinates. It was during this period of decentralization of the public police that Pinkerton emphasized the centralization of his business. Detective administration emerged as important as detection itself for Allan Pinkerton.[1]

The agency was very small at first. Agency lore claimed that Pinkerton started his business in 1851. Between 1851 and 1855, Pinkerton was a troubleshooter; he was an occasional agent for the Treasury Department, a special agent for the Post Office Department, a deputy sheriff for Cook County, and a sometime agent for the railroads. He was a loner, handling all of his cases personally. His career was more firmly nailed down with the creation of the North West Police Agency in 1855. For the first year Pinkerton had a partner, an attorney named Edward A. Rucker, a valuable asset when operatives made their first important accusation and courtroom testimony in the Oscar Caldwell affair. That partnership lasted only one year, after which Rucker left to follow in his father's footsteps and became a judge. Four operatives—James Yost, B. F. Benedict, Samuel Bridgeman, and Peter West—worked the trains and discovered Caldwell's crimes in the summer of 1855. Yost was a clerk for Rucker's father and earned extra money working for Pinkerton. Samuel Bridgeman had been a policeman in New York, as Benedict had been in Buffalo. Peter West, a painter, had already left the agency by the time of the Caldwell trial.[2]

After Rucker's departure in 1856, Pinkerton hired three assistants who figured importantly in the early organization. Kate Warne convinced Pinkerton, who probably had an eye for females anyway, that women could be useful spies on the trains. By 1860, Warne superintended a small number of women operatives in Chicago, even acting in the capacity of a dormitory keeper for the ladies. Women were an important part of the detective agency throughout the founder's life. On several occasions critics, even within his own family, claimed that Pinkerton kept concubines and was having a love affair with Warne.[3] After his death women vanished from the agency, probably because of the overt policies of his sons, who suspected their father's philandering. George H. Bangs and Timothy Webster were guards at New York's Crystal Palace in 1856. Bangs had been a reporter for his father's newspaper, the *New York Era,* before turning to police work. In time he became general superintendent of the agency. His son, George D. Bangs, assumed the same position in the 1880s, making two generations of the family in the agency hierarchy. Bangs and his son, neither of whom had any real detective experience or leanings, represented the beginnings of the professional managerial class in the agency. Webster, an English immigrant, came to America in 1833 and, because he lacked political influence, failed to enter the city police department. Along with George H. Bangs, Webster moved to Chicago to be a Pinkerton man. During the Civil War, Webster became the agency's first martyr. In a familial gesture, which characterized the early days of the agency, Webster's remains were interred in Pinkerton's burial plot at Chicago's Graceland Cemetary.[4] George H. Bangs and Warne were later buried there too.

Prerequisites for being a detective in the nineteenth century were vague and the training was informal. Honesty and morality, from the beginning, were important. Pinkerton was certain that common sense, rather than any mysterious powers, made the good detective, so operatives came from a variety of backgrounds. William Norris bought and sold produce in Chicago before he joined the agency in 1858. H. K. Knipe was a bootmaker before the war. Knipe was one of Pinkerton's military secret service spies and continued as detective after Appomatox. Before joining the agency in 1863, John Bauer, an immigrant from Germany, had been a wine merchant. T. A. Holland migrated from England and became a clerk for the Rochester police force before joining Pinkerton in 1863.

As the new offices opened, recruitment became even more important. In New York, the editor of the *Police Gazette,* an ex-police chief, George Matsell, suggested men to George H. Bangs, as did personal and business friends of Pinkerton. The largest recruitment, however, grew out of the December 21, 1865 advertisement in the *New York Herald Tribune* for "men of all Professions and Trades. To engage in an enterprise out of the city. . . ."[5] R. H. Ackerman was a prize, it was felt, because he previously worked as a brakeman for the Illinois Central. Operative O. R. Willard was a U.S. tax commissioner, and Thomas McDonald was a schoolmaster before becoming a detective. Theodore Quakenbush had been a stencil cutter, as well as a seventeen year old resident of a reform school, before he started testing conductors.[6]

One promising operative, S. McNair, eventually was considered for the superintendent of the Philadelphia office. In 1872 McNair was thirty-six years old and a father of seven children. His father had been a member of Congress and young McNair had many influential friends. Between 1854 and 1861, he was a governmental clerk but went south during the war and had a grocery business in Richmond. After the war he was a ticket agent for the Richmond-Danville Railroad then moved to New York to work on the Long Island line before joining Pinkerton's. George H. Bangs was impressed and thought McNair "as capable a man as we have had in the institution for a long time."[7] Operative McNair did not get the Philadelphia post. Instead it went to Benjamin Franklin, who had been chief of detectives in the Philadelphia police during the war. Simply put, Franklin's connections in Philadelphia and his tested administrative abilities seemed more advantageous for the agency. This selection was a calculated gamble too. Franklin had been dismissed from the police department because of a drinking problem, a problem that led to his dismissal from Pinkerton's in 1879.[8] Shortly after Franklin's selection, McNair resigned.

Employment was fluid; operatives came and went with regularity. Pinkerton provided work, it seems, for those caught between jobs or those wanting to test out a new vocation. F. H. Reeves, a bartender, worked twelve weeks as a Pinkerton before moving to Brooklyn to open a hotel. Before returning to his carpentry trade, H. T. Nash was a Pinkerton for six months. Leather cutter James P. Lloyd flirted with detective work before going on to open an advertising firm.[9] Wives of many operatives supplemented family income by occasionally spying on conductors. Mrs. Hunt, who worked out of the New York office, made it clear that she was only working to make enough money to open a dress pattern business.[10] Numerous operatives used the Pinkerton experience as preparation for a career in public police departments. Horace M. Elliott worked for Pinkerton in Chicago until Cyrus Bradley appointed him to the newly created police detective bureau in 1861. Owen Bowen came to Chicago from Ireland in 1867. Between 1868 and 1873 he was a Pinkerton detective and then joined the Chicago police detectives in

1874. Another Irish immigrant, Patrick Tyrrell, after service with Pinkerton during the war, came to Chicago in 1869. After two years testing conductors he joined the police department.[11] In Philadelphia, William Hulfish was a Pinkerton from 1869, until joining that city's police detectives in 1875. One of his comrades, James Tate, was a detective for the Philadelphia police in 1876, resigned to be a Pinkerton for two years, and then returned to the police department in 1879.[12]

One operative, Thomas E. Lonergan, had an interesting career which charted the occupational fluidity of the early detective. Born in Lockport, Illinois, in 1844, his education at Notre Dame was interrupted by the Civil War. After a short time as a postal clerk in Chicago, he joined Pinkerton's staff. He moved up the hierarchy quickly, and by 1866 he was a trusted aid to George H. Bangs in setting up the New York and Philadelphia offices. In 1867 Lonergan left the agency and became the editor of the *New York Era* and a professor of military tactics at the People's College of New York. After a year he returned to Chicago to be an editor for the *Chicago Republican* before becoming chief operative in the Western Division of the U.S. Secret Service under H. C. Whitley.[13]

Low pay might account for some turnovers. The operative's paycheck in New York, for example, ranged between thirteen and sixteen dollars per week at a time when the city detectives were making twenty dollars per week plus a percentage of the reward money.[14] Ten years later, though, in 1875, George H. Bangs claimed that the Pinkerton operative made more in salary than the New York police detective.[15] Pinkerton feared the corrupting influences of "blood money" and made it a cardinal rule to refuse all rewards. Some of the turnover was due to the standards set up by Pinkerton for employee behavior and performance. Many left simply because they were asked to leave! In addition, as the agency became more firmly attached and dependent upon the business establishment, which at this time was the railroad and express industries, the fluctuations of the economy threatened layoffs. Clearly, the agency was in flux, and Pinkerton wanted to be in better control and at the same time project an image of professionalism to clients and public alike.

This sharp increase in the number of employees came at a time when it was widely held that it took a thief to catch a thief. Pinkerton, thus, had two tasks to consider. One, was to create a favorable, and to Pinkerton's way of thinking, a correct public understanding of private detectives in American society. In short, he needed to professionalize the private detective industry by articulating an appropriate philosophy for private detectives and by creating proper role models for potential detective entrepreneuers. Second, though it is linked to the above, was to professionalize the occupation itself. He needed to educate his own operatives as to proper detective work. In any vocation, managers need standards by which to make decisions as to good or poor work performance, but in a new vocation, especially such a controversial one as private detection was becoming after the Civil War, workers needed to be given guidelines for proper action. They needed concrete rules not only as to task, but also as to behavior.

As early as 1864 Pinkerton was distributing his *Special Rules and Instructions to be Observed in Testing Conductors*. Operatives must be so circumspect that their actions and motives could never be questioned. They were never to speak to other operatives, never to frequent hotels where railroadmen congregate, or even go into saloons. As pseudo-passengers, they were to watch the conductor collect and stamp tickets. To avoid suspicion, long and detailed reports were made from memory, noting the number of passengers in the car, when they got on and off the train, how much fare they paid, and the personal conduct of the employee.[16] Many railroad executives were already suspicious of their workers, a suspicion that increased in the 1880s, and employees were discharged on the flimsiest of information. So the operative's report became very important. How much of it was fact or fiction depended upon the skill and honesty of the operative and the philosophy of the agency.

Pinkerton elaborated his managerial philosophy and tried to set the perimeters of operative behavior in 1867 with the publication of the *General Principles of Pinkerton's National Police Agency*. All employees were required to study the pamphlet, and additional reprints were made in 1869 and 1873. An agency official, at this early time one of the superintendents, would review the *General Principles* with the new operative and then supervise the early reports of the employee.[17] Contrary to prevailing attitudes that it takes a thief to catch a thief, "the profession of the detective is a high and honorable calling," he told his operatives. "Few Professions excell it."[18] The possibility that "spotters" were fabricating scare reports to reaffirm the implicit suspicions held by management apparently concerned Pinkerton and he counselled that

The Detective must, in every instance, report everything which is favorable to the suspected party, as well as everything which may be against him. The object of every investigation made by this Agency, is to come at the whole truth, in all the cases that are submitted to it. There must be no endeavoring, therefore, to over-color or exaggerate anything against any particular individual, whatever the suspicion may be against him.[19]

Sometimes such high-minded principles got in the way of task efficiency. Management suspected dishonesty or they would not have hired the private detective in the first place. The danger of self-fulfilling prophecy was always present, and, on occasion—in the name of operational shortcuts, careless mistakes, or personal status seeking—the operative found dishonesty where it might not actually exist.

Detectives, Pinkerton declared, fought society's enemies with the tools of deception and secrecy. In fact, secrecy was the prime condition of detective skill; it was the main strength the operative had beyond that of an ordinary man. Customers were never to see the operative, as all business arrangements were to go through the superintendent. Too much exposure made the operative useless and the agency ineffectual, it was believed. Such devices and procedures were delicate and vulnerable issues in a society that at least gave lip service to the canon of honesty and openness. All businesses, of course, did cloud some activities in secrecy, but one dedicated to that principle could expect considerable criticisms. "Moralists may question whether this be strictly right," he observed, "but it is a necessity in the detection of crime, and it's held by the Agency that the ends being the accomplishment of justice, they justify the means used."[20]

The notion that the constant association between detectives and criminals had a corrupting influence was denied. Crime was foreign to human nature and was analogous to a disease that infected those with weak resistence, thought Pinkerton. Exposure to the seamier life was not dangerous to those who cultivated a "moral power." In order to develop and insure this moral power—to be wholesome and honest—certain restraints and guidelines were placed upon the operative. Excessive drinking was prohibited unless it was in the line of duty. Exorbitant expenditures of money were regulated. Every employee made daily written reports of all expenditures of time and money whether on duty or not, a policy that superintendent George H. Bangs felt to be the best possible safeguard against employee dishonesty.[21] Since all employees were on call seven days a week, the line between professional life and private life was blurred. What was done with leisure time was a reflection of personal character and an indication of what might be done during working time. Therefore, each operative served a trial period while his character and work habits were scrupulously checked. After that, George H. Bangs declared in an interview later, "we . . . pay him liberally, and stand by him. He can find no better friend than his employer."[22]

Pinkerton was not only adopting the life style but also the managerial philosophy of those classes he represented—America's business leadership.[23] There was a danger, of course, that ambiguity and hypocracy might result if the operational tasks of the institution were in tension with the stated philosophy. Mixed messages were already being sent to the general public, a problem which Pinkerton would try to rectify later. Equally dangerous was that Pinkerton employees might create a dichotomy between the agency philosophy and its operational performance. Allan Pinkerton and his sons, for example, were hardly teetotalers, and like many reformed drinkers, they became obsessed over the dangers of intemperance. In 1874 Pinkerton confessed to his youngest son, Robert, that until forty years old, "I used to take a drop now and then, making me cross, and I had trouble with everybody.[24] William Pinkerton, the founder's eldest son, was known for his social life, and Pinkerton worried about "Willie's" excessive drinking.[25] Saloons and theaters, he believed, were not only a waste of time, but dangerous to one's character as well. At the same time, in one of Pinkerton's typical contradictions, William was encouraged to become educated about Chicago's criminal classes by frequenting The Store, the notorious saloon and gambling house of Mike McDonald.[26]

The stated policy was that those suspected of drinking or dishonesty were to be quickly dismissed. But exceptions were sometimes made. Henry E. Thayer, superintendent of the Philadelphia office in 1869, drank to excess. He had already angered George H. Bangs because of his unprofessional flippant style of business correspondence.[27] Intemperance, it was believed, kept Thayer from repaying a loan to Pinkerton, but, instead of dismissal, his salary was controlled by the office bookkeeper. Pinkerton got his money and retained a capable detective administrator for a time.[28] The competent administrator of the Protective Patrol in Chicago, Captain Fitzgerald, was excellent when sober, but, according to Pinkerton, "everyday, drinking, drinking, drinking."[29] In 1875 the trusted

George H. Bangs went on a drinking spree that embarrassed Pinkerton and prompted him to scold, "Oh! Shame, Shame! That any of my officers should get so debased as to drink whiskey to steady his nerves. The Agency is disgraced by such doings, and drinking to any extent will drag down any man."[30] Bangs had been discovered roaming the streets of Philadelphia at 9:00 A.M., stone drunk. "Mr. Bangs, you know very well how I adhere to the rule that no drunkard shall be employed in this Agency, but how does it look to see the General Superintendent drunk(?)"[31] Thayer, who had been drinking with Bangs, was discharged at last.

Dishonest operatives, especially those who had excessive expenses, were a problem, and numerous men were fired. Operatives Knapp, Ackerman—the one who had been so prized earlier, and Dempsey were fired because of excessive expenses.[32] One operative was known to be falsifying his expense account in 1870. That same person was reported going into saloons and theaters in 1873, but Pinkerton remained reluctant to fire him because he knew too much about the business.[33] Surely a disgruntled ex-operative might go to the competition and disclose the agency's secrets. The crowning embarrassment at this time was Henry Davies, the assistant superintendent to George H. Bangs in New York. Between 1870 and 1873 Davies stole $3,000 from the agency's accounts. The embezzlement-chasers had an embezzler within their ranks! Davies was discharged but quickly rehired so as to pay back the stolen money. But Davies continued to drink heavily and perplex the agency until he was finally fired a second time. The ex-Pinkerton superintendent then went off to form his own agency, but he continued to get in trouble.[34]

It looked as though the spies needed to be spied upon, and, by 1874, Pinkerton was thoroughly disgusted with all the "machinations and tricks and plans" going on in the offices.[35] Pinkerton's organization was going through the same growing pains of other businesses and was experiencing the same problems that called the agency into existence in the first place. The number of deceitful employees threatened to verify the suspicions increasingly held by the public. Strains were placed upon the management personnel—strains similar to those that perhaps drove George H. Bangs and Thayer to drink—to project a respectable image and maintain an efficient organization. Operational efficiency was clashing with idealistic pronouncements. There was a difference between the real and the ideal within Pinkerton's ranks. In 1875, the same year

George H. Bangs praised the employee-employer relations in the agency, Pinkerton wrote: "In my employ every person is watched. I hire them all on the supposition that they are honest, but it does no harm to see that they are not unduly exposed to temptation; so they are carefully watched, and rarely do they even have an opportunity to be dishonest, even were they so inclined."[36] Of course, Pinkerton did not hire outside people to check on the honesty of his own employees, but apparently internal surveillance became important. Mrs. Stanton, who took Kate Warne's place when the latter died in the early 1870s, supervised the "female department" and spied on all personnel, reporting directly to Pinkerton.[37]

In spite of occasional crises with employees, Pinkerton's testing program continued until 1872. Sluggish times occurred around 1869, a portent of the depression soon to come. Actually these were tougher times for Pinkerton than the depression itself. By then he was busy writing detective stories and investigating the Molly Maguires. Throughout the five years after the war, the Philadelphia office was in debt. Money was drained from the other offices, especially Chicago, to sustain the flagging operation in Philadelphia. Some subordinates resented this and William Pinkerton even suggested that it should be closed. Instead, Allan Pinkerton farmed out some Philadelphia operatives to New York and busied the remainder with drumming up business. George Smith, the superintendent of the Philadelphia office, got so depressed that he eventually resigned, an act that led to the hiring of Franklin in 1872.[38] The slowing down of the postwar economy plus the drains of the the Philadelphia office put the Chicago office $9,967 in debt in 1870. Many operatives passed out advertisement circulars and collected bills the next year when over $17,000 was owed the agency.[39]

Another crisis occurred at this time with the exposure of the spotter system. A successful spy system depends upon secrecy. The three embezzlement trials—Caldwell in 1855, Hill in 1864, and Van Daniker in 1867—revealed the Pinkerton spy. The Order of Railway Conductors was organized in 1868 and alerted the worker to the detective menace. Such incidents did not threaten the agency's effectiveness. Rather effectiveness was enhanced. Belief that a spy was near, but uncertain as to who it was, acted as a deterrent. It was only when the individual spotter was spotted that his effectiveness was lost. As specific operatives became known, their effectiveness ended and they were either dismissed or given other duties. Sometimes

dismissal resulted because exposure indicated poor work performance. But in November 1872, the entire spotter corps was laid open
and the test program jeopardized. Ten miles outside Jersey City,
New Jersey a spotter stuck his head out of the train window as it
crossed a bridge. A girder struck and pulled him out of the railroad
car and into the river. When he was found, the papers on his body
revealed him as a Pinkerton detective in charge of testing Erie
Railroad employees.[40] Furthermore, enough clues were evident that
representatives of the conductors' unions, in a piece of detective
work of their own, were able to locate secret Pinkerton offices. Those
who had been spied upon for seventeen years began to spy upon the
spies. Since Pinkerton offices were conspiciously placed in Chicago,
New York, and Philadelphia, two secret gathering places had been
set up for operatives to get instructions, write up reports, and rest
from their travel. Soon the Pinkerton secret office in Jersey City,
temporary homebase for all the eastern testing programs, was
found.[41] Another secret office was discovered in Dayton, Ohio, by the
aggressive railroad men.[42] George H. Bangs moved the Jersey City
office in the middle of the night, and the Dayton operatives went to
new offices somewhere in Cincinnati.[43] Agency officials realized that
they were being watched by railroad union men as much as they
were watching the conductors. After 1872 Pinkerton scaled down his
testing services. It never assumed the importance it had in the 1860s.
An ex-Pinkerton operative, Gus Thiel, even opened an agency in St.
Louis and slowly began to monopolize most of the railroad testing
programs.[44] Pinkerton remained concerned over employee loyalty
and honesty and even occasionally ran a test for an old friend, but
by mid-decade, threats of collective and conspiratorial violence out-
weighed individual acts of employee dishonest.

Times were difficult for Pinkerton, but some of the economic edge
was taken off of the recession of the early 1870s. The New York office
held its own by working on the Cuban case in 1870. Cubans revolted
against Spain in 1868, and considerable support for American intervention on behalf of the rebels occurred. President Ulysses S.
Grant's secretary of state, Hamilton Fish, tried to hold such senti-
ment in check, and Pinkerton's was hired to investigate any breach
of neutrality laws and uncover potential filibuster expeditions.[45]
Spain pacified the rebels by 1878, and the issue over Spain and Cuba
did not emerge again until the late 1890s.

The Chicago office investigated the robbery of the Third National

Bank of Baltimore. In the summer of 1872, a gang of burglars rented an office next to the bank and during the night tore down a wall and took $150,000 from the vault. This became a characteristic technique in the robbery of urban banks in the 1860s and 1870s. The case was never solved, but it did precipitate a crisis between Allan Pinkerton and his son William. William Pinkerton spent two years on the case, even travelling to Europe on an investigation, and enraged his father with his drinking and expensive socializing. Allan overlooked the invaluable contacts William made at Scotland Yard and the Sûreté, and confided to his other son Robert that Willie was "not the man that I could ever put in charge of an office."[46] The debt-ridden Philadelphia office came into its own now. Franklin solved some minor coal robberies, collected a few overdue bills, and got involved with the celebrated Charley Ross abduction case.[47] When the Philadelphia police seemed so incapable, a committee of concerned citizens collected a fund to bring the Pinkerton agency in on the case. Everyone got in everyone's way and neither Ross nor his abductors were found. The case went unsolved. More important, Franklin supervised the Philadelphia office during the Molly Maguire exposures.

The general economic slump, however, devitalized Pinkerton, and it took a crisis to bring him new zest. In October 1871, the offices of the "Vidocq of the West," as Pinkerton was called by the *New York Times,* were gutted by the Chicago fire. All of his criminal records, estimated at 400 volumes, were lost. A rare set of the *Records of the Secret Service of the Army of the Potomac,* which the government had tried to purchase earlier, were destroyed too.[48] Losses were great, but Pinkerton felt exhilarated and the tragedy seemed to yank him out of some sort of lethargy. He wrote to Salmon Chase that he was back into the habit of working on Sunday and that generally "I think I have been benefited by the fire.[49] Since the number of Chicago policemen (around 310 in total) was inadequate, Pinkerton helped police the burned district. A shoot-to-kill broadside was quickly published warning all thieves, burglars, and looters away. Pinkerton men then protected property as a massive rebuilding program began in the city.

Pinkerton rebuilt also, and within a year he wrote a good friend and boast that his new office was "one of the best any where in the United States." The appearance of success, especially in the midst of the economic slump, seemed all the more important. He described his new building in great detail.

I occupy a Building about thirty-six (36) feet by ninety-five (95) feet. It is fitted up most beautifully. The first floor is my "Preventive Watch," we now have nearly eighty men and probably by the end of the year we shall have a hundred. Right in the front of it is a spendid lamp . . . and over all is an Eye. The all seeing Eye under which are the words "We Never Sleep." On the stairway, up to our detective's room, is another beautiful lamp and that also has the inscription under the Eye, "We Never Sleep," and why friend Harvey do I say so, because as one of the force goes to bed, another one gets up. Everything is in motion and the Eye is looking after them all the time.

Upstairs is the Supt.'s office, a fine office indeed. Then comes the Gen. office of the assistant Supt., Cashier, Bookkeeper, Recording Clerk, and the Chief Clerks, all in motion. The next is the Detectives, one room for business, and one for sleeping. The next room is the Detective's Watch, for Captain and Lieutenants, during the day it is also my office for seeing that everything progresses well. The next fartherest away, where all is quiet, is my office. There I survey everything that is going on, everything must come under my supervision. . . .

Upstairs are the ladies rooms, everything will be fitted up there in fine style, but we have not got time, to do that now.[50]

The office now was not just a place of business; it was meant to be a symbolic expression of the Pinkerton style of private detectives. It was meant to be familiar and compatible to the client, the successful businessman. More importantly, it was to provide the proper businesslike atmosphere for Pinkerton employees—an orderly, logically arranged place for those whose work function took them willy-nilly across the land. The three-floor building was well lighted, replete with authoritarian symbols, and distinctly organized with both work function and office hierarchy placed in ascending importances. Pinkerton's offices were his corporate expression of detective business. Three years later, in 1875, a reporter visited the New York office. Its appearance was meant to "frown away everything but business of the most serious nature," he felt, and altogether the office and general superintendent George H. Bangs had "the dull business air of a lawyer's ante-room."[51]

Still aglow with optimism, Allan Pinkerton wrote his son William that, in spite of money problems and competition, he would win: "You see Willie my idea is never lose heart, never think a moment of giving up the ship, I am bound to go through, to sink or swim. I shall win at last."[52] Two years later, Robert, always the more businesslike son, wanted to expand and establish offices in New Orleans and San Francisco. Later such ambitions would lead to a rift between father and favorite son, but at this time, in 1874, Allan Pinkerton liked the idea and vetoed it only because there were not enough good men to superintend additional offices.[53] The very thought of expanding in the midst of the depression, which started the year before, is an indication of the personal and business enthusiasm of Pinkerton and his agency.

Shortly after the office building was completed, Pinkerton began making weekly visits to his land in Onarga, Illinois. Four thousand maple trees, five thousand evergreens, and over one hundred thousand larch trees—hence the name Larches—were planted. Larch farm was a show place, a model farm, and a visiting reporter claimed in 1882 that it had "no equal in the West, and no superior in the United States."[54] The main house, surrounded with twelve acres of lawn and laced with serpentine walks, resembled an antebellum plantation. A small fortune of paintings, mainly depicting various Civil War scenes and portraits of General McClellan, were on the walls. Pinkerton's special private place was the "Snuggery," a modest dwelling a short distance from the house. Here he met with old friends and trusted subordinates to unwind. Its walls were covered with large canvas murals highlighting events in Scottish history. The entire farm looked like a self-contained village or manor with an additional twenty-four out-buildings for the ten to twenty caretakers who lived there year round. Pinkerton could, and frequently did, count himself as a successful man, a Scottish nobleman transplanted to the prairies of Illinois.

Pinkerton's business continued to decrease, but his optimism did not. Perhaps he was still caught up in the booster psychology of so many Chicagoans who were creating new opportunities out of the old burnt rubble of the city. Nontheless, when the depression hit in 1873—the worst in American history to that date—and lasted until 1879, it was not as ruinous to Pinkerton as might have been expected. The previous recession proved that his personal success could not be tied too closely to the success of the business community. Earlier he had avoided the capriciousness of local politics and maintained his independence by expanding and diversifying. Though still connected to the business world, as recession skidded into depression Pinkerton found new activities that transcended economic fluctuations. It was during this depression that he discovered un-American conspirators, such as the Molly Maguires and the Communists. Such menaces, whether real or not, were easier to find perhaps because of the depression. Capitalism was challenged and causes needed to be found. He also used such discoveries to enhance his position as spokesman for the private detective profession. To do so he took to a career of writing.

CHAPTER 4

Private Detectives
and Public Images

FROM THE BEGINNING, Allan Pinkerton had been concerned with society's acceptance of the detective. After the Civil War the tools so necessary for detective success—spying, secrecy, and deception—came under increased criticism. These arts of detection had been feared before, and detective bureaus were slow to develop within the newly founded police departments. War-weary Americans, however, sensed an increase of detectives and detective operations in urban society. Such activities seemed contrary to America's historic ideals of openness, candor, forthrightness, and trust, and were particularly sensitive issues to a people trying to mend the wounds of a rebellious war. As the number of detectives (both public and private) increased, feelings arose similar to those against all secret combinations. Hostility, much in the same vein as found earlier toward anti-Masonic, anti-Catholic, and anti-Mormon movements, resulted. Therefore, the Pinkerton agency, and other private detectives in general, became vulnerable to the larger societal distrust of the basic premises of detection.

Concern over government's role in the life of private citizens also touched the detective issue. Fears and expectations were colored by the obvious differences between French detectives (highly secret and effective crime fighters who were frequently used by the state to suppress civil liberties) and the English detectives, who were more visible and ineffective investigators in the 1870s and 1880s. In fact, many people in England, it was revealed in 1884, went to "private inquiry offices," the English equivalent to America's private detective agency, because the London detectives failed so often.[1] In 1884, William Pinkerton, looking for European models that best exemplified the main thrust of his father's business, declared a kinship with the French police. Such a statement was only partially correct. Pinkerton's had much in common with English detectives as well. Actually, the London police was much more structured and controlled than the American police. There was a much tighter internal discipline in London than in New York, for example. It is more accurate to say that by the 1870s and 1880s the Pinkerton agency more clearly resembled both the French and English police systems than it did those of America. This was only palatable to business leaders because it was the flexing of governmental muscle, not business muscle, that they most feared. These same business leaders would have been aghast if public officials at this time declared such linkages to the French or English models. To Pinkerton management, the public police detective in America resembled most nearly the English model, while the country's largest private police detective agency resembled and respected the French Model.[2]

Lafayette C. Baker wrote, two years after he retired as head of the United States Secret Service in 1867, that a detective bureau was "contrary to the spirit of . . . republican institutions in time of peace." Official spy systems were tolerable during the wartime, but after peace was restored, government detectives were quickly confined to chasing counterfeiters, a job that previously had been left to privately hired detectives. Baker touched base with most Americans when he argued that the idea of a national detective police belonged to European monarchies, with their greater distance between ruler and ruled.[3] A rule of thumb was taking shape. In dictatorships, privacy and freedom from spying and interference were monopolized by the rulers at the expense of the citizenry. On the other hand, in a democracy the rulers were to be watched and the citizens cornered the rights to privacy. Of course Baker was talking of a national detective system and such views, with the exception of the treasury and postal inspectors, stalled the development of government detection. The Federal Bureau of Investigation within the Justice Department would not be created until the twentieth century. The new name of Pinkerton's business, the National Detective Agency, took on greater meaning because no such official system existed. As was quite common in the nineteenth century, the private sector simply did what the public sector could not or would not do. On one hand, Pinkerton profited from such a situation. He was hired to investigate possible American violations of the neutrality laws because there was no government system to do so. At the same time, Pinkerton was caught up in the general distrust of all detectives.

Fear of a national detective system was tied closely to fear of spies. The Civil War sensitized society to the presence of secret agents, and soon old notions that equated all detectives with spies were reaffirmed. Spying, at this time, was the most important tool of the detective trade, and certainly the first training a Pinkerton operative received was shadowing. Testing programs were simply spying programs. Pinkerton's undercover operations were challenged in 1867 at the trial of John Van Daniker. Judge John P. Vincent cautioned the jury that evidence presented by any private detective needed strong corroboration. The man who becomes a detective, Vincent noted, no matter how meritorious his motives, must expect public suspicion because

the character of the detective—and it is simply another word for spy— has always been, and always will be, an unpopular one. There is an element in human nature—and it is an element that humanity may be proud of and not ashamed—which looks with suspicion necessarily upon that calling in life and that kind of business, because there is necessarily connected with it more or less deception and deceit.[4]

One concerned New Yorker noted in the late 1860s that "men are watched and tracked about the city by these gentlemen, and one cannot tell when a spy is on his track."[5] One Pinkerton operative in New York City so unnerved some express company employees upon whom he was spying that he was reported to the police.[6]

Some of those concerns pivoted on the notion of secrecy. To what extent should the detective operate in secrecy? As the name implies, the stock-in-trade of the private detective was privacy and secrecy, precious commodities for the circumspect client. Pinkerton advocated complete secrecy of operatives and operations to protect both the agency and the client. Others disagreed. For many urban dwellers, openness was needed "not only for the exposure of criminals and the advertisement of their movements and of every suspicious circumstance, but for purpose of holding the Police themselves to a faithful performance of their duties."[7] One thinker, T. D. Woolsey, in a paper presented before the 1870 meeting of the

American Social Science Association, pondered the police image in a democratic society. In dictatorships, where nighttime visitations, censored mail, and spying upon the discontented were common, contempt for the police was understandable. Urban police did not do such things in America, yet public hatred and suspicion in the post-Civil War period increased. Generally, he believed, the police represented the growing power of the government and possible restraints upon citizens' natural rights. Detectives, especially, were "moral scavengers" who frequently became as low as the ones they pursued. Society's guardians, for the protection of society, needed to be watched.[8]

On numerous occasions it seemed as though a conspiracy was afoot to undermine and to neutralize the effectiveness of the police detective. Newspaper and magazine stories constantly ruined any chance of detective anonymity. This revealed and highlighted a turnabout on a basic American truism. Success was determined by the efficient use of resources, be they personal or business resources, but such notions were ambiguous in the realm of government when efficiency threatened basic liberties. Thus police departments in general, and their detective bureaus in particular, had been created with some misgiving. Spectacular events—mob disorder and riot, sensational crimes, and youth gang warfare—had forced the modern police into existence in the 1870s and 1880s, creating a potential monster. Safety seemed to exist in obstructing its growth and preventing it from running amuck and trampling civil liberties. Therefore, inefficiency could be tolerated; indeed, inefficiency, within limits, was a safeguard. As long as this ambiguity existed, the private detective had extraordinary opportunities to grow and to prosper.

Furthermore, such tendencies to limelight detection highlights a difference of opinion about the detective's role in policing. The creation of detective bureaus within police departments indicated that detectives were to be visible bureaucrats. In the business of crime detection, they were to be reactive. Their function was to collect, analyze, and interpret facts for solution of crime. Except for extraordinary times, when radicals might be a real threat, the need for undercover operations was never compelling. Though they might not agree, the police officials, more than Pinkerton officials, had to operate within such public expectations.

A number of organizations to combat vice arose to complicate matters. As early as 1870, the Association for the Prevention of Gambling had a staff of detectives watching and reporting on the frequentors of gambling houses. Employers, business partners, and wives, for a fee of $50, were notified of the gamblers' activities. The association was taken to court in 1870 for falsely accusing one businessman, but the practice continued throughout the century.[9] Anthony Comstock's Society for the Prevention of Vice did much the same thing in the 1880s. Criticism against the practices of these latter-day Puritans resulted in "spy bills" being introduced in 1882 and 1885 in the New York legislature. Numerous judges and attorneys, as well as people like Comstock and Pinkerton, reacted against such attempts to tie the hands of detectives in favor of the criminal. A young state legislator, Theodore Roosevelt, led the pro-detective and pro-spy forces and successfully killed the spy bills, as detectives and private detectives continued to raise difficult questions as to the proper policing of American society.[10]

One characteristic of the new police systems developing in America was that the men were salaried. Public parsimony, however, allowed for private rewards to creep into policing. Working for rewards, many felt, was an incentive to better effort. Probably nothing destroyed the efficiency of detective work more than the practice of offering rewards. Police detectives were spurred into activity or inactivity depending upon the amount of reward offered. "They became intent upon gaining rewards rather than upon performing their duty as public officers," declared the *New York Times* in 1878, "and where a compromise is offered, they devote themselves to recurring remuneration, possibly from both sides to the transaction."[11] After reviewing the problems of the New York police detectives in 1874, Police Commissioner John R. Vooris was not surprised that "the dissatisfaction of businessmen with the present system of the Detective Office has been steadily increasing."[12] Detectives became go-betweens, cultivating bartering skills within a network of criminal acquaintances, rather than investigators, cultivating detective skills within the criminal justice system. Jonathan Wild had come to America! Urban detective police were criticized throughout the period because "to the average citizen the very name detective [carried] with it a sensation of mingled dread and admiration, tinged, it must be confessed, with a little aversion."[13]

One of Pinkerton's earliest business policies was refusal to work for rewards. Clients, regardless of the success of the investigation, paid a prearranged fee of $6 or $8 per day for each operative. Such fees were high enough to be selective, and only large businesses, governments, or the very rich could employ Pinkerton. In 1881 he wrote that his agency was "an organized ally of the correctional laws, to be hired and paid for stated operations. . . . My officers are not accidents, but chosen, salaried associates who have therefore no motive either for dalliance with crime, or favoritism to criminals."[14] They were motivated by more than the desire to forestall greed and opportunism. Pinkerton knew that operatives working for a set wage more closely resembled other respectable laboring men; this was a link in his attempts to create a similarity between his profession and other nineteenth century businesses. After all, "my operations are based entirely upon a distinct understanding and agreement of a business character," he wrote in 1880.[15] Such sentiments endeared him all the more to the business community.

At first blush, the antidetective police ideology rebounded to the private detective's favor. Those who felt the police detective to be of little worth might hire private detective firms. This occurred frequently, and, as if in response, the number of private detective agencies increased. By the time Pinkerton died in 1884, Chicago alone had fourteen established private detective businesses.[16] Growth in other cities did not match Chicago's, but the nationwide increase was steady. Problems resulted. Competition increased and frequently the competitor's practices and philosophies were antithetical to that of Pinkerton's. Such a fledgling profession needed watching, and, if possible, directing by the pioneers. As the number of private detectives increased, the already sensitive occupation became too visible. Public tolerances diminished. Private enterprise in police work began to share more consistently in the negative image once nearly monopolized by the public police detective.

Pinkerton was most concerned with the public image of the private detective. Earlier on he had impressed his clientele, the business community, with his intrinsic worth. Crime detection was a business, Pinkerton maintained, with established rules of conduct and responsibility. The operative was not and should not be a loner; he was instead, a small part of a vast coordinated network of men working together to solve a crime. Crime solution was to be bureaucratic and methodical rather than mysterious and miraculous. The businessman was dealing with something quite familiar—an agency with the same organization and philosophy as his own—which was contrary to the dark, back-stairs agencies criticized in the press. In fact, William Pinkerton claimed in 1884 that the best detectives might most likely come from the ranks of the business community.[17]

Business leaders in the railroad and express industries felt Allan Pinkerton and his police to be a necessity. Pressures from an increasingly competitive market, plus ambitions to expand his own business, meant that Pinkerton had to keep his name respectably prominent. But after the Civil War and gaining special intensity throughout the 1870s, others became more critical of private detectives. In spite of Pinkerton's early efforts of avoiding politics and of obtaining adequate personnel for his agency, many began to echo John Wentworth's old arguments that the private detective was evil. Opinion makers, such as newspapermen and politicians, were more critically vocal. The business community remained fairly safe, though Pinkerton still wanted to win contracts over competitive firms. At this time, lower classes, including organized labor, were relatively unimportant. But other considerations pressured Pinkerton to seek out larger audiences, especially those people who never came into contact with his agency.

Pinkerton and other private detectives in those formative days enjoyed considerable freedom from restraint and regulation. Police detectives had considerable freedom and discretion too, but they were public servants and not private entrepreneurs. Theoretically, there was more structured accountability for police detectives than private detectives.[18] The lack of governmental regulation and accountability might be license for irresponsible deeds. Increasingly, people were made aware that to clothe men with public powers without any recourse to public restraint seemed a step back into feudal times, a metaphor that would grow in popularity in the next decade. Edward Crapsey, a New York police reporter, believed that private detectives were "harpies of the city" who had a vested interest in disorder. The ultimate success for many private detectives meant proving a client's suspicion, a process often leading to deception, exaggeration, and criminal collusion.[19] They were a mockery to legitimate police power and undermined respect for law, he maintained, and though

> there are probably some [private detectives] who endeavor to pursue their calling with all possible honesty.... it is difficult to deny that as an institution they are wholly unnecessary and evil in their influence. The

little legitimate detective duty they do would be much more likely to be justly and well done by the regular officers of the law. The tracking of a criminal for gain by a person unauthorized to arrest him when found, breeds indifference to the demands and forms of law, which is calculated to breed contempt for the law itself, and this leads to the serious demoralization of the community which permits it.[20]

One thinker advocating the necessity of a federal police in 1880, argued that

The individual efforts that have been made to prevent and punish crime by the organization of private police corporations, styled "detective agencies," have but too generally succeeded in defeating the purposes for which they were created. For being under no control of the government, and owing no reports to the law, their whole aim and object has been to make as much money as possible—an aim and object utterly incompatible with the conception of a true police-system.[21]

It was painfully evident to Pinkerton and his disciples that politicians, especially on the local and state levels, might respond to the pressures of media and unions and impede the profession's growth. At any rate, Pinkerton needed to project a proper image to the public and to other detectives, and clearly to set himself apart from the more disreputable agencies.

Although the number of detective agencies increased, Pinkerton's near monopolistic position aroused jealousies and animosities. As early as 1868 these tensions made headlines when George Johnson tried to kill Pinkerton in Windsor, Canada. At first Johnson startled the local press by claiming he was just a Pinkerton operative assigned to get publicity with a phony assassination plot. This seemed plausible enough, since at the same time Pinkerton's part in the Baltimore assassination plot on Lincoln was being questioned in the New York papers. But after a day or two of grilling in one of Pinkerton's back offices, Johnson said he was ordered by the U.S. Secret Service to kill the private detective. Further interrogation, however, revealed that Johnson was actually in the hire of a Detroit private detective. Sam Felker, an ex-Secret Service agent, had a small detective agency in the Detroit area. He represented everything Pinkerton felt blighted the profession. Felker had boasted that his only concern was making money, and he rushed into every case that offered large rewards. He was notorious for using evidence to blackmail suspects as well as helping criminal clients escape the jurisdictions of the courts. Resentment of Pinkerton's presence in the Detroit-Windsor area prompted Felker's desire to get the "old Scotsman out of the way," claimed Johnson.[22]

This "war of detectives" drifted from the backrooms to the courtrooms and newsrooms. Johnson went to prison but Felker escaped indictment and continued to be a small success in Detroit. Damage had been done, Pinkerton felt. Much of the publicity, from Pinkerton's perspective, was uncontrolled and unwanted. Pinkerton certainly seemed respectable compared to Felker, but generally the publicity was negative. All private detectives, rather than just Johnson and Felker, seemed to be on trial. Public suspicions appeared confirmed, and though Felker was released, the entire private detective profession seemed indicted. To avoid guilt by association, all unprincipled detectives, Pinkerton told his superintendents, had to be avoided.[23] Throughout the rest of his life Pinkerton resented the growing number of detectives who sought newspaper notoriety to win public confidence "while all their mind and energies [were] bent upon secretly increasing their acquaintance and intimacy with known and unknown burglars and forgers, to whom they unblushingly offer their services to arrange settlements and secure immunity from punishment."[24]

Divorce detectives were also important in the growing hostility toward the entire private police system. The first American divorce case involving a private detective agency occurred in 1860 when a successful Chicago banker, Isaac Burch, brought suit against his unfaithful wife. The outcome of the trial seemed certain until the wife hired Cyrus Bradley's agency to investigate the banker's past. Bradley produced witnesses willing to testify that Burch was a seducer and whoremonger. The evidence was incredible, but Burch, sickened over the scandal, settled out of court. John Wentworth, the unremitting enemy of Bradley, was outraged and criticized a profession that was "capable of getting up testimony to convict the purest man of any crime in the world."[25]

Between 1867 and 1886 the number of American divorces went from 9,937 to 25,535 per year, a 157 percent increase.[26] Such a rise was really due to liberalization of divorce laws, especially in the Midwest, and to the growth of some divorce colonies—places where divorce was extremely easy to obtain. But many blamed the private detective. In those places where divorce remained difficult, like New York, unhappy couples had few alternatives. Desertion, the most common choice among the lower classes, was unsatisfactory for those in the middle and upper classes who either lived together miserably or maintained separate abodes.[27] Crowded out of the market by large detective firms or the public police, locally based agencies began offering solutions to the matrimonial dilemma. By spying on unfaithful mates, evidence of scandalous conduct might be obtained or fabricated, and divorces secured. The number of divorce detectives increased in this period, and one New Yorker thought the "sudden explosions in domestic life, the dissolution of households and family separations, originate[d] in this system."[28] In March 1873 a Brooklyn detective was declared a perjurer in a divorce case. Convinced that divorce lawyers could not win one case in one hundred without the aid of detectives, the *New York Times* called for an end to such "disreputable traffic."[29] In the spring of 1880 another divorce case was thrown out of court because two private detectives perjured themselves. Those who were appalled demanded that an example

be made of dishonest detectives who, in divorce cases, have repeatedly sworn ... to statements wholly without foundation. It has long been customary here for men wishing to obtain a divorce from their wives, to employ detectives to furnish testimony against them in court. The detectives, knowing what was wanted, would be different from the average of their order if they did not produce it. In consideration of handsome pay, they would pretend to have seen what had never happened, and by their perjury, innocent women would be put away and stamped with infamy.[30]

The reputation of "the spy in social life" became so notorious that by the end of the 1880s most states required corroborated evidence before a private detective's testimony could be accepted in matrimonial cases.[31]

Pinkerton's was directly responsible for much of the criticism aimed at private detectives in the 1870s and 1880s. Besides its growing strike service, some heavy-handed detective work tainted the Pinkerton image. In 1873, for example, George Bangs and three Pinkerton operatives were arrested in Boston for intimidating, without proper legal authority, the wife of an alleged mail robber. The agency was sued for $10,000.[32] In November of the same year Robert Pinkerton was hired by the New York district attorney to bring a Jersey City, New Jersey, resident to New York as a witness in litigation. Carelessly, Pinkerton had failed to get the necessary papers for the arrest, and he was charged with assault and kidnapping. The *New York Times* complained that "the utility or morality of the private detective system we regard as extremely doubtful, but there seems to be little doubt as to the propriety of their employment by a public prosecuting officer when public detectives are at his disposal."[33]

The first armed train robbery in the United States occurred at Seymour, Indiana, on October 6, 1866. The Reno brothers robbed the Adams express car of the Ohio and Mississippi Railroad of $15,000. For the next two years they looted trains and county treasury offices throughout the Midwest. In 1867 Pinkerton operatives infiltrated Seymour and kidnapped the leader, John Reno. Frank Reno took over the gang and led a robbery spree into Iowa, where William Pinkerton captured them in 1868. The outlaws escaped from the Council Bluffs jail and returned to Indiana to steal $96,000 from the Ohio and Mississippi Railroad at Marshfield. Then Frank Reno fled to Canada, his two brothers hid in Minneapolis, and the rest of the train robbers continued their crimes until they were caught and lynched in July 1868. Also that month, Pinkerton detectives arrested William Reno and Simeon Reno in Minnesota. Allan Pinkerton followed Frank Reno to Canada, during which time the attempt on Pinkerton's life was made by Johnson and Felker. After a long extradition battle, Pinkerton returned the outlaw to Indiana in December.[34]

Much of the same pattern was demonstrated in subsequent cases. Early in 1868, Allan Pinkerton went to Canada to arrest Ike March and Charles Bullard for the Hudson River Railroad robbery. Then in 1871, William Pinkerton and Robert Pinkerton chased the Farrington brothers from Kentucy to Missouri and Illinois.[35] Clearly, the railroad industry valued the Pinkerton agency as a police unburdened by political boundaries or restraints. Furthermore, the Pinkerton adventures seemed heroic, and, as if to give a stamp of approval, rustic citizens quickly lynched the Reno brothers in 1868 and the Farringtons in 1871.[36] After nearly ten years of successful and glamorous detection of railroad bandits, Pinkerton's then had a crisis.

In March 1874, two Pinkerton operatives, Louis Lull and Joseph Wickher, were murdered by the Jesse James gang. Allan Pinkerton was enraged. "I know that the James and the Youngers' are desperate men," he wrote to Bangs after Lull's burial at the Pinkerton family plot, "and that when we meet it must be the death of one or both of us . . . my blood was spilt, and they must repay, there is no use talking, they must die."[37] Nine months followed, and the criminals made a mockery of Pinkerton's attempts to force a capture. Then on the night of January 26, 1875, Pinkerton operatives, responding to a rumor that the James brothers were hiding at their mother's farm surrounded the home and threw a fire bomb in order to light up the interior. The train robbers were not there, and a member of the household pushed the incendiary into the fireplace to avoid starting a fire. The bomb exploded. A little boy was killed, and the outlaw's mother was severely wounded.[38] A pistol marked with the agency's insignia was found at the farm, and immediately the Pinkerton's were linked to the affair.

Allan Pinkerton never denied the raid, and, in fact, he felt quite justified for such action, because two of his men had been murdered by the outlaws.[39] Revenge, at least on this issue, was a part of his system of justice. Others, however, were appalled and regional newspapers condemned all detectives who "hunt for hire" under the semblence of the law. Even the Missouri General Assembly voted for an investigation, but the railroad interests quashed it.[40] Chicago newspapers declared the incident an example of "moral ruins" which turned popular sympathy to the criminals. The entire episode confirmed many suspicions that private detectives were as menacing as the bandits.

Railroad robbers, especially the James brothers, emerged now as romantic, glamorous, and somewhat justified in their actions. America had its first real "social bandit," a special form of outlawry, that represented peasant protest and rebellion against oppressive authority. Jesse James represented crucial elements in this "social bandit" mythology of noble robbers, righteous avengers, and postwar Confederate insurrectionists. "Their fame has become national, aye, world-wide," declared a Kansas City newspaper in 1875. "Ever since the war closed, and left them outlawed, they have borne themselves like men who have only to die, and have determined to do it without flinching. For the last two or three years, the whole country has rung with daring and hardihood." The villain was an abstraction: the railroads or eastern big money that was invading Kansas and Missouri. At least Pinkerton could personify that evil. As Jesse James became an American Robin Hood, Pinkerton became its sheriff of Nottingham.[41] Cult villains as well as cult heroes were being created, something that had to be counteracted by Allan Pinkerton. One way was through detective literature.[42]

In the decade between 1874 and 1884, Allan Pinkerton was responsible for the pulication of sixteen detective books: three in 1875, one in 1876, two in 1877, two in 1878, one in 1879, one in 1880, two in 1881, two in 1883, and two in 1884. The secret of such rapid productions was that Pinkerton, still suffering from the stroke that had occurred in 1869, did not write them. Instead he dictated some incidents and anecdotes to a stenographer who gave the notes to a professional writer. After the story was completed, Pinkerton edited the manuscript. In 1876 alone he had four men working on his books.[43] Pinkerton's books, like his detective business, were corporate and cooperative enterprises. He merely substituted organizational skills for literary ones. His books were an attempt to bolster the agency's prestige and assure Pinkerton's place as spokesman for both the private and police detective profession. Equally important, they were an attempt, in this general period of waning prestige, to salvage the detective profession from the exaggerated glamor put on detectives by pulp writers, and remove the stigmata put on detectives by dishonest detectives and critical newsmen. The time was also appropriate to tap the growing popularity of the detective and crime story genre.

The detective story and the crime story were well established by the time Pinkerton published his first book in 1875. Pinkerton was not merely riding the crest of that popularity, though he certainly had a talent for opportunism. Rather, he was writing in response to detective literature, hoping to correct some of the misconceptions fostered by the literary products of the previous thirty years. For example, Edgar Allan Poe's short stories had created many of the conventions of the detective mystery story and titilated such a wide following that he has been called the father of such literature. "The Murders in the Rue Morgue" (1841), "The Mystery of Marie Roget" (1842), and "The Purloined Letter" (1844), were vehicles for Dupin, an eccentric private citizen, to show remarkable deductive thinking. Written at a time when New York was beginning to create its city police system, Dupin represented the private citizen in police work. Much like Sherlock Holmes later in the century, Dupin was never interested in the average unimaginative crimes, which the police were adequate to solve. Instead, Poe's detective was interested in the more bizarre difficult crimes which, with a remarkable set of intellectual calisthenics, he solved without leaving his home. Being above the common mind, Dupin, in a celebration of reason, explained the solution of the mystery at the end of each case. Pinkerton's stories and skills never attained the quality of Poe's works. But in the real world of crime detection, Poe was too heady. Emphasis upon headwork over legwork was misplaced. Detection was not all spectacular deductions or leaps in logic; instead it was plain common sense. The detective had to be demystified.[44]

Still another influence on Pinkerton was the "pulp literature" industry. One important part of this industry was the police gazette. When Pinkerton started publishing in the mid-1870s, three police gazettes existed. The *California Police Gazette* in San Francisco, the *Illustrated Police News* in Boston, and the more important *National Police Gazette* in New York. Eventually all drifted into sensational sex exposés and sporting news, but until the late 1870s they emphasized crime reporting. The *National Police Gazette,* founded in 1845 by George Wilkes and Enoch E. Camp, was most aggressive in identifying the criminal classes. The paper featured such regular articles as "The Lives of the Felons," a series of criminal biographies drawn from the police records. In its first issue, the *National Police Gazette* presented its mission as stripping the criminal

of the advantage of a professional incognito, by publishing a minute description of their names, aliases, and persons; a succinct history of their previous career, their place of residence at the time of writing, and a current account of their movements from time to time.[45]

In 1866 the *National Police Gazette* was sold to George Matsell, former police chief of New York and a personal friend of Allan Pinkerton. Eleven years later it was purchased by Richard K. Fox, and sporting news became the main feature of this barber shop and barroom literature, leaving a vacuum in the field of crime reporting.[46] The role of reporter of criminals and criminal ways needed to be recast by the late 1870s.

The dime novel was a part of this pulp literature industry as well. In the 1860s, Erastus Beadle's publishing house won a large youthful audience with its inexpensive western and sea adventure stories.[47] George Munro, a bookkeeper at Beadle's, established his own business in 1866 to publish a magazine, the *Fireside Companion,* and a series of dime novels. As a competitive challenge, Munro serialized

Harlan Page Halsey's "Old Sleuth, the Detective" in 1872. This story of a youth assuming the disguise of an old man and performing astonishing detective feats was very popular, and the Old Sleuth Library became a part of the dime novel industry. Soon "Old Sleuth in Philadelphia" appeared. Encouraged by the success of Old Sleuth, the *Fireside Companion* ran two or three detective stories regularly, and a new detective hero appeared in 1881. If Old Sleuth represented the importance of disguise, "Old Cap Collier" dramatized the mysterious nature of the detective. Frequently at odds with the police, Old Cap was described as surrounded by "a veil of mystery which was simply impenetrable." Old Cap's popularity was so great that his name headed a list of detective novels numbering several hundred titles describing the adventures of every kind of mystery. There were "Lightening Grip, the Cautious Detective," " 'Piping' the Nathan Murder Mystery," and "Young Ironclad, the Keen Detective," to name just a few. Where Old Sleuth and Old Cap left off, "Young Badger," a junior partner of Sleuth, now out on his own, commenced.[48]

These dime novel stories did not tax the readers' intelligence. The detective's main preoccupation was rescuing heroines from abductors and assuming disguises to befuddle the police and the criminal world. Both Old Sleuth and Old Cap used violence and trickery more than intellect. Allan Pinkerton felt that these detective adventures, with their emphasis on theatrics and mysterious exploits, cheapened his profession.[49] In 1884, William Pinkerton blamed the "yellowback" literature for the flood of romantics that tried to become detectives.[50] As early as 1871, Allan Pinkerton considered writing stories from his detective files, but refused the suggestion by the Dick and Fitzgerald publishers that they be dime novels.[51]

Another style was open that tapped the detective and crime story genre, exploited the serialized dime novel's audience, and provided a medium for elevating the image of the profession. In 1873, Gen. R. B. Marcey, father-in-law of Allan Pinkerton's good friend George McClellan, wrote a laudatory article about the agency in *Harper's Magazine*.[52] One Chicago newspaper responded by declaring Allan Pinkerton to be "Chicago's Vidocq, or shall we call Vidocq the Parisian Pinkerton."[53] He had already been called the "Vidocq of the West" by the *New York Times* in 1871.[54] Pinkerton limited such comparisons, because Vidocq had been a criminal whose detective successes were attributable to his knowledge of criminals and criminal ways. Of course, much of Pinkerton's sucess depended upon such knowledge too, but the readiness of Americans to suspect police of criminal collusion limited the appeal of that theme. The link to Vidocq, however, continued to be suggestive in terms of literary endeavor. Pinkerton had not the imaginative genius of Poe, nor did he approve of the dime novel. But Vidocq's popular memoirs, written in 1828, was neither a fictional puzzle nor a sensationalist caricature. The *Memoirs* was dramatized fact based upon real life occurrences. Imitators soon sprang up. For example, LaFayette C. Baker wrote a history of the U.S. Secret Service in 1867 after the Lincoln assassination undermined that agency's image. George P. Burnham did the same thing in 1872, but it was less auto-biographical and more institutional history than Baker's. Dick and Fitzgerald's pulishing house, regretting their spurning of Pinkerton's literary ambitions four years earlier, marketed five detective memoirs in 1875.[55]

Using the Vidocqian model, Pinkerton produced his first book, *The Expressman and the Detective,* in January 1875. Within the first sixty days 15,000 copies were sold, and he was encouraged to write more.[56] Literary reviews of the *Expressman* were good, but also they pointed up the ambiguous position of private detection in American society. Pinkertonism was both praiseworthy and perplexing. Pinkerton's detective ability as seen in the book was craftlike and admirable. The story, as Pinkerton had wanted it, was long, minute in detail, and skillfully narrated. Such revelations would warn and deter criminals from their deeds, felt one Chicago reviewer. But, unintended by Pinkerton and his writers, sympathies slowly turned from the pursuers to the pursued. Vigilant and relentless attempts to bring the felon to the point of self-conviction, attributes Pinkerton felt commendable, were seen by the reviewer to be "revoltingly cold-blooded and cruel." Perhaps touching upon the feelings of many of his contemporaries, the critic wondered: "True, it is in the pursuit of justice, and crime must be ferreted out and punished for the salvation of society; but the tender conscience obstinately puts the inquiry, Does the end justify the means?"[57]

Pinkerton's books fell into two categories. First, there were those stories that tried to portray, in a favorable light, the adventures of the Pinkerton detective and show that detection and punishment inevitably followed the commission of a crime. These detective stories, based upon true Pinkerton cases, varied from good to very bad. Another group of books, smaller in number but better in quality and in importance, allowed Pinkerton to assume the position of chief expert and public teacher of crime in America. Foreign conspiracies, criminal personalities, and felonious techniques were called to public attention. By identifying public enemies, Pinkerton hoped to become a public hero, something J. Edgar Hoover would do fifty years later. As defender of the private detective, Pinkerton justified his own agency's past history, while as public educator he assumed the role of America's expert crime fighter. In both ways, in an increasingly competitive market, he assured his position as America's foremost private detective and opened up new areas of business development.

The incidents portrayed in Pinkerton's detective stories occurred between 1851 and 1880. Most cases, however, transpired in the period before the Chicago fire, when the agency's criminal record file was destroyed. Consequently, the stories depended upon Pinkerton's memory, with fictional dramatization and digression dominating historical fact. All of the stories shared a common formula. Rarely, as in *The Model Town and the Detective* and *The Bank Robbers and the Detective,* was there a detective problem or mystery to be solved. Generally, the criminal was already known, and the story concentrated on the methodical tracking down of the suspect or the accumulation of evidence for a conviction. In *The Expressman and the Detective* and *Bucholz and the Detective* the culprits were known very early, and Pinkerton's task was securing a confession.

In the early days, Pinkerton investigated the cases personally, and he was a bit theatrical. The agency had a wardrobe of disguises, and Pinkerton frequently made his appearance incognito. In *Model Town* he appeared as a farmer. In "Mr. Lafferty's Guest," a short story in *The Rail-Road Forger and the Detectives,* he was an Irish laborer. As head of the official spy service during the Civil War he operated under the name of E. J. Allen.[58] Female detectives assumed an important place in the Pinkerton story, but they were never used to lure or seduce confessions out of criminals. Instead, they posed as widows, female companions, or wives of criminals in order to win the confidence of the suspect's wife. In the name of Victorian propriety, female operatives only dealt with female suspects. Invariably the male operative assumed the garb of a criminal or in some way gained the confidence of the suspect. For weeks or months the detective played a role, then emerged in the end to make the arrest or give evidence in court—to the astonishment of the criminal. This acting ability became fundamental to investigations, and Pinkerton felt that "nine-tenths of the actors on the stage . . . would do well to take lessons in their own profession" from the operative.[59]

Of course, such offstage acting was interpreted by many as crude deception rather than art. The testing program experience was conspicuously absent from any of the stories. To safeguard the agency's reputation, Pinkerton inserted biographical sketches emphasizing the respectable antecedents and the noble intentions of the disguised operative. But he needed also to legitimize his activities that bordered on the devious by convincing his readers that a real criminal threat existed besides the occasional activity of the casual criminal. In short, an entire criminal class needed to be exposed, and his importance in fighting these enemies to society needed to be affirmed.

Pinkerton's best books were those in which he posed as America's foremost expert on foreign conspirators and professional criminals. The first book to indicate this trend in Pinkerton's thinking, *The Molly Maguires and the Detectives,* was published in 1877. It revealed the alleged Irish terrorist fraternity in the Pennsylvania coal fields and suggested his concern over foreign ideas infesting the American worker. Significantly, *Molly* was printed the same year as the wide-spread railroad strikes, and Pinkerton was so affected that he published *Strikers, Communists, Tramps and Detectives* in 1878. Since there was some growing sympathy for labor, Pinkerton went to pains in recalling his working-class origins as a Chartist. At the same time he preached the standard Protestant ethic and called upon his own life experience and the ideas of his clients. Pinkerton believed that hard work, frugality, and perseverence would guarantee a fair share of life's amenities and pleasures. Strikes were unnecessary, worthless, and probably Communist inspired.[60] Reluctant to condemn the ordinary worker for the flurry of strikes in America, Pinkerton blames Communism, which he thought to be another word for scoundralism. Such foreign ideas augmented by a restless class of tramps and vagabonds were the reasons for labor disputes. The leadership of the Knights of Labor was an amalgam of Molly Maguires and refugees from the Paris Commune.[61] Specifically, he singled out the Brotherhood of Locomotive Engineers as the fomenter of the great railroad strikes of 1877. Operatives who infiltrated the union and publicized all its ritual and ceremony, therefore, were doing the country a great service. In addition, the strikes of the late 1870s proved the inability of the urban police. Local, state, and national leaders lacked the nerve and were stymied. Private interests and private police, once again, were left to preserve the orderly progress of business.[62] Such musing provided the rationale for him and the like-mined for the strike decade of the 1870s when the Knights of Labor and the knights of capitalism jousted along the picket lines of America.

Still another threat to the business community, and, to Pinkerton's way of thinking, to the entire American society, was the professional criminal. Burglars, sneak theives, and pickpockets, to name a few, made their entire livelihood from crime and embarrassed the police and threatened business operations. Labor problems, as he had defined them earlier, represented a foreign conspiracy. No such intrigue existed in the world of professional criminality; notions of Mafia and Cosa Nostra were fifteen to twenty years in the future. Instead, the rise and success of professional criminals in the 1870s and 1880s were associated with police ineptitude and business naïveté. Basically, Pinkerton's agency had been concerned with casual criminals, those people who, when sufficiently tempted, took advantage of an opportunity and committed a crime. His exposure of professional criminals was minor compared to the casual criminal. Railroad and express robbers and bank burglars made up a small amount of work for Pinkerton's at this time. Later, in the 1880s and 1890s this changed and Pinkerton's sons could speak with much more authority. Generally, the public police detective specialized in the professional criminal and the private detective specialized in the casual criminal.

In some ways professional criminals were easier to detect; criminal techniques and styles were more identifiable and predictable. Besides the lackluster successes of the police, the private detective had another free-wheeling advantage. They could trace-and-chase crooks across the country, paying little heed to jurisdictional lines, while the urban police were reluctant to venture out beyond city limits. Furthermore, much private property—such as department stores, hotels, and sporting facilities—became public places in need of policing. More importantly, so much of the professional thief's success depended upon the business community's lack of security sophistication. Many banks, jewelry stores, department emporiums, and hotel rooms were vulnerable, especially at night. The simplest of tools opened most doors in America.

An early awareness and exploration of this problem was reflected in the 1873 pamphlet by Pinkerton called *Bankers, Their Vaults, and the Burglars,* written to arouse the banker to a "livelier sense of pending danger." The problem was a general "want of proper caution," he believed, and after a short description of burglars and burglar techniques, bankers were told to "have less faith in your vaults and safes, and more in your watchmen and their revolvers."[63] With the publication of two books, *Professional Thieves and the Detectives* (1880) and *Thirty Years a Detective* (1884), Pinkerton provided an encyclopedia of crime and criminals in the mid-1880s. Others soon followed Pinkerton's example. In 1886, Thomas Byrnes, chief of detectives in New York, also vying to be the nation's chief crime fighter, compiled the admirable *Professional Crimminals of America,* adding photographs to that outlined by Pinkerton. Such books became rogues gallerys and were useful tools to various police departments. But for Pinkerton, at least, it was certainly an attempt to expand his market. He wanted to be the nation's crime expert. He told clients and potential clients of a crime threat and of the necessity of his agency in meeting that threat. As the number of private detectives increased, so did competition. Pinkerton was simply seeking new markets to monopolize, and at the same time, garner new prestige. As reward for his efforts, in 1883 the Jewelers Security Alliance, a confederation of jewelers concerned over professional crime, placed Pinkerton on retainer to wage war on burglars and sneak thieves.

One of the recurring themes throughout Pinkerton's books was the necessity and respectability of detective work. His work, unjustifiably had been "dragged down by unprincipled adventurers until the term 'detective' was synonymous with rogue." But he quickly added that "there are quacks in other professions as well as mine, and people should lay the blame where it belongs, upon the quacks, and not upon the profession."[64] Those sentiments had been uttered in his first major book. In one of his last books he reminisced that the romantic sleuth was gone and that the detective's "calling has become a profession."[65] Clearly, he was a businessman in quest of profit. But also his role was lending respectibility to the detective vocation and making it a profession. Large numbers understood and applauded his efforts. In a memorial given at Pinkerton's funeral in

1884, Luther Mills, a prominent Chicago attorney and states attorney for Cook County between 1876 and 1883, declared Pinkerton to be a reformer fighting against the evils of society. Mills eulogized that "the profession in this country of which in its true dignity, he was the honored founder, is no mean profession. It is a social protector."[66]

PART TWO

THE MIDDLE AGES

THE PINKERTON BROTHERS
AS ROBBER BARONS

CHAPTER 5

Knights of Labor vs.
Knights of Capitalism

BUSINESS BUILDING and image building in the last years of Allan Pinkerton's life occurred against a backdrop of familial conflict. The courtship habits of his daughter, Joan, for example, so offended the sensibilities of the prudish father that she was forced to leave home and live with her brother Robert in New York. Only with her final marriage to William Chalmers, who would help establish the famous midwestern ironworks, Allis-Chalmers, was there a reconciliation.[1] In 1878, in "one of the largest and most stylish weddings that ever took place in Chicago," Joan Pinkerton married. "There never was such a throng of people at a wedding in Chicago and these from the best society circles of the West Side,"[2] the *Chicago Tribune* reported. The Pinkerton family had arrived. This was at a time when Pinkerton was carrying on a platonic love affair by mail with a Mrs. Sargent in Denton, Texas. She was even promised a position in the agency if she moved to Chicago. There is no evidence, however, that she ever left her husband and moved to the Midwest. William Pinkerton's drinking problems continued and a "water cure" for the eldest was always being considered. Instead, he was kept close to home under the watchful eye of his dominant father.[3] William's outgoing jovial life-style, which so frequently disturbed his father, actually worked to the credit of the agency. The eldest son slowly became a resident expert on America's underworld and earned the nickname The Eye. His day would dawn at the turn of the century.

But the greatest heartaches came at this time from the favorite son, Robert, especially after longtime associate George H. Bangs died in 1883.

Of the eight children born to Pinkerton, only three survived. Mary Pinkerton, at two years three months, died in 1854. The first Joan died in 1855 when she was seven years old. Isabella lived to be nineteen before she died in 1863. The other two died earlier in the marriage and records are lost. Joan Pinkerton never became involved in the agency. Robert Pinkerton, born in Dundee, Illinois, in 1848, was the youngest son. William Pinkerton, two years older than Robert, received much of his education in the field and immediately went into the family business. Robert's talents for administration were soon evident, and before joining the agency in 1865, he was sent to the University of Notre Dame to take business courses. Throughout Allan Pinkerton's life, the power center was in Chicago. Unlike his Chicago-based brother, Robert went to New York and was out from under his father's direct control. The trusted lieutenant, George H. Bangs, supervised Robert, but soon the young man demonstrated some independent thinking. Robert was eager to expand and to create new offices as early as 1873. Even though he went through an apprenticeship as a detective, by the 1880s Robert was convinced that the future fortune of the agency was in the Protective Patrol.[4]

The Protective Patrol, the watchman component of the agency created in 1858, was confined to Chicago. The patroling functions of the big city police departments were still inadequate, but Allan Pinkerton's aversion to big city politics forestalled the patrol's expansion. Robert Pinkerton saw, however, that suburban policing and especially race track policing could provide a lucrative market, and, perhaps, skirt boss politics. Throughout the late 1870s and early 1880s, especially as labor strife increased, Robert began to pressure for expansions of the guard service. After repeated requests were denied by the irascible old man, Robert threatened to resign and open a new agency. William was unhappy enough under his father's control, and pliable enough to Robert's influence as well, that for a season it looked as though both sons would leave. A shakey truce resulted just to keep the family and the agency together. George H. Bangs was expected to keep Robert in line.[5] After Bangs' death, the New York and Philadelphia offices quietly came under Robert's control, and the center of power shifted eastward.

After Allan Pinkerton died in 1884, both brothers headed the agency—William in Chicago and Robert in New York. William followed the logic of his life and continued to build a reputation as The Eye. He carried on the detective emphasis set forth by his father. To Allan Pinkerton, the Protective Patrol was merely an afterthought, though in terms of business, it brought in a steady income. To father and eldest son, the National Detective Agency was to be concerned with detection. But at this time, and for two decades after the founder's death, Robert Pinkerton's personality and policies guided the agency. The agency remained largely a railroad police, but to the detective's spying was added the watchman's guarding of railroad property. A decade of contention and controversy occurred due to the labor strife, and in the 1880s and early 1890s, Pinkerton's became an industrial police. Many railroads, taking cues from the monopolistic policies of notable industrial leaders like John D. Rockefeller, owned coalfields and ironworks. Appropriately enough, as industrial owners and managers increasingly equated crime and disorder with collective bargaining and work stoppages, Pinkerton's opportunities enlarged. The Homestead disturbances and subsequent congressional investigations then forced a realignment of the agency's leadership and business emphasis.

A railroad police is a mechanism within a particular company's management structure that has the responsibility of detecting crimes against the railroad and protecting company property. The personnel, popularly called "cinder dicks," got their police power from the state legislature but were recruited, paid, and controlled by the company. They were created in response to the growing crime problems of the post-Civil War period and the lack of any official police mechanism outside of city limits. Train robbers, for example, continued to plague the railroads. The Burrow brothers in Alabama, the Daltons in Kansas, and the Sontags in California were just a few of the numerous kinship gangs menacing the Midwest and Far West. Pinkerton's, still smarting under attacks due to the Jesse James incidents, tried to minimize their bandit chasing. A sensitive nerve was retouched in the late 1880s when Newton Watts, a train robber captured by William Pinkerton, died in prison amidst retrials. To an assembly of five hundred mourners, Rev. John M. Caldwell attacked the notion that detectives were a necessary evil and placed the blame for Watts' death on "Pinkerton deviltry."[6] Train robbery became so epidemic that William Pinkerton called upon the government to do something about the "Highwaymen of the Railroad." It was wrong to force large corporations to finance their own protection, he maintained.[7]

Criminally inspired train wrecks were always a problem. One group of travelers in 1872 suggested that a private society be created to protect their property and lives when traveling. Such fears were justified, because in the next five months, over one hundred attempts at malicious derailment were reported.[8] Then, especially during the times of economic depression like the 1870s, tramping became a problem. In July 1878, for example, nearly two hundred vagabonds boarded a Chicago and Alton Railroad in St. Louis.[9]

— At first Pinkertons monopolized railroad policing, as railroads were slow to develop their own police systems. In the formative years of railroad development it was less expensive to hire private detectives when need arose than to have an ongoing staff of police within the corporate structure. Pinkerton's was expensive, however, and as crime increased it became more economical to have a permanent business police. Furthermore, as private detectives became more notorious, it seemed necessary to tie control and culpability closer to railroad management. So in these years—1870s and 1880s—when railroads were consolidating into mega-companies, the modernizing of management meant sluffing off of dependence on Pinkerton detectives.[10] They were still used, but only in dire circumstances. This forced Pinkerton's to reconsider their market position and reemphasize the necessity of their organization in American society.

Beginning in 1865, the Pennsylvania legislature allowed state railroads to endow some employees with police power. Massachusetts provided for a railroad police in 1871, as did Maryland in 1880, and New York in 1890. Others followed, and by 1896, the Railway Association of Special Agents of the United States and Canada organized to encourage cooperation of the diverse railroad police systems.[11] These railroad policemen were increasingly identified as enemies of labor. For Pinkerton's it had started with the testing programs, but the Molly Maguire incident, more than any other single case, was seen as a declaration of labor war.

The Molly Maguires, a radical Irish group that arose during the potato famine in Ireland in 1846, were alleged to have come to the Pennsylvania coalfields in the late 1860s. The Irish of the time were too readily identified as America's "dangerous class" anyway, and as fifty inexplicable murders occurred between 1863 and 1867 in

Schuylkill County, a conspiracy was suspected. Franklin B. Gowen, president of the Philadelphia and Reading Railroad, had been an attorney in Schuylkill County in the 1860s and had caught the Molly fever. His railroad also controlled the Philadelphia and Reading Coal Company, and in an attempt to break the Irish crime group or weaken the growing power of his coal workers, he called upon Benjamin Franklin, the Philadelphia superintendent of Pinkerton's, in 1873. Allan Pinkerton was jubilant over the opportunity and immediately set one of his operatives, James McParlan, to studying the history of the Molly Maguires. Then McParlan was selected to infiltrate the secret order.[12]

McParlan came to America from Ireland in 1867 and worked for W. S. Beaubien's detective agency in Chicago before joining Pinkerton's in 1871. After an apprenticeship spying on railroad conductors, he was chosen to go to the Pennsylvania coalfields. With his name changed to James McKenna, he posed as a hard-drinking, hard-fighting miner with a shady past and was shortly asked to join a group of workers he reported to be the Molly Maguires. Since he could write, he was made secretary of a local lodge, and for over two years he sent reports to Franklin and Allan Pinkerton warning of several planned arsons and murders. When a secret membership list was made public, the lodge leadership suspected a spy. Then, early in 1876, a conductor for the Philadelphia and Reading Railroad recognized and exposed McParlan as a Pinkerton. The Pinkerton undercover agent fled the coalfields, and his testimony and reports later were responsible for sending thirteen men to the gallows.[13]

The Molly Maguires became a household word. Protest meetings and demonstrations were held in Philadelphia during the trials by the Workingmen's Party.[14] *The Irish World,* a nationalistic publication in New York, denied the existence of any secret fraternity in Pennsylvania. Such an organization was the invention of railroad leaders and the Pinkertons, it believed. The *Labor Standard,* the official newspaper of the Workingmen's Party, felt the Pinkerton detective was an *agent provocateur,* a theme echoed for years by Terence Powderly of the Knights of Labor.[15] In 1889 Powderly, looking back to the Molly Maguire incident, was sure that "that plague spot on American civilization, the Pinkerton detective, had entered the council chambers of the workingmen of Schuylkill County, and, under the guise of friendship, urged the men on to deeds of desperation and blood."[16] On the other hand, many felt the Mollies were a genuine un-American menace. One lawyer, along with most railroad executives, believed the Pinkerton agency "accomplished one of the greatest works for public good ... achieved in this country and in this generation."[17]

Management was already sensitive to the growth of unions and to the increase in the number of strikes. It seemed that the Protestant work ethic was being challenged. Business leaders already suspected that uppity labor was advocating principles detrimental to free enterprise, the foundation of America's economic progress. The economic depression of 1873–1879 had weakened some business confidence when the Molly exposures occurred. Labor seemed cloaked with the trappings of radical and criminal conspiracy. The Molly Maguire incident aroused fears of labor radicalism, especially the infiltration of foreign ideas into American unions. The railroad strikes of 1877 confirmed those fears. It seemed, after celebrating its centennial, that America was to enter its second hundred years challenged by foreign radicalism.

In the summer of 1877, West Virginia, Maryland, Pennsylvania, Illinois, and Missouri had railroad strikes, which to those who remembered the bloody days of the Paris Commune in 1871, seemed to resemble a general strike. In Europe a general strike immediately preceded revolution. Communism entered the American vocabulary. There was no question, if one read Allan Pinkerton's book *Strikers, Communists, Tramps and Detectives,* where the blame was to be placed. Violence in Chicago was understandable, Pinkerton felt, because that city "contained as pestilential a crew of communists as any city in the world." The Brotherhood of Locomotive Engineers, he was sure, was controlled by foreign Communists.[18] Organized labor and organized strikes were judged upon the criterion of Communist affiliation. Pinkerton had a new crusade: to make American safe from Communism.

Furthermore, the railroad strikes of 1877 proved the inadequacies of America's mechanisms for crowd control. Not only the American economic system but the American political system was caught off guard. For political reasons, city mayors and county officials were hesitant to use local policing units. Neighbors policing neighbors, in this instance, could be politically volatile. There were no state police systems. State militia were also inadequate. Shortly after the strikes, the president of the Pennsylvania Railroad complained that only five of the thirty-seven states had effective militia.[19] The militia either was too sympathetic to the strikes or too severe, often precipitating violence such that the regular army had to be brought in to restore order. In fact, the regular army, called in from garrison or Indian fighting duty, was a significant tool used in the summer of 1877. But in June 1878 a national law was passed restricting the use of the army during strikes. Lawmakers balked in the face of such an efficient and potentially dangerous manifestation of national power in local affairs.

One response to the strikes was the national guard movement. In August 1877 the *National Guardsman* began publication, and the National Guard Association was founded two years later to coordinate the various new national guard groups.[20] Local businessmen, fearful of further disruptions, took an interest in the national guards. They subscribed and supported, for example, the building of armories. By having official repositories for guns and munitions, businessmen did much to undermine the constitutional excuse for citizens to have guns in the home and thus guns in the street. One Illinois colonel, speaking to a convention of the National Guard Association in 1881, told that Chicago's guard

grew out of our riots of 1877, previous to which time we had no cavalry in the State. During the riots it was found necessary to have cavalry, and we hastely organized a battalion of cavalry among our business men who had seen cavalry service during the war. Our cavalry was not equipped by the state. It belongs to the National Guard, but was equipped and uniformed completely by the Citizen's Association of the City of Chicago. This association is composed of business men, who look after the best interests of our city.[21]

The National Guard became involved as violence occurred, and between 1877 and 1892 they were used in thirty-three labor disturbances and fourteen riots. Another response, especially during the peaceful phases of a strike, was the greater use of private detective agencies. Of course, a possible strategy might be to use the private watchman to precipitate violence hence bringing in the National Guard or police to break the strike.

In 1880 there were 762 strikes, and for the next two decades the smooth operation of business was disrupted on 22,793 occasions.[22] As early as September 1866 Pinkerton guards protected the coal miners during the Braidwood, Illinois, strikes. They returned in 1874 against the wishes of both the sheriff and the mayor of Braidwood.

Instead, the mayor appointed and deputized a committee of 72 miners who were to prevent violence and to protect property. Rebuffed, the agency stayed out of strike work until the late 1870s.[23] Then between 1877 and 1892 the Pinkerton's were involved in seventy strikes, most of which clustered in the 1880s. As Robert Pinkerton testified later, this was a small percentage of the total number of strikes. But they were some of the biggest, and Pinkerton's won the hatred of organized labor.[24]

The Pinkerton agency, especially after the founder's death and under the administration of Robert Pinkerton, offered two services to distressed businessmen. First, detectives infiltrated labor unions and exposed their secret plans to employers. The practice was so widespread by 1888 that at the convention of the Brotherhood of Locomotive Engineers in Richmond, Virginia, a committee was appointed to search for hiding places that might conceal a spy. When a newspaper reporter was found they resolved to hold all meetings behind closed doors. Even note taking was forbidden, because detectives might find scraps of information. Such anxiety was justified, but the precautions were futile. Two Pinkerton operatives officially attended as delegates from Reading, Pennsylvania. They composed elaborate reports on all the issues and discussions at the convention.[25] Then in 1889 union fears were fully confirmed when a Pinkerton confidential circular became public that suggested that

at this time when there is so much dissatisfaction among the laboring classes and secret labor societies are organizing throughout the United States, we suggest whether it would not be well for railroad companies and other corporations, as well as individuals who are extensive employers of labor to keep a close watch for designing men among their own employees, who, in the interest of secret labor societies are inducing their employees to join these organizations and eventually to cause a strike. It is frequently the case that by taking a matter of this kind in hand in time and discovering the ringleaders and dealing promptly with them, serious trouble may be avoided in the future.[26]

A second service offered by Pinkerton's was the guard system. If detectives were hated because they were invisible, the guards were hated because they were too visible. Founded in 1858, the Pinkerton Protective Patrol was confined to Chicago until 1881 when a similar branch was opened in New York due to the prodings of Robert Pinkerton. Further expansion of the patrol did not occur until Allan

Pinkerton's death. It was a uniformed military organization designed to prevent crime by guarding certain businesses at night.[27] Occasionally, the patrol provided police protection for areas like Coney Island. In the 1890s and 1900s the guard system was used extensively at race tracks, but in the 1880s it was used primarily to protect property during strikes.[28]

The public made no distinction between the detective or the guard, and both were referred to simply as "Pinkertons." There were differences, however, which Pinkerton management tried to make clear. The detective branch, which had suffered considerable bad press, was identified by Pinkerton executives as a small permanent elite corps, composed of men of intelligence and character. In contrast, guard work was seasonal with rapid hirings and layoffs every year. Long lists of reserves were kept, but during emergencies, many men were recruited indiscriminately off the street. Occasionally, seedy characters with short, volatile tempers became guards and rashly precipitated riots. The Knights of Labor were not so generous. It thought violence was more a matter of Pinkerton policy than individual action.

Violent incidents did occur, and labor claimed it was due to the presence of the detective agency's guards. In 1885, the Knights of Labor drew up a platform calling for the exclusion of all detectives from labor disputes. When a bomb was thrown killing several policemen at Chicago's Haymarket Square in 1886, the anarchist agitators were arrested. Most workers, however, believed that Pinkerton agents provoked the incident. A brother to Albert Parsons, one of the condemned anarchists, claimed he had evidence linking the Pinkertons to Haymarket. A reporter for the *New York Star,* it was asserted, was bribed away from Chicago because he knew that a Pinkerton threw the bomb.[29] Years later, Gov. John Altgeld pardoned the remaining convicted anarchist and placed the blame for the bombing upon the city's failure to jail Pinkerton guards for shooting workers.[30]

Terence Powderly, head of the Knights of Labor, was dismayed over the general timidity of politicians during the strikes, and he called upon state governors to be readier to bring in the state militia to police strikes. Sensitive to the growing criticisms, the Pinkerton agency responded to Powderly. The spokesman for the agency, New York superintendent Robert Linden, claimed that the Pinkerton detective was used only when and where needed. In the New York newspapers, Linden advised Powderly that it was useless to look to the state governors for redress, because they had nothing to do with a strike. A strike, Linden maintained, was purely a private matter between those wanting to destroy property and those wanting to protect it.[31] Of course, the Knights of Labor and the knights of business jousted elsewhere besides in the pages of the newspapers, and some political officials began to disagree with the Pinkerton policy. The strike was simply causing too much public turmoil to be defined as a private matter.

The number of indiscriminate shootings by Pinkerton guards increased. In the autumn of 1886, a Pinkerton guard killed an innocent bystander during the Chicago stockyard strikes. Powderly, hearing of the shooting, reflected "that if the men did remain absolutely quiet and sober, some agent of the packers or Pinkerton's could be depended on to start trouble." But, in this case, the workers did not remain quiet and a riot occurred. T. B. Barry, friend and colleague of Powderly, cryptically reported on the resulting state of seige in Chicago. "Eight hundred Pinkertons here. Four of them were beaten today. One of them was stripped of his clothes, and to put it mild, hell was knocked out of the four of them; they are all in the hospital"[32] Leo P. Dwyer, state representative for the Fifth District of Cook County, promptly introduced a bill at Springfield to prohibit the interference of private police in strikes. It was labeled "whimsical" by the newspapers and defeated by the legislature.[33]

In January 1887, another Pinkerton guard killed a boy during the Jersey City coal wharves strike. The entire city was aroused, and the mayor attacked the Pinkerton system as medieval barbarism. The killing led to national exposure through a vitriolic article in the *Nation*. Pinkerton's became a symbol of America's internal weaknesses. It represented a retrogression to the lawlessness of the eleventh and twelfth centuries when the absence of a public police caused the creation of feudal armies. In effect, the *Nation* noted, the presence of the private detective meant that "American mayors and sheriffs and governors have refused, at the demand of Labor, or through the fear of Labor, to give American citizens protection for either life or property."[34] Henry Ledyard, president of the Michigan Central Railroad, wrote a friend during the debates in Indiana over an anti-Pinkerton bill that it was useless "as experience has shown us, for corporations, especially railroad companies, to trust to the local State authorities for protection in time of trouble." That is why, he went on, the railroads needed Pinkerton's.[35] With a vicious circularity, Americans were confronted with the dilemma that the state could not or would not preserve the peace, and in their attempt to maintain order, the business community's private police caused disorder.

In the midst of this climate, Pinkerton's dramatically demonstrated its capacity to destroy a major strike. During the Burlington Railroad strike of 1888, Pinkerton's emphasized another service—providing substitute workers or strikebreakers. Scabs had been provided as early as 1874 during the Braidwood strike but never in such quantity nor with such impact. Now added to the detective and guard service was the recruitment of scabs. In March 1888, eleven engineers were brought to Chicago from New York by Pinkerton's. Later in the month, twenty-three more arrived heavily protected by detectives. On April 2, fifteen Pinkerton guards met ninety-three switchmen coming from the East.[36] The scab became a source of frustration as union coffers were drained in an attempt to buy off the strikebreakers. On April 5 a watchman was attacked, and the strikers began damaging machinery. Then in June and July, John A. Bauereisen, head of the Aurora division of the Brotherhood of Locomotive Engineers, began dynamiting railroad property. When Pinkerton detectives finally arrested him, the Burlington strike dissolved into a miasma of ill feeling. Hatred persisted, and in 1889 the Brotherhood of Locomotive Engineers formed a committee to lobby for national legislation to abolish Pinkerton detectives. They also drew up model bills for state legislators to prevent the conferring of police power on Pinkerton guards.[37]

This labor unrest of the 1880s stimulated the growth of the private detective profession. Established agencies expanded rapidly, and new firms came into existence. Robert Pinkerton had always believed in expansion, and within ten years of his father's death in 1884, he added six new offices. James McParlan, flush from the success of the Molly Maguire exposures, was made superintendent of the Denver office. The labor troubles of Colorado and Idaho were his specialty, especially after the Wobblies arose early in the twentieth century. In 1888 and 1890, the Boston and Kansas City offices were opened. Finally, the Portland, St. Paul, and St. Louis offices were functioning by 1893. Mooney and Boland's detective agency expanded into Kansas City and New York in the same period, while Gus Thiel formed his fiefdom in Missouri and the Far West. By 1892

Chicago had twenty-two detective agencies. In 1893 New York had "more than a score such establishments," while Philadelphia had increased from eight in 1881 to seventeen by 1892.[38] These new agencies were a response to the strike decade. Matt Pinkerton, exploiting the similarity of his name, opened the U.S. Detective Agency in the 1880s and provided guards for the Bay City, Michigan, lumber strike in 1885.[39] The Veteran's Police Patrol and Detective Agency demonstrated a more obvious connection between the detective and strike. Based upon the principle of employing only veterans and sons of veterans, this Chicago agency was established by John Manning on May 1, 1886. One week later the veterans supplied over one hundred men for the Western Indiana Railroad strike. An additional thirty men worked the Wabash strike.[40] Many of these agencies attempted to siphon-off business by making the Pinkerton name part of their letterhead and logos. Robert Pinkerton spent much time in the court obtaining injunctions against such pretenders.[41] Then, too, this increasing number of detectives forced the "Pinkerton" name as a generic term. Public shorthand tended to label all detectives as Pinkertons, hence inflating the sense of strike involvement by the Pinkerton agency.

By 1890 the growing number of detective agencies involved in strikes provoked some sympathy for organized labor in Congress. Disgusted with the presence of Pinkerton Guards in the New York Central Railroad strike, Congressman John Quinn presented a resolution for the investigation of detectives in labor strife. Nothing happened until Thomas Watson, the Populist representative from Georgia, steered a similar resolution to the floor in January 1892. Watson declared the existence of private detectives to be symbolic of the weaknesses of public police. William Jennings Bryan echoed the same sentiments more eloquently: "Governments are organized to protect life and property. These functions should not be transferred to private individuals and hired detectives until we are ready to acknowledge government a failure," he reasoned. "Let public order be preserved by public authority." The resolution was passed, but no investigations occurred until the violence at Homestead, Pennsylvania, compelled Congress into action.[42]

Homestead, a small town of 10,000 people seven miles east of Pittsburgh, supplied the labor force for the Carnegie, Phipps Steel Company. Dissatisfaction over wages moved the workers to strike in 1889, and they turned back one hundred sheriff deputies who were to guard Carnegie property. When a new strike threatened in 1892, the plant manager, Henry Clay Frick, bypassed local police authorities altogether and hired Pinkerton guards. As anticipated, the strike materialized, and on July 4 an ominously symbolic date indeed, 376 Pinkerton guards secretly left Chicago, New York, and Philadelphia. They met at Youngstown, Ohio, and sailed to Homestead by barge. When the Pinkertons arrived, the strikers thought they were an army of scabs and fired upon the boats. The Pinkertons returned the fire, and a twelve-hour siege occurred before the guards surrendered. Three guards and ten workers were dead.[43] Homestead became one of the most famous strikes in American history, touching political, economic, and popular culture. A ballad, "Father Was Killed by the Pinkerton Men," was written and published by William Delaney in 1892, with the stirring chorus

> God help them tonight in the hour of their affliction
> Praying for him who they'll ne'er meet again
> Hear the poor orphans tell their sad story
> Father was killed by the Pinkerton men.[44]

Following a traditional scenario, neither state nor federal authorities interfered at Homestead until all local attempts were exhausted. Gov. Robert E. Pattison waited until July 16 before he placed Homestead under martial law, verifying to some that such political timidity created the need for private detectives.[45] But hesitant minds found resolution as the private police of Gus Thiel, a former Pinkerton, was used in the Idaho coalfields, and violence resulted on July 11. Congress was also concerned, and almost providentially the Coeur d'Alene strike occurred as Thomas Watson predicted a crisis for the republican form of government. Amidst warnings that America was entering the Dark Ages, a congressional investigation was instigated by Watson, who became a persistent enemy to all detectives.[46]

The House committee began its investigations in July, spending all its time in Pittsburgh. The Senate waited until November and traveled to Pittsburgh, Chicago, and New York. In both cases Congress seemed to be playing a political game. The hearings were filled with anti-Pinkerton rhetoric, but the final reports gave only conservative recommendations. The issue seemed to revolve around the constitutional use of police power. Should private persons, asked most congressmen, have police power without public accountability?

To what extent should bodies of armed men be allowed to cross state lines? Fears of standing armies, an old standby in nineteenth century political rhetoric, were aired once more. References were made to Aaron Burr's military activities at the beginning of the century, as were remarks equating Pinkerton's to the Hessian mercenaries of the American Revolution. For those of an even more historical bent, Robert Pinkerton resembled a medieval baron with an army for hire. Several union men testified, but the highest ranking labor leader to appear was Terrence Powderly of the Knights of Labor. Powderly, whose hatred for the Pinkerton's was kindled by the belief that his wife had been murdered by a Pinkerton man, felt the private detective to be a menace to good government. Hot tempers always flair during a strike, but the presence of a Pinkerton detective guaranteed violence and ultimate class warfare, Powderly believed.

Indeed, Pinkerton's seemed armed for war. It was discovered, for example, that most large agencies maintained private arsenals. Pinkerton's kept about 250 rifles and 500 revolvers in the Chicago office alone. The Mooney and Boland agency stocked nearly 200 firearms, and Thiel admitted to possessing numerous guns. In addition to guns, the Pinkerton guard was trained and drilled with military discipline. Contrary to repeated denials, many guards were hired without consideration as to good character. Robert Bruce, a private detective who investigated the Pinkerton's for the strikers, regarded most of the guards as "the scum of the earth." Bruce claimed that one Pinkerton superintendent had been an ex-convict, but it was discovered later that in fact the suspected man had been at one time chief of police in Cincinnati. Bruce was prejudiced, but, to be fair, at least one Pinkerton guard admitted that no one ever asked him for references. Furthermore, the guards at Homestead were not deputized and most were not even residents of Pennsylvania. In short, the Pinkerton invasion of Pennsylvania indeed looked like the work of a mercenary army.[47]

Numerous private detectives also paraded before the congressmen. If the investigation into the Homestead labor violence accomplished anything, it was acquainting the country with the extent of the private police industry in America. Not only Pinkerton's, but the entire private detective profession was investigated. Charles French of the Thiel Detective Agency, Matt Pinkerton and Ross Pinkerton of the U.S. Detective Agency, William Sutherland and Emil Sandmeyer of Mooney and Boland's Detective Agency, and Thomas Thompson of the Illinois Detective Agency all talked of their part in the labor strife of the previous ten years.[48]

Of all of the friendly witnesses, greatest weight was given the testimony of Robert W. McClaughry, perhaps one of the most important law enforcement men of the late nineteenth century. At the time McClaughry was chief of police in Chicago and founder of the World's Fair Police. In addition, McClaughry had been warden of the Illinois State Penitentiary and later headed the Leavenworth Federal Prison. He had been instrumental in bringing the Bertillion system of criminal identification to America and would do the same for dactylography later. McClaughry echoed the sentiments of so many others at the hearings: the rise of the private detective agency was due to the inadequacies of the public police systems. The watchmen were useful because it was "impossible to provide a police force large enough to meet all the wants of business . . . we have found that [they] work very well in connection with our police service." In spite of concerns over a too paternalistic government, the private watchman should be regulated by the police departments, McClaughry maintained. Frank Hitchcock, U.S. Marshal for the northern district of Illinois, agreed with McClaughry and felt that "the system of the Pinkerton National Detective Agency, for its legitimate purposes [ferreting out of crime] is the best system in the world."[49]

Of course several Pinkerton men were called to testify. Superintendent of the Chicago office, Frank Murray, told of the general organization of the business. He went to pains, as did others, to distinguish between the detective and the watchman. In addition, reaffirming his own level of respectability, he told of his years as chief of police in Joliet, Illinois, and, previous to that, his work for the Illinois State Penitentiary. More important was the testimony of Patrick Foley, head of the Pinkerton Protective Patrol. Foley had been an officer in the Union army during the Civil War. From 1866 to 1877, he was a lieutenant in the Protective Patrol. He was made the captain in 1878. Contrary to charges of irresponsible conduct, the watchmen, according to Foley, were sober responsible men. Every watchman signed a contract pledging that he would not drink liquor. Drunkenness was punished by dismissal and forfeiture of two weeks' salary. The men were smartly dressed in blue flannel blouses and vests with dark pants. A "McClellan"-type slouch hat with gold cord and tassel was worn. Silver buttons with "Pinkerton Protective Agency" stamped on them identified and decorated the costume. Though unstated, the implication was clear; the uniform itself was a sign of accountability and responsibility. As to the necessity of private policemen, Foley was asked

> Now, captain, from your long experience in this sort of work, what reason can you give, that is satisfactory to yourself, why your sort of men here in Chicago, should be employed to preserve the peace and suppress riots in other states of the Union?

Foley's reply was not just personal opinion; it was the rationale of the Agency's existence. "The authorities in those states are unable to give protection to the people," he stated.[50]

Throughout the hearings it was obvious that Robert Pinkerton was the spokesman for the agency. He had gotten the Homestead contract in the first place. Even when William Pinkerton was testifying, Robert interrupted to make or remake a point. Once again, to congressmen astonished over the prevalence of the private police system, Robert described the extent and purpose of the agency. There were six hundred employees in the eight Pinkerton offices. Contrary to growing public opinion, the guards did respectable work. In 1888, in fact, the U.S. government hired twenty Pinkerton guards for the presidential inauguration. In twenty years, Pinkerton's had been involved in seventy strikes. Only three people had died before the Homestead incident, hardly a casuality list worthy to be called a class war. The guards were not armed during their transport to Homestead. Guns were on the boat but were not to be distributed until the men were deputized; this was agency policy. The deputy official was on the boat, but in the flurry of activity after the first shots were fired from the shore, he forgot to deputize the men. The fault lay with the deputy and not with the agency or the Pinkerton guards. Just as his father before him, Robert Pinkerton claimed to have no quarrel with organized labor. Workers have the right to strike peacefully, he maintained, but those workers who choose not to strike have the right to work unmolested. The Pinkerton duty was to protect property and the worker. There was considerable disagreement in Congress, in the press, and on the streets. But most, based upon their own various perspectives, would agree with Robert Pinkerton's assessment of the larger significance of Homestead.

We have reached a point in the history of the State where there are but two roads left to us to puruse. The one leads to order and good government; the other leads to anarchy. The great question which now confronts the people of this country is the enforcement of the law and the preservation of order.[51]

In spite of their findings, the Senate and House reports issued in February 1893 left the remedies to the states. Both reports agreed that hiring of private guards was due to the inability of civil authorities to render protection to persons and property. But any attempts at mitigating the evils of the private detective system had to come from the states and not the federal government. There had been several attempts at regulating the private policeman before 1892. In 1885, state legislator Andrew C. Robertson tried to end the "Pinkerton System" in Pennsylvania.[52] He was unsuccessful as were similar endeavors in Illinois during the 1887 and 1889 legislative sessions. However, in 1889 both Montana and Wyoming made constitutional provisions forbidding the importation of nonresidents for police work. That year Missouri passed similar legislation and Georgia followed in 1890. Then in 1891, New Mexico, Minnesota, Washington, and Kentucky restricted the freedom of detectives not domiciled in their states. New York and Massachusetts passed kindred laws in 1892, shortly before the Homestead violence. The labor strife of the late 1880s had stimulated considerable antidetective feeling.

In response to the congressional investigations, a flurry of anti-Pinkerton bills appeared and became law. On February 25 and 28, 1893, West Virginia and North Carolina passed laws forbidding armed detectives from entering their states. On March 4, South Dakota passed a similar law, and the day before the District of Columbia stopped the federal government's policy of hiring private detectives. In April, both Nebraska and Wisconsin passed anti-Pinkerton legislation, as did Texas and Pennsylvania in May, and Illinois in June. By 1899, six more states followed, and a total of twenty-four states plus the District of Columbia forbade armed guards from entering their jurisdiction. These laws applied only to the guard, and very little was done to restrict the plain-clothed detective. Only Maine, Colorado, Pennsylvania, and Massachusetts attempted to regulate the detective by licensing laws by 1895.[53] Of course, such laws probably had little practical effect on private policing. All an agency had to do to circumvent such legislation was establish an office in the state and recruit people for the watchman corps within the state. Nonetheless, the anti-Pinkerton laws were public notifications that the previous decades of unregulated activity by private policemen were over.

Pinkerton's emerged from Homestead with a loss of $15,000, a battered image, and a stronger alignment to the business community. Organized labor continued to denounce "Pinkertonism" while business leaders felt the detective a legal alternative to inadequate state authority. Public hostility toward organized labor remained high.[54] But the cumulative effect of the thirty years after the Civil War posed a problem for the image-conscious Pinkerton's. Linked so closely to the railroad world, the agency prospered during the period. It solidified opposition as well. The all-seeing eye and the motto "We Never Sleep" may have been emblems of the Pinkerton agency, but they also became societal symbols. They came to symbolize the divergent attitudes growing toward the entire detective profession. To those in the business community whose interests were watched and protected, the eye meant security and safety. But a growing number of persons, besides the criminal and the union member, thought the eye meant spying and lack of faith. To those who resented the expansion or exploitation of the railroads, the train robber took on a Robin Hood image while the detectives personified villainy. The "testing" of employees was construed as tempting honest men into crime. At best, the spotter was a nuisance. Finally, though the war on organized labor did not necessarily win converts to unionism, it did raise some more doubts over the presence of private armies in a modern republic.

Matthew Mark Trumbull, the old English Chartist who emigrated to America in 1846, was a prominent attorney in Chicago by 1892. Trumbull, however, had taken quite a different path than his old comrade Allan Pinkerton and became a spokesman for labor. After Homestead, Trumbull reminisced in his radical magazine that

Among the prominent Chartists of the North was a young man whose name was Allan Pinkerton: and when the Government was busy fining, imprisoning and transporting Chartists, Pinkerton made his escape to the United States where, in bitter irony, grim fate made him establish the most dangerous order of spies that ever preyed upon social freedom in America: and it became his unlucky destiny to give his name to an army of illegal soldiers not under the command of the nation or the state, an impudent menace to liberty; an irresponsible brigade of hired banditti, equipped with rifles and threatening every American working man.[55]

The strike continued to be a threat between 1895 and 1905, but the Pinkerton's minimized their strike work for that decade. Of prime concern was salvaging their public image and solidifying their business position. During Allan Pinkerton's lifetime, this had been done in terms of creating a professional mystique about the agency. Robert Pinkerton and William Pinkerton, especially after Homestead, were equally image-conscious. Under their direction, the agency still worked for the business community but in less controversial ways. At the time the Pinkertons were decreasing their work for the railroads, they began concentrating on the professional criminals plaguing jewelers and bankers. In their own way, Robert and William were creating a positive image of Pinkerton's as a specialized police force against sneak theives and burglars. Though Robert Pinkerton would remain important in New York, especially in setting policy in regards to the Jewelers Security Alliance, there was, after Homestead, a subtle shift of influence to William Pinkerton, "The Eye."

CHAPTER 6

Professional Criminals
and Crime Prevention

BY THE 1890s, many people saw the Pinkertons and all private detectives as inexcusably evil. Others, because of inadequate public policing, saw the private police as necessary. Homestead, however, was a critical event. Robert Pinkerton's "watchman" orientation of the 1880s proved nearly disastrous. Of course, many business leaders still felt that private police were useful, and numerous detective agencies arose in response to the "striking menace." But to Pinkerton management, precedents had been set. The possibility of future congressional investigations and governmental regulations were painful realities. The real work function of the agency for the previous forty years had been challenged. Dishonest employees and recalcitrant union members remained a problem, and on occasion, the Pinkerton agency handled "sensitive assignments for friends of the Agency." But Homestead indicated that support from economic elites was not enough. Political leaders seemed to be becoming more responsive to organized labor. Official Pinkerton policy for the next several decades after Homestead was to minimize strike services. When one work function or speciality gives way, an organization will seek out another to take its place. That is simply organizational survival. A new emphasis for the agency occurred in the 1890s.

Professional criminals had always been of some concern to the agency. Whenever a client was victimized by thieves, burglars, and railroad robbers, Pinkerton operatives were brought into action. Careful public relations accented these activities. For a business committed to the notions of privacy for clients, secrecy of operations, and inconspicuousness for personnel, considerable publicity was generated over the problem of professional criminality. This was all a mask for the real function of the agency. Pinkerton's served a specialized clientele. The needs of the business community dictated the kinds of criminals the agency pursued. Up until the 1890s, the deterring and apprehending of amateur criminals was the main concern of the Pinkerton detective. Amateur felons were ordinary people, overwhelmed by life's frustrations and temptations, who succumbed to a criminal opportunity. They were not full-time criminals, and in fact, many probably did not think of themselves as criminals at all. Certainly union leaders and strikers resented being put in such a category. During the 1860s through the 1880s, the agency maintained high visibility in matters of minor concern (the professional criminal) and low visibility in matters of major concern (the amateur criminal). This orientation ended after Homestead as the agency began to direct its energies towards the professional criminal.

Professional criminality pointed to some problems in public policing. In the past a rather flimsy division of labor had occurred. City police, though mainly concerned with patrol and class control, had some detectives who specialized with varying success on the professional criminal. Now the Pinkertons were moving in. Pinkerton private detectives and police detectives were brought closer together than previously. Robert Pinkerton and William Pinkerton not only fought crime, but they also became more involved with reforming police procedures. In reference to their business clients and police colleagues, the Pinkerton brothers, much like their father had done twenty years earlier, posed as America's experts on crime and crime control. They tried to refurbish their post-Homestead image, and at the same time, solidify their business position in an increasingly competitive market by alerting the business world to new problems and forging new relationships within the leadership ranks of American policing.

Professional criminals may be divided into two broad categories. Vice lords and ladies operated the brothels, gambling palaces, and saloons of the cities. Unlike the more aggressive criminals, the vice criminal generally remained in specific geographic areas protected by politicians and police and awaited the arrival of the victim. This was the golden era of the red-light district. The police sought to regulate and contain, rather than to suppress, these criminals. Frequently, as in Chicago under the rule of vice lord Michael Cassius MacDonald, the politicians and police were closely tied to the gamblers. On numerous occasions gamblers were politicians. John Morrissey of New York, for example, was a gambling prince and U.S. Senator in the 1860s and 1870s. Later, when he was a state senator, he set up gambling operations in Saratoga Springs.

Occasionally, a reformist city official became angered by the symbiotic relationship among politician, police, and professional criminal. On August 9, 1882, for example, the New York district attorney used eleven Pinkerton detectives to raid the gambling syndicate of the Simmons brothers. The city police were not notified of the offensive, and the *Times* considered the snub justified; the city detectives, it was believed, had protected or neglected the vice districts for too long.[1] In 1903, the detective agency of Frederick Adams, out of Indianapolis and Kansas City, was brought into New York by police Commissioner Greene to investigate both the gambling houses and the police.[2] Outraged Puritans always called for the cleansing of the sin districts. Anthony Comstock and Charles Parkhurst were just two of many Galahads who waged medieval-like crusades against evil. In 1887 Comstock hired the Pinkerton agency to raid three horse-racing poolrooms in New York.[3] The next year some blue-ribbon founders of New York's jockey clubs got the Ives Anti-Poolroom Law passed, and Pinkerton's busied itself investigating illegal bookmaking. Pinkerton's main exposure to gamblers came about when the jockey clubs tried to crush the poolrooms.

After the Civil War, jockey clubs, "made up of men of the highest reputation for honor and integrity in the business world," sought to improve the breed of horses through tests of skill and endurance.[4] By the summer of 1896, after nearly two decades of great involvement in labor turmoil, the guard service was fully committed to the jockey clubs of New York. Security services, for example, were provided for the Westchester Racing Association, Queens County Jockey Club, the Brooklyn Jockey Club, and the Coney Island Jockey Club. The New York Steeple Chase Association paid $483.00 in 1896 for gatemen, ushers, and nightwatchmen during its three-day meeting. Crowd control at sporting events by private police had come into its own.[5] To a lesser degree the situation was similar in Chicago. Races were held between May and October each year, and on-track betting was encouraged to increase gate receipts. The New

York legislature legalized the new gambling scheme called book-making in 1887, and the jockey clubs were held responsible for its regulation. Much of Pinkerton's early work at the tracks was the surveillance and control of these bookmakers.[6]

Off-track gambling, however, remained more sin than sport. Accommodating those gamblers not journeying to the suburban tracks were a large number of urban-based gambling establishments called poolrooms. Here people gathered together during lunch breaks or stolen moments from work to form a pool of gamblers on a particular race. Gambling was permissible for those who could afford the money and leisure to be at the track, went the logic of the clubmen, but those who could least afford to lose the money should be forbid-den poolroom opportunities. Reformers like Comstock closed the poolrooms in 1891, but they quickly reopened claiming that Western Union telegraph lines to the tracks linked them to the bookmakers. Poolrooms were merely urban agents for the bookmakers, argued the city gamblers.[7] Fearful that the poolroom would keep people from coming to the races, the jockey clubs restricted access of Western Union to the tracks.[8]

War between poolroom gamblers, headed by Pete DeLacy, and jockey clubs resulted. Pinkerton detectives discovered and destroyed secret telegraph lines linking the tracks with poolrooms. Some began to question the criminal connections with Western Union. Men with binoculars who spied on the races from nearby trees were exposed, and women coming to the tracks with carrier pigeons beneath their petticoats were expelled.[9] The battle of the racetracks remained ongoing throughout the 1890s and 1900s, after which the jockey clubs became caught up in the general antivice crusades, which eventually closed many tracks, annihilated most red-light districts, and prohibited alcoholic consumption. By the turn of the century only three states (Maryland, Kentucky, and New York) still allowed racetrack betting, and New York prohibited it in 1910. In the meantime, Pinkerton's had shifted to other kinds of professional criminals.

Jockey club contracts always made provision for numerous oper-atives to mill among the crowds looking for suspicious characters. Pickpockets increasingly exploited the congested places in America, such as theaters, busy streets, railroad terminals, and street cars. Many pickpockets, or dips as they were called, traveled throughout

the country following circuses, wild west shows, and political cam-
paigners. One Pinkerton informant reported in 1901 that "several
bands of pickpockets were ... being got together for the purpose of
following President McKinley on his jaunting trip."[10] Such thievery
was common at sporting events, and William Pinkerton reminisced
in 1905 that "when we first undertook the policing of race tracks it
was considered almost legitimate for a pickpocket to operate on the
tracks."[11] When a pickpocket was discovered, Pinkerton operatives
forced him to run the entire track carrying a sign proclaiming "I am
a pickpocket."[12] Some years later one pickpocket, Chic Conwell,
believed that the "private police generally cause more trouble for
the professional thief than the city police do. When the Eye [Pinker-
ton's] are brought in to protect a race track or an exposition, that is
bad," Conwell concluded.[13] In terms of real involvement, however,
the safe burglar and sneak thief became of special interest to the
Pinkerton agency.

In the nineteenth century jewelry salesmen and jewelry stores
were easy prey to the wandering strong-arm thief. Representatives
of urban-based wholesale jewelers, for example, were sent throughout the countryside with valuable samples of jewels in trunks and
suitcases. Gangs of thieves simply followed salesmen and robbed
them at their leisure, as in 1873 when five salemen were plundered
within two months.[14] Big city merchants responded in 1878 by establishing the Jewelers' Protective Union to safeguard traveling salesmen. Henceforth, robbers of traveling salesmen were singled out for
special treatment by the private detectives hired by the protective
union.

Small town jewelry stores were also victimized by professional
criminals like Gilbert Yost. Between 1865 and 1883, Yost terrorized
western New York, Pennsylvania, Ohio, Michigan, and Indiana.
Many small town jewelers purchased valuables on consignment; this
meant that several big city wholesalers received no money until a
sale was made on the local level. In short, a robbery in a small town
had an impact on the big-town jeweler. Fearful of overreaching its
abilities, the Jewelers' Protective Union refused to extend its protection to the small store, and in April 1883, seventeen members bolted
to establish the Jewelers' Security Alliance. As if in affirmation of
this deed, on the same day Yost was captured by William Pinkerton
in Indiana. Shortly thereafter the Pinkerton agency was retained as
the official detective corps for the alliance.

In simplest terms the purpose of the alliance was to provide a specialized detective service for jewelers molested by robbers. Pinkerton's was to do for the jewelers what it had done for the railroads in the 1870s and 1880s. The criminals were menacing and the police were ineffective, and so a special interest group simply took matters into its own hands. The alliance was a revolutionary concept. A St. Bernard dog perched upon a traveling trunk was the organization's emblem, and the motto was "Prevention, Pursuit, Prosecution, and Punishment." This was more than forced alliteration. The prevention of crime, so went Robert Pinkerton's philosophy, depended upon unrelenting pursuit, rigorous prosecution, and stiff punishment. For all too long the business classes favored the return of stolen property over the apprehension and prosecution of criminals. Return of property remained important, but no longer did it guarantee immunity from the law.[15]

Although not part of the motto, "preparation" became equally important as Pinkerton's quickly involved the jewelers in preventative measures. The success of the thief, jewelers were told, was due to the laxness of the individual businessman. Robert Pinkerton, still in his prime as the main force in the agency, issued long lists of suggestions to help prevent robberies. Bulletins informing jewelers of the new types of robbery schemes and new criminals at work were published and issued regularly. Finally, membership signs, which were really warning signs to the criminal, declared the premises to be "Protected by the Pinkerton National Detective Agency." Every member received one and was urged to keep it visible as a deterrent.[16]

The alliance seemed remarkably successful—no member was attacked in 1884 or 1885. G. W. Fairchild and Son, a jeweler in Bridgeport, Connecticut, was robbed in 1886, but Pinkerton's quickly arrested "Kid" McManus, Joe Dollard, and George Feyeth. Between 1887 and 1890 only one member was burglarized. Five members were robbed in 1891, but the thieves were shortly apprehended. By 1894, when the next such experiment occurred, it appeared that the jewelers and their particularly tough philosophy ended the jewelry thief threat. As in days of old when the hue-and-cry brought neighbors together to meet a crisis, so it was obvious trade associations could do the same. Two unintended consequences resulted.

Success of the private sector in fighting professional criminality encouraged those of a more conservative bent. The lesson of private detective history was reaffirmed: there was an alternative to the public police in America. Initially, the police had been created for the wealthier urban residents. Working-class and lower-class people, within limits, were allowed to handle their own criminal justice problems. It was the downtown and residential property of the middle and upper classes that was to be protected. Thomas Byrnes, chief of detectives in the New York police, even had treaties with the underworld in order to safeguard the Wall Street area. There were some tensions, of course, over police toleration of brothels and gambling halls, which gave rise to such do-gooders as Comstock in New York and Arthur Burrage Farwell in Chicago. More importantly, however, crime did not decrease downtown. The police, it seemed, failed to provide the necessary protection and detection, and the private agency became more attractive. Then, as city bosses increasingly controlled the police, a certain ineffectiveness and inefficiency was tolerated because other crime fighting services existed.[17] Another response, which seems to have more tangible historical evidence, was within police leadership. Although police detectives were concerned with professional criminals, the major function of police departments in the previous fifty years had been "class control." Dangerous classes were more often ethnic groups, class groups, and youth groups rather than professional criminals. By the late 1880s, greater commitments were being made to "crime control" orientation. The activities of the Jewelers' Security Alliance was part of the reason and so was the rise of the American Bankers' Association.

Rapid business growth occurred in the last third of the nineteenth century, increasing the importance of banking. The number of state banks, for example, grew from 754 in 1883 to 3,579 in 1893. Roughly in the same time period national banks increased from 2,733 to 3,706. The American Bankers' Association was created in 1875 for the exchange of ideas and the pursuit of common goals in Congress.[18] Bank robbery—the holdup during the day and the break-in during the night—was one of the common problems discussed periodically by the members of the association. Holdups occurred more often in rural areas, where police protection was minimal, while safe burglary and sneak theivery were more common in urban banks.

Safes, at first, were merely wooden boxes lined with metal stripping (hence, "strong boxes"), which could be easily opened with crowbars and wedges. The cast-iron "Lilly Burglar Proof Safe," constructed in the late 1860s, changed burglar tools to drills and gunpowder. When Langdon Moore decided to learn about Lilly Safes, he visited the company's plant in Troy, New York, and observed all the stages of construction. Maximillian Shinburn, as a newly arrived immigrant in the 1860s, worked for the Lilly firm and learned a great deal about the construction of vaults and safes.[19] Both Moore and Shinburn turned such information to profit as they vied for the crown of King of Burglars during the late nineteenth century. George White, in a flash of innovation, simply went to the bank executive's home and at gun point forced him to return to the bank and open the safe. Between 1866 and 1880 some one hundred robberies were committed in the same manner. The technological response was the invention of electric alarm systems and time locks. Safe makers each year developed new "burglar-proof" safes, and safe breakers each year found new ways to open them. Shinburn, the nation's most notorious burglar, felt it was "nip and tuck between the safe makers and the crooks, as to which should gain the upper hand." By the mid-1890s, with the use of nitroglycerin, the burglars seemed to have won the contest.[20]

Criminal expertise was matched with the bankers' lack of security sophistication. Interior arrangements and business procedures favored the criminal. Bank cashiers and tellers were frequently not caged, and money lay in accessible stacks. In 1888, Charles O'Connor entered the Fifth National Bank of New York City, and using a soapbox as a step ladder, he simply reached over the counter and stole $3,000. Later the same day O'Connor did the same thing at the Commercial National Bank in Wall Street and took $7,700.[21] In rural banks, which became increasingly favorite targets as the century progressed, the number of employees was small. A teller could be easily diverted by a sneak thief gang and money stealthly stolen. Safes, left open to expedite quick transactions of business, were inviting to sneak thieves like George Carson, Walter Sheridan, Billy Coleman, Horace Hovan, and Adam Worth. Safe manufacturers sold all safes and vaults with a standard combination, which was easily learned by burglars. Bankers who failed to change the combination or kept the combination "on the half cock" (running through the combination sequence with the exception of the last number, which was off a few tumbles) suffered from nighttime attacks. Burglars like George Leslie, Ned Lyons, Ike Marsh, Langdon Moore, George White, and Shinburn had rich pickings in the last decades of the century.[22] Throughout the period bank thievery continued at a quickened pace, and, by the last decade of the century, it was commonly accepted that "in the sneak-thievery and safe-burglary line the Yankee has outstripped all other nations."[23]

Robert Pinkerton, as early as the mid-1880s, suggested that the American Bankers' Association imitate the Jewelers' Security Alliance and organize against the professional criminal.[24] The American Bankers' Association had created a protective committee in 1881, but because of inadequate funds, it was limited to issuing occasional warning circulars.[25] In 1889, G. A. Van Allen, president of the First National Bank in Albany, New York, failed in an attempt to establish a fund within the association for the conviction of criminals.[26] The growing number of sneaks, burglars, and forgers caused enough concern in 1891 that the association gave the protective committee $2,800 to offer as rewards for apprehending criminals.[27] Names like Joe Killoran (sneak thief), Max Shinburn (safe burglar), and Charles Becker (forger) were becoming too familiar. In addition, the committee was asked to present a plan on how bankers could meet the criminal crisis. Little was done, however, until 1894, when the flurry of criminal attacks appeared to the association's president to be "so great that [cooperative mutual protection] seems a necessity."[28]

Robert Pinkerton continued to pressure the bankers. In April 1894, he published an important article in the *North American Review* repeating much of his father's book, *Thirty Years a Detective*, written ten years earlier. But unlike his father's advice to hire more watchmen, Robert Pinkerton proposed an alliance much like that used by the jewelers. If each member of the American Bankers' Association paid a small retainer fee, declared Pinkerton, and hired a private detective agency that adhered to the "no compromise" principles of the Jewelers' Security Alliance, the threat from professional bank thieves would soon end.[29] The article caused quite a stir and was widely quoted at the next annual convention of the association.[30] In addition, letters were sent to the association's officers requesting support for such a bankers' union against criminals. Pinkerton was convinced that "one or two convictions of leaders of these forgery bands, brought about by a Bankers' Protective Union, would do much toward stopping criminals from engaging in professional forgery."[31] On November 19, 1894, the protective committee announced that it was henceforth to be an aggressive agent in fighting crime and that the Pinkerton Detective Agency would be the detectives for the American Bankers' Association.[32] The partnership lasted fifteen years.

Pinkerton's was dramatically successful, especially in the first six years of their formal connection with the bankers. As with the jewelers, the bankers received quarterly bulletins, warning circulars, and albums of photographs to safeguard the business and eradicate the lax procedures that characterized banking for so long. Small metal signs, which were thought to be deterrents, were distributed to bank members declaring them to be protected by Pinkerton's. From the beginning, in somewhat of a historic countertwist to Pinkerton practice, the agency only pursued professional criminals. Petty crimes and employee dishonesty were blamed on the individual banker's negligence and not considered the proper concern of the association. The agency would investigate such crimes if requested, but they were not covered by the membership fee. Instead, it was handled like any private matter brought to the agency. By virtue of being the association's official detectives, most bankers automatically went to Pinkerton's with other problems. This was so profitable a position that the agency did not allow any change in policy by the association in spite of growing appeals by bankers.

Pinkerton detectives quickly captured the most feared bank criminals. On May 31, 1895, Joe Killoran, Charles Allen, and Harry Russell were arrested by the agency for the sneak robbery of the First National Bank of Plainfield, New Jersey. All three, however, escaped the Ludlow Street Jail in New York and fled to London. In June 1895, Shinburn, "the King of Burglars," was arrested for the robbery of the National Bank of Middlebury, New York. Then in May 1896, Charles Becker was arrested by Pinkerton operatives for his forgery on the Nevada Bank of San Francisco. He was sentenced to seven years in San Quentin, concluding what the leading trade journal thought to be "the most important piece of work ever done for the bankers of America in the prosecution of criminals."[33]

Five hundred new banks became members of the association in 1896, bringing total membership up to 2,188. President E. H. Pullen believed that "the protective feature of our work has been this year the greater factor in attracting new members."[34] The next year, in an article entitled "The Eye That Never Sleeps," the *Chicago Eagle* lauditorily claimed that "no institution in the United States [was] of such great benefit to the business community as the Pinkerton National Detective Agency."[35] Criminal attacks continued but they shifted to nonmembers. A burglar in 1900, after criticizing the "four-flushin" activities of the New York police, told Josiah Flynt that

> the guns leave the Big Man's [Pinkerton's] territory alone, if they can. If there was two banks standin' close together, an' one o' them was a member o' the Bankers' Association an' the other one wasn't, the guns ud tackle the other one first. The Big Man protects the Bankers' Association banks.[36]

Every year the agency presented statistical data extolling its successes as protectors of member banks. At the same time the criminal threat was shown to be constant as nonmember victimization skyrocketed. In such ways the agency indicated both its continued success and its continued necessity as a crime fighter. Between 1895 and 1900, for example, nonmember banks lost $664,000 to sneaks, burglars, and forgers while members lost $65,000. It is difficult to determine just how much of this was statistical manipulation to pacify members and to encourage nonmembers to join. At no time during Pinkerton's tenure as the detective service for the American Bankers' Association did a majority of the nation's banks belong to the association. Crooks had many other banks and jewelry stores to rob. Nonetheless, so successful did Pinkerton's feel, or at least wanted to appear, that William Pinkerton, in 1902, declared that "professional crime among intelligent men is largely extinct. We have no great burlgars or forgers in the United States today."[37] By that time the social make-up of jewelry and bank thievery changed; the change would affect the agency. Besides the success against the professional criminal, another reason for restored Pinkerton confidence after the crisis of the 1880s was a closer working relationship with the nation's chiefs of police.

Pinkerton's increasing involvement with professional criminals in the last twenty years of the nineteenth century put the agency in greater contact with the public police. On one level, the success of the private police seemed connected to the weaknesses of the public police. Some scene stealing was going on. After studying the *World of Graft,* Josiah Flynt concluded that "the Pinkerton Detective Agency . . . could protect Chicago for less than two-thirds of what police departments now cost the taxpayer, and the protection would be real and thorough." One Boston criminal told Flynt that the "reason that the [private] agencies have so much to do is because the town coppers can't be relied on, or are too lazy to get down to business."[38] On some occasions heated rivalry occurred between the public police and the Pinkerton agency. The New York police, for example, seemed to be a perpetual enemy. During the Lexow hearings on police corruption in 1894, the New York police were accused of favoring the Wilkinsen Detective Agency in an attempt to push Pinkerton's out of the city.[39] All too often rival chiefs, owing their careers to political considerations, worked at cross purposes in a scramble for notoriety. William Pinkerton was enraged in 1906 when the St. Louis police claimed credit for the arrest of the Hedspeth gang. The San Francisco police, working with Pinkerton's, had made the arrest while

the St. Louis Police, like all other Police Departments, accomplish very little themselves, but they grab everything they can from other people so as to get their names in the newspapers. . . . The St. Louis Police Department, and all Police Departments for that matter, act like a lot of hogs, and cheat the Agency out of all the credit they can, and I wonder they don't fall down in the monumental gall they show at times.[40]

Charles E. Felton, onetime head of the Chicago House of Corrections and secretary to the Illinois Board of Charities, was one of the more perceptive observers of American policing. As a member of the National Prison Association, Felton chaired the Committee on Police, and every year he reported on the state of the police. In 1888, for example, Felton criticized the police for being purely local organizations. The previous year a popular magazine praised Pinkerton's for its work for foreign governments. With some exaggeration it was reported that "the Canadian government looks to the Agency entirely, and there is a constant correspondence between Robert A. Pinkerton at the New York office and the police authorities of London, Paris, Berlin and other great European cities."[41] America's urban policemen seldom went outside the city limits unless the crime was especially heinous or the reward was especially large, Felton believed. More attention was given to the recovery of stolen goods than the conviction of criminals, a condition which made the police and thief allies. Exchanges of information and police cooperation rarely occured. Felton, as early as 1888, singled out the Pinkerton agency as particularly noteworthy for its far-flung network of offices and its uncompromising crime control philosophy. The growth of the private detective industry was simply due to the failure of the city police to fight crime. Felton believed the police forces needed more unity of action.

Detective agencies have branch agencies in all the large cities, or they exchange courtesies and business among each other, to the end that the criminals they want may be captured. Take the Pinkerton force, for instance. Its information of the movement of criminals is so perfect that, at headquarters, they can instantly tell you in what part of the country, or abroad, many of the known gangs of thieves may be found. Their detectives in remote cities advise the main office of every change of location made; and if a crime against property is committed, and the agency is employed, the capture of the criminals, or a return of the property stolen, is most certain to follow.

Two years later he declared that the employment of private detectives was a public criticism of the ability and honesty of the official police. Felton then called for legislation to organize national police cooperation because "some system must be devised whereby at least as great efficiency can be obtained in tracking and arresting fugitives by officials as by detective agencies within a state or outside a state."[42]

By the early 1890s the successes of the professional criminal on one hand and the private detectives on the other forced police administrators to rethink the issue of national cooperation, especially in regard to the problem of criminal identification. Historically, successful detective work largely depended on a quick eye and retentive memory. Weekly "line-ups" were held as early as 1851 in Boston so that police personnel could memorize the features of the felons.[43] Much detective duty consisted of milling in crowds looking for suspicious characters. Pinkerton management made sure that all criminals visiting the agency were seen by as many operatives as possible, and several detailed descriptions were quickly written.[44] "Rogues galleries" were kept by most large police departments and the Pinkerton agency, and photographs were grudgingly shared with others. New York chief of detectives Thomas Byrnes published a book of pictures in 1886. It was somewhat of a breakthrough in cooperation, but many believed his motives leaned toward profit rather than professionalism. A major innovation was the introduction of the Bertillon system in 1887 by Richard McClaughry, warden of the Illinois State Penitentiary. Anthropometry, the science of body measurements, was applied to criminal matters in France by Alphonse

Bertillon in 1883. Certain boney portions of the human frame, it was believed, did not vary between adolescence and old age. By taking extensive measurements of the body, accurate identification of professional criminals was possible. McClaughry became chief of police in Chicago and established a Bertillon based identification bureau in 1888.

As early as 1871, James MacDonough, chief of police in St. Louis, called a conference of police officers. One hundred and twelve police administrators attended MacDonough's National Police Convention and listened to reports on "Photography and Exchanges of Same" and "Detective Information." Allan Pinkerton was invited to attend and participate in the meetings at St. Louis. As head of the nation's largest detective agency he was to speak on detection. Unable to attend because of the press of business, he sent an essay, "The Character and Duties of a Detective Police Force," which was published in the transactions. The threats of professional criminals and the benefits of national cooperation were more novel than compelling, however, and attempts to make the organization permanent failed.[45] Twenty years later, after jewelers, bankers, and police chiefs became more concerned with professional criminality, cooperation seemed more appropriate. McClaughry, for example, feared an invasion of pickpockets at the World's Columbian Exposition in 1893. He sent out a call to the police departments of every major city in the United States and Europe for detectives to attend the exposition. McClaughry amassed over two hundred men and formed the Secret Service of the Columbian Exposition. Over 800 arrests were made as national and international detectives mingled in the crowds to "spot" the visiting criminals.[46]

Perhaps inspired by McClaughry's call for the world's fair police, and certainly concerned over the needs of the smaller police departments, William Seavey, chief of the Omaha police department, sent 385 invitations to police chiefs throughout the nation to meet in Chicago during the World's Columbian Exposition to organize a national association of police administrators. Fifty-one police officials, a much smaller number than those who met in St. Louis twenty years earlier, assembled on May 18, 1893. Seavey was elected temporary president, and the National Association of Chiefs of Police was organized. Milwaukee police chief J. T. Janssen, a former private policeman for the Chicago, Milwaukee, and St. Paul Railroad, nominated Robert Pinkerton and William Pinkerton as honorary members, the only private detectives so honored for the next ten years.[47]

The chiefs immediately passed a resolution to assist each other on all occasions by arresting and detaining criminals who fled across city and state boundaries. Just as the far-flung activity of the professional criminal forced jewelers to associate, the chiefs of police united in the war on crime. As they adjourned, with commitments and organization to meet the following year, the chiefs immediately began honing future policy by visiting the Chicago police department's identification bureau. The issues of the professional criminal, national police cooperation, and criminal identification were joined. The Pinkerton brothers would play a considerable part in the early days of the National Association of Chiefs of Police.

The necessity for a central clearinghouse of information for criminal identification became a major issue in the National Association of Chiefs of Police. After the second annual meeting, a petition sent to Congress asked for such a facility within the Justice Department. Fearful of the possible presidential abuse of such a police state mechanism, Congress refused the petition, and, in response, the association appointed a committee in 1896 to create a central bureau of identification within their own organization. William Pinkerton was on that committee. The following year a bureau was opened in Chicago with Bertillon expert George Porteous as administrator. A six-man board of governors was appointed to manage the bureau, and William Pinkerton served on that board until his death in 1923. He was also responsible for getting the bureau an official magazine specializing in matters of police work and criminal identification. In time the publication, the *Detective,* became regarded as the official organ of the National Association of Chiefs of Police.[48]

Not all policemen were enthusiastic about the new police organization or its mission of more effective criminal identification. New York detectives, under Thomas Byrnes, believed the Bertillon system to be useless. These old-style detectives thought that if criminals were known enough to be measured, they were already sufficiently known to the detective. Detective science, it seemed to them, was simply getting in the way of detective craft. Some believed that Byrnes feared his book, *Professional Criminals,* would not sell as well if police departments had access to an identification bureau. The New York police department, therefore, did not establish its

Bertillon bureau or actively participate in the proceedings of the National Association of Chiefs of Police until Byrnes was displaced and a reform commissioner, Theodore Roosevelt, came to power in 1897.

Many members of the police chiefs association did not accept the Bertillon bureau concept. In 1897 only fifteen police departments subscribed to the services of the newly opened bureau. By 1900, only thirty-nine of the total ninety-seven members of the association subscribed. The main problem was money. To use the facilities of the organization's identification bureau, a police chief had to pay a yearly fee, which was separate from the general membership dues of the association, based upon the size of his city's population. The assessments ranged from $10 to $100, and the bureau was quickly in financial difficulty as less than half of the association's members participated. There was a vigorous effort by the leadership to stimulate support, and the identification bureau soon became recognized as the main purpose of the association. William Pinkerton enthusiastically advocated dues be tripled to assure the bureau's success. Others balked and reminded the private detective of their stricter budgets. Police chiefs were then asked to pressure their congressmen for federal support of the bureau.[49]

Some members were divided over the proper control of the bureau. One group, headed by a core of midwesterners who sat on the board of governors, felt it unlikely that Congress would ever approve of a federal bureau of identification. Philip Deitsch of Cincinnati, Joseph Kipley of Chicago, and J. Janssen of Milwaukee, wanted the police chiefs to concentrate on building up the association's Chicago-based bureau. Even if Congress created an identification bureau within the Justice Department, Deitsch maintained, it would be soon ineffective because of politics. McClaughry, who was by now the warden of the United States penitentiary at Levenworth, Kansas, disagreed and resigned his seat on the board of governors in 1900. The board, according to McClaughry, was a "closed cooperation." Richard Sylvester, chief of police at Washington, thought the identification bureau should be in his city. Both the association and its identification bureau were national in scope, Sylvester maintained, and should be in the national capital acting as a prod to Congress to create a federal bureau of identification.[50]

In 1901 Sylvester was elected president of the association, a position he held for the next two decades. The name of the organization was changed to the International Association of Chiefs of Police, and Sylvester began to campaign to put the bureau in the Washington police department. If Congress was to continue to resist creating a federal bureau, at least indirect federal support would come if the association's bureau was within the Washington police system. Funds for the Washington police came from Congress. Robert Pinkerton remained uninvolved, but William Pinkerton, as a member of the board of governors, sided with the McClaughry and Sylvester faction. In 1902 these three proponents for federal responsibility in criminal identification testified before the House Judiciary Committee's hearings on a national bureau of identification. The committee reported favorably, but the bill was killed in the Senate. It would be 1908 before the federal government would have a police mechanism in the Justice Department that might provide a nationwide identification network. Not until the 1920s, however, would the Federal Bureau of Investigation have a major identification bureau. In the meantime, the International Association of Chiefs of Police continued to ponder the problems of criminal identification.[51]

While McClaughry, Sylvester, and William Pinkerton were pressuring for national recognition and sponsorship of the association's Bertillon bureau, the notion of Bertillonage was being challenged. Scotland Yard adopted fingerprinting for criminal identification in July 1901. The Pinkerton brothers, who had a thirty-year friendship with the superintendents of Scotland Yard, became acquainted with fingerprinting at about the same time.[52] Then in 1903 two prisoners at McClaughry's Leavenworth penitentiary were discovered to have the same body measurements and the same name—William West. Warden McClaughry felt the "Will West Incident" meant the end of Bertillonage and began changing over to fingerprinting.

The International Association of Chiefs of Police, also in 1903, set up a committee of three to study fingerprinting as a means of identification. Michael Evans, superintendent of the association's bureau of identification, W. G. Baldwin, of the Baldwin Railroad Detectives, and William Pinkerton, served on the committee. Baldwin toured European police departments in 1904 and reported favorably on the technique. The next year William Pinkerton went to England and declared that Scotland Yard had reduced criminal identification to a matter of bookkeeping.[53] For the next five years, William Pinkerton, as a member of the association's board of governors, worked to get more widespread police acceptance of fingerprinting.[54] By 1910 sixteen police departments supplemented Bertillonage with finger-printing. After 1911, when fingerprints were accepted in court as the sole incriminating evidence in the Caesar Calla case, fingerprinting became the main tool of criminal identification.[55]

The 1890s were crucial years for the Pinkerton Detective Agency. After decades of very mixed feelings, the Homestead strike and investigations threatened to stigmatize the agency. Homestead accelerated the agency's drift toward greater specialization on professional criminals. Increased involvement with the managers of the police occurred and quickly Pinkerton's seemed a part of America's official police establishment. William Pinkerton, socializer and convention-going type, was the more active. His attendance at the annual meetings was regular and he delivered numerous speeches. For example, he read a paper titled "The Yeggman" to the assembled chiefs of police in 1904 and presented "Forgery" in 1905, "The Professional Sneak Thief" in 1906, and "The Porch Climbers" in 1908. To the police administrators of America, he posed as a model crime fighter. His agency was the best example of efficient crime fighting. At the same time, in the name of operational efficiency, Pinkerton's became more intimate with criminals, a practice that threatened to reaffirm old notions that perhaps after all, "it takes a thief to catch a thief."

CHAPTER 7

Professional Criminals and Criminal Apprehension

MOST ORGANIZATIONS, especially during entrepreneural stages, are reflections of their leaders. Business empires of the last three decades of the nineteenth century were extensions of such personalities as Andrew Carnegie, Jay Gould, John D. Rockerfeller, and Commodore Vanderbilt.[1] Some historians even personified this period as the era of the "robber barons." The Pinkerton agency certainly was no exception during the life span of the founder and his two sons. Until his death in 1884, Allan Pinkerton was the Pinkerton agency; his personality dominated policy and procedure. Robert Pinkerton's influence prevailed during the strike decades of the 1880s and early 1890s. It was, however, in the last decade of the nineteenth century and the early twentieth century that William Pinkerton's style began to emerge. That could be seen as William played an important role in the formative years of the International Association of Chiefs of Police.

Also, the Pinkertons took cues for procedure and behavior from their clientele. At least at management levels Pinkerton people thought of themselves as businessmen and acted accordingly. Services were rendered for a set fee, subordinates were held accountable, discretion was minimized as much as possible, and proper "work demeanor" were important attributes of the agency. This set the Pinkertons apart from most other private detectives and police departments and comforted clients who felt their sensitive matters were being handled by detectives who understood the importance of business, businessmen, and business ideology in American society.

The fact that the Pinkerton brothers, who were not police chiefs, could join and be active in the International Association of Chiefs of Police indicates that they did not think of themselves as common private detectives. They were business administrators and they were police administrators.

One other influence affected the Pinkerton organization and most assuredly affected public police departments as well.[2] All police mechanisms apprehend criminals, and a legitimate tension between law enforcers and lawbreakers results. But for a variety of reasons (some of them good and some of them bad) arrangements or alliances are made between police and criminals. On one hand such accords may aid police efficiency; on the other hand they may result in corruption as a flurry of police scandals at the turn of the century attested. No matter the reasons, these symbiotic relationships have an effect on the operation and organization of the police and upon the public's view of crime fighting. During the two decades that bracketed the turn of the century, Pinkerton involvement with the professional criminals and the professional police changed the agency and its image. In many ways William Pinkerton personfied this shift.

William Pinkerton was different from his younger brother. Robert Pinkerton very soon demonstrated administrative ability. While William helped his father with the spying business during the Civil War, Robert went off to the University of Notre Dame to study business courses. In the late 1860s Robert was apprenticed to George H. Bangs, superintendent of the New York office, and in that freedom from his father he blossomed. It was from the eastern office that connections and contracts were made with industrialists, jewelers, and bankers. The late 1880s and early 1890s were the heyday of the eastern office, and Robert continued to represent the role of "detective as administrator" until his death in 1907.

In contrast, William Pinkerton stayed in Chicago under the direct and stern tutelage of his father. After the war William also went to the University of Notre Dame and then took some courses in a business college in Chicago. A business education was the best preparation for that hyphenated world of detective and detective-administrator. William was not studious and was soon back in the business. Initially, he was made a clerk as Allan Pinkerton wanted his son to move quickly into the management levels of his business. Soon, however, he was on the streets. William was not ready for desk jobs.

At first, he wandered the aisles of the great State Street emporiums watching for pickpockets and shoplifters. Then it became his duty and delight to frequent notorious saloon hangouts and keep informed on the activity of the underworld. Mike McDonald's saloon, The Store, became William Pinkerton's university, and many lifelong friendships were made with professional criminals. Soon he became a walking rogues' gallery, and to both criminal and policeman alike William Pinkerton became affectionately known as "The Eye."[3]

There had been considerable tension between Allan Pinkerton and his elder son. For example, in 1872 William went to England in search of the burglars of the Third National Bank of Baltimore. Soon the bankers dropped the case, but the young detective lingered in Europe to frequent the pleasure resorts of Paris and London with his new friends at the Sûreté and Scotland Yard. An angry father quickly summoned him home with a scolding for his mishandling of money.[4] The next year William returned to Europe and this time captured the forger Stephen Raymond. Exasperated again by William's apparent profligate ways, Allan Pinkerton feared that his oldest son would someday be paralyzed by riotous living and talked of sending him to a "water cure."[5]

When Allan Pinkerton died, the administration of the agency was divided between Robert in New York and William in Chicago. Kinship ties, apparently, were stronger than any aggravations the old founder felt toward his elder son. Theoretically both brothers had equal power in the agency. Very soon, however, it was obvious that Robert Pinkerton was the guiding light in business and administrative matters. On numerous occasions Robert sent letters instructing his brother on appropriate managerial skills and procedures. William Pinkerton's main contribution remained that of acquaintanceship with the criminal and sporting classes. Charles H. Hermann, owner of Chapin and Gore's Saloon, was a close friend in the 1890s. Joseph Martin (gambler and politician), "Big Top" John Ringling (circus owner), John Ryan (head of a betting ring at Washington Park racetrack), and Pat Sheedy (gambler) were part of William's inner circle of friends in Chicago.[6] His heavy-set frame (he weighed over 200 pounds), black mustache, and dark eyes were well known by the lesser lights of the levee as well. In 1903, for example, when the *Chicago American* satirically suggested a day of honor for the numerous criminals recently released by the State Board of

Pardons, it was recommended that William Pinkerton give a luncheon for the felons at the "Crooks Club."[7] Such facetiousness had elements of truth. Max Shinburn, the noted bank burglar, confided in 1910 that while both Pinkerton brothers were respected by the professional criminal, William Pinkerton was a particular favorite because he was such a "good mixer."[8] When William Pinkerton died in 1923, it was estimated that most of the mourners were from the underworld.[9]

Friendship with professional criminals, those whom I chose to call the "gentlemen burglars," was characteristic of the Pinkerton agency, especially as William Pinkerton's influence became more apparent. William Pinkerton liked to refer to them as the "silk hat" or "silk glove" men.[10] Gentlemen burglars were those burglars and sneaks of the late nineteenth century who were nonviolent mechanics of crime. It was a common belief in the Pinkerton establishment that if these "cracksmen" had applied their talents to legitimate endeavors they would have been successful craftsmen. They would take weeks to plan a crime, and perhaps days to execute it. Elaborate machinery and devices, amply described in books by Thomas Byrnes and Allan Pinkerton, were used to pry and rip safes apart. Jimmies, sledges, rachets, braces, and pullers, were part of the professional gadgetry of these criminals. It was a considerable operation just getting the tools of the trade to the crime site. Certainly part of the growing sophistication of these thieves was the compacting of these devices, a process that was pretty much completed by century's end. After a successful robbery, the felon could be found in one of the capitals of the world operating a fashionable saloon or otherwise living in luxurious idleness. Though their activities were dramatic (robberies amounting to one million dollars were common) their planning and execution took time, and considerable breathing spells between robberies resulted. Furthermore, these burglars with signature *modus operendi,* were relatively easy to identify. The Pinkertons, with their nationwide detective system, frequently outshone the city-limits-locked police departments of the nineteenth century in capturing the "gentlemen burglars." Perhaps that is why the Pinkerton brothers were so readily accepted by most chiefs of police in the their national organization.

In the late 1860s such gentlemen thieves as "Hod" Ennis, Charlie Rose, and Charlie Bullard stole over one million dollars in bonds in New York. In 1878 "Rufe" Miner smuggled $300,000 in securities from the New York brokerage office of James H. Young. Joe Killoran was thought by Robert Pinkerton to be "one of the best managers of Bank sneak thieves" in the United States.[11] By gambling and dissipation, Killoran squandered an inherited fortune and turned to crime to maintain his expensive habits. On August 1, 1883, he stole $10,000 from the First National Bank of Coldwater, Michigan. After spending some time in prison, Killoran took $5,000 in Lewisburg, Pennsylvania, in 1891. Then in 1894 he attacked the First National Bank of Plainfield, New Jersey, for $22,765. Killoran's career illustrates that as the large urban banks became more security conscious and better protected, the professional criminal turned to small-town America.[12] Many of these great thieves and burglars lived in the criminal districts of the major cities and commuted to the rural areas to commit their crimes.

Landgon Moore was released from prison in 1890 after a burglary career that earned him an estimated two million dollars in the 1860s and 1870s.[13] George White robbed a bank in Cadiz, Ohio, for $300,-000 in 1866. In June of 1869 he obtained $2,550,000 from the Ocean National Bank in New York. Captured in 1876 and imprisoned for fourteen years, White appeared on the scene in 1890 and returned to robbing banks and jewelry stores.[14] The most notorious bank burglar, however, was Max Shinburn. William Pinkerton, writing to Scotland Yard, declared Shinburn to be "the smartest burglar, both bank, vault and safe, that we ever had in this country."[15] Born in Germany in 1835, Shinburn migrated to New York in 1861 and quickly established himself with the sporting classes. In 1865 he joined George White and robbed the Walpole Savings Bank. When arrested he bribed police officials from a large reserve fund he kept for such purposes. After several years of burglary in the East, Shinburn returned to Europe in 1883 and was imprisoned for sixteen years after attempting a theft in Belgium. He was released in 1892 and returned to America where he successfully burglarized the Middleburgh National Bank at Middleburgh, New York on April 16, 1895.[16]

Compared to the total number of professional criminals in the United States, forgers were a small elite group of little over two dozen in the last decade and a half of the nineteenth century. Equipped with artistic talent, the latest scientific knowledge, and superior organizational ability, the professional "pen man" was considered the aristocrat of the underworld by criminal and policeman alike. The three most common methods of such bank swindling consisted of raising or altering authentic drafts, forging the signature of a depositor or payee, and gaining the confidence of bank officials to get money for totally bogus checks. The forgery gang was elaborately organized with a capitalist or backer who found and financed the forger. A middleman acted as liaison between the forger and the presenter of the forged paper so that exposure of the artist would be kept to a minimum.[17]

Charles O. Brockway swindled $10,000 from the First National Bank of Chicago in 1879. The next year two banks in Baltimore provided him with an additional $10,000. In 1880 George Wilkes confessed to a U.S. consul in Milan, Italy, that he and his associates obtained nearly four million dollars by forgery in the decade of the 1870s. New York chief of detectives Thomas Byrnes credited Wilkes with creating the first international band of swindlers and declared him "King of Forgers."[18] There were, however, other claimants to the throne, including George Engles and Charles Fisher. But no one had as great a claim to fame as the forger Charles Becker.

Born in Württemberg, Germany, in 1848, Becker came to America as an apprenticed engraver. Impatient with the monetary successes of his craft, he turned to forgery for money to win the hand of a sweetheart. The engagement was aborted when his crime was discovered, and he fled New York to engage in forgery professionally. In the 1870s and 1880s, he divided his energies between America and Europe, even spending some time in a Turkish jail. In these two decades Becker's expertise increased to such an extent that he was compared to Michelangelo, Rembrandt, and Whistler in artistic talent. One bank official felt that the only difference between Becker's forgeries and authentic notes was that the forgery bettered the original.[19] Beginning in February 1892, Becker began a forgery raid that lasted three years and victimized nearly forty banks. On December 18, 1895, his gang swindled the Nevada Bank of San Francisco. The presenter, A. H. Dean, rented an office in San Francisco and deposited $2,500 in the bank. He then purchased a $12.00 draft and gave it to the middleman, James Cregan, who passed it to Becker. With the aids of acids and aniline colors Becker raised the $12.00 draft to $22,000, and it was successfully passed. When the discovery was made several weeks later, it was one impetus for the American Bankers' Association to declare war on crime.[20]

On one level, Pinkerton's relationships with these gentlemen criminals was severe; a high degree of tension was maintained. The "no compromise" policy of the Jewelers' Security Alliance and the American Bankers' Association established tactics of aggresive pursuit, certainty of prosecution, and swiftness of punishment as an overall strategy of deterrence. Professional criminals were calculating, and deterrence, if it were to work at all, would do so best against them. These professional criminals, especially the gentlemen burglars of the late nineteenth century, were easier to deal with than the amateur crooks.

Part of this "get-tough" posture was manifested in the campaign against excessive executive pardons. By the last decade of the century most police officials felt pardons were too accessible. The average prisoner, it was calculated, served only 51 percent of his sentence. When President Benjamin Harrison freed the notorious safe burglar Yank McLaughlin in 1891, Robert Pinkerton was enraged and contemplated writing a public letter of protest.[21] Six years later William Pinkerton attacked the parole system of America at the National Association of Chiefs of Police convention. In response, a resolution was passed declaring official disapproval of parole for murderers, burglars, robbers, and arsonists.[22]

Crime, especially for the professional criminal, often took on the appearance of a game. These dishonest people determined their respect or lack of respect (their fear or lack of fear) of the criminal justice establishment based upon the integrity of that system. Many criminals divided the police into two groups: "square coppers" and "burglar coppers." One crook claimed that an honest policeman was seldom seen, and that "almost all members of the special details in large cities are burglar coppers . . . they simply do not want to catch thieves except to get some money from them."[23]

On numerous occasions the Pinkerton policy of deterrence worked well. Harry Russell, for example, reported to a Pinkerton detective that his gang almost robbed a bank in 1901, but at the last moment he saw the little sign all member banks of the American Bankers' Association displayed. Russell, so the story goes, immediately put his finger to his eye to warn the rest of the gang that the bank was protected by "The Eye," and they went elsewhere.[24] One criminal in 1904 wrote a Pinkerton friend that none of his criminal acquaintances wanted to antagonize the agency.[25] Such deterrence had some effect. Between 1894 and 1909, when Pinkerton's was the official detective agency for the American Bankers' Association, 194 members were robbed for a total loss of $147,065. During the same period 1,062 nonmember banks were attacked at a loss of $1,468,879.[26]

On another level, Pinkerton relationships were based upon altruism. There was a real humanitarian impulse going back to Allan Pinkerton's abolitionist days. Shortly before his death in 1907, Robert Pinkerton wrote his brother that he had always been glad to help those criminals "who are sincere in their desire to reform, and help themselves."[27] Later, William Pinkerton told a reporter that he was prouder of the fact that he had helped a few criminals to become honest than of all the work he had done in putting them behind bars.[28] The Pinkerton family, it would seem, worked hard to put criminals in jail, and then worked hard to keep them out.

One of the earliest attempts at rehabilitating crooks was directed at William Forrester, the accused murderer in the celebrated Benjamin Nathan case in 1874. Allan Pinkerton believed Forrester was merely a scapegoat for a blundering New York police department. Forrester proclaimed his innocence in a public letter and advised the police to turn the entire case over to the Pinkerton agency.[29] Charges were dropped against Forrester in the Nathan case, but he eventually went to prison in the late 1880s for burglary. The Pinkerton brothers sent him food and clothing, and after his release, Forrester went to Chicago where William Pinkerton helped establish him in a shoe repair business. Soon Forrester tired of the reformed life and took to the road on a robbery spree. The Pinkerton brothers lost faith in Forrester but not in reforming criminals.[30]

Robert Pinkerton felt the existing prisoner aid organizations ineffective, and in 1887 he advocated the creation of a National Prison Reform Society. Only a small fraction of the first offenders were beyond reform, thought Pinkerton. Even professional criminals might stabilize their lives if only corrupt and overzealous city detectives would stop hounding them.[31] Both Pinkerton brothers called for a national organization with agents throughout the country to care for ex-convicts. These agents would protect the released prisoner from unscrupulous detectives, provide financial aid, offer advice and encouragement, and furnish employment during the early months of adjustment. "When the convict could feel that there was someone to protect his rights it would probably do more than anything else to inspire him with confidence and give him encouragement," Robert predicted.[32]

Such a National Prison Reform Society never materialized, and instead, the Pinkerton brothers aided their old enemies in three ways. Most often they gave small amounts of money to destitute felons. Convicts made numerous requests to the Pinkerton brothers to pressure public officials for pardons or reductions of sentences. But more importantly, the agency used its influence to get ex-convicts employment. Frequently all three forms of assistance were given to the same individual.

Giving money, of course, was the least troublesome. Whether taking it out of their own pockets or charging it to the American Bankers' Association, the Pinkerton brothers were generous to a fault. Frank Seaver, a member of the Becker forgery gang, got a railroad ticket from Chicago to New York and $10.00 cash when he was released from prison in 1899.[33] Sneak thief Patsy Flannigan received magazines, food, and underwear while incarcerated. Occasionally, Flannigan's poverty-stricken family got money from the agency also.[34] William Boyce not only avoided robbing members of the American Bankers' Association but convinced many others that it was not wise to anger the Pinkerton's. Consequently, when Boyce got out of prison, William Pinkerton sent money until he was established in a new job.[35]

Flannigan's plight specifically illustrates the effort the Pinkerton brothers were prepared to expend in aiding a criminal. Flannigan, a sneak thief, robbed the Pinkerton-protected Yonkers Saving Bank in 1897. When he discovered the bank to be a member of the American Bankers' Association, he quickly turned himself over to the Pinkerton's expecting a light sentence. But Flannigan received the severe punishment of eleven years at Sing Sing. The Pinkerton brothers immediately worked for a reduction.[36] Superintendent Seymour Beutler traveled to the prison frequently and got Flannigan transferred from a hard job in the laundry to the prison library.[37] Contrary to his own antipardon position, Robert Pinkerton wrote letters to the judge, the victim, the warden, and the governor of New York in an attempt to get the sentence lessened.[38] Finally, in December 1902, Governor Benjamin Odell pardoned Flannigan and the Pinkertons gratefully promised to keep him honest.[39] But after his release Patsy called on William and borrowed a railroad ticket to the Southwest, where he joined another gang. Three years later Flannigan was killed during an attempted bank robbery in Texas.[40]

Pardons from prison and financial aid did not guarantee rehabilitation. Some sort of steady employment had to be provided. Even that proved disappointing. The James Dunlap case demonstrates the extent to which the Pinkerton brothers helped a felon and the extent of their frustrations. On January 25, 1876, masked men robbed the Northampton, Massachusetts, National Bank of nearly one and a quarter million dollars. Pinkerton's was hired, and within eight months Robert Pinkerton captured William Edson, Robert Scott, and James Dunlap. Edson turned states evidence and went free, but Scott and Dunlap received twenty year sentences.

Robert Scott died in prison and his widow declared war on the private detectives responsible for his capture. She printed several articles attacking the Pinkerton agency and called for Dunlap's release from prison.[41] In the meantime, Robert Pinkerton had not forgotten Dunlap. A Thanksgiving turkey was sent to the prisoner annually and Pinkerton began pressing for a pardon in 1889.[42] Between Mrs. Scott's fiery articles and Robert Pinkerton's subtle pressures, Dunlap was released in December 1892.[43] Mrs. Scott tried immediately to convince the ex-convict to appear in a theatrical production of the bank robbery in which "the villainy and perfidy of certain private detectives [would] be exposed."[44] Of course, the image-conscious Pinkertons were against such a play. Even the governor of New York felt such theatrics would corrupt the youth, and he warned Mrs. Scott to abandon the skit. She refused.[45] To escape Mrs. Scott's influence, the bewildered Dunlap was taken to Chicago where he was introduced to the chief of police by Pinkerton officials, and plans were made so that overzealous city detectives would not molest the ex-convict. William Pinkerton then gave Dunlap $2,000 to open a day-saloon in the business district of the city.[46] The saloon soon failed and Dunlap, hungry for more excitement than a day-saloon could provide, pressured the Pinkerton's for money to open a gambling hall. William Pinkerton felt that Dunlap could not operate as a gambler and instead got him another saloon. After the second saloon failed also, Dunlap joined Paddy Ryan, Jerry Driscoll, and Ed Finley to establish a gambling den in 1893. The Pinkerton's had no further dealings with Dunlap, and six years later he went to prison for burglary.[47]

Numerous other discharged prisoners were aided. Joe McCluskey, a former member of the Becker forgery gang, worked a short time for the Pinkerton's at the Coney Island Jockey Club racetrack.[48] William Pinkerton got burglar William Maher a job as a doorman at George Considine's gambling house.[49] When the international sneak thief Horace Hovan returned to America, Robert Pinkerton gave him $50 for clothes and $200 to invest in his brother's business.[50] Joe Killoran returned from Europe old and infirm. William tried unsuccessfully to employ the old sneak thief as a watchman. He finally set Killoran up selling pipe reamers, but the old rascal soon grew restless and returned to Europe where he committed suicide in 1913.[51] In prison Becker conceived a forgery-proof paper and ink, and Robert tried to interest several paper firms in the new formula.[52] Nothing came of Becker's invention, and he was employed as a Pinkerton guard at the racetracks, a position he held until his death in 1916.[53] After a period of hostility, even Max Shinburn called upon the Pinkerton's for help. Shinburn, a mechanical wizard, developed new ideas for automobile wheels while in prison. William Pinkerton gave the ex-convict money and introduced him to several automobile manufacturers.[54] The inventions were rejected and William finally got Shinburn a job as a janitor. The agency also commissioned the burglar to write a history of safe robbery, and William Pinkerton declared it so revealing and instructive to the novice criminal that its publication was forbidden. Then in 1913 William introduced Shinburn to writer Hugh Weir, who paid the exburglar $1,500 for a series of articles for the *New York Sun*.

Pinkerton aid to ex-convicts was a bittersweet mixture of failure and success. There was no established policy. Instead it was merely an intuitive altruism based upon the brothers' feelings toward a particular felon. News of Pinkerton generosity quickly spread throughout the underworld, and the agency became a stopping-off place for many ex-convicts. Those who were reliable sources of information were highly regarded. Long-time acquaintances, as well as those disabled by old age or disease, consistently found a sympathetic response from the Pinkerton family. Shortly before his death in 1907, Robert wrote to William of the child-like helplessness of the newly released prisoner and marveled "that of all the men we knew in our early days eventually the most of them came back to us."[55]

In contrast, those "enemies" who persistently attacked Pinkerton patrons, cheated the agency out of information, or published scurrilous books condemning private detectives were disliked.[56] When "Big Ed" Rice was paroled from prison in 1898, William refused him aid because of his disparaging remarks about the agency.[57] In 1908 Bob Turner tried to make book on a midwestern racing track, and William Pinkerton voiced the family's philosophy as he chased him off. "I have no objection to urging these people to get along on the right lines whenever we can, and [I] think it is our duty to do so, but this Turner was the lowest, dirtiest, lying thief I ever had anything to do with."[58]

Pinkerton aid to criminals, therefore, was a selective process. At best it presented a further dilemma that undermined the agency's effectiveness. Very few released prisoners were capable of working outside of their criminal specialty, so they were hard to place in respectable jobs. Unfortunately, the kinds of jobs the Pinkertons could provide were hardly rehabilitative. Work at saloons, gambling-houses, racetracks, and circuses was not conducive to reform. Whether the ex-convict was sincere or not, backsliding was often inevitable and gave the impression of criminal collusion rather than reform. One case, however, illustrates the practical pay-off of maintaining friendly ties with the professional criminal. It also shows the willingness of the agency to go public as long as it had control of the facts.

One of William Pinkerton's favorite saloons in Paris was the American Bar, owned and operated by Adam Worth. Most of the famous thief-takers—Thomas Byrnes of the New York police, John Shore of Scotland Yard, and William Pinkerton—agreed that Worth was the "brainest thief of the century."[59] Born to German-Jewish immigrants at Cambridge, Massachusetts, in 1844, Worth ran away from home and was a bounty jumper during the Civil War. After the war he bacame a sneak thief and took part in a series of crimes that culminated in the famous robbery of $450,000 from the Boylston National Bank of Boston. With Charles Bullard, his partner in crime, Worth fled to Europe and opened the American Bar. Thereafter periodic forays throughout Europe, Africa, and Turkey amassed for them an estimated fortune of $3,000,000. Worth avoided apprehension by cultivating respectable and influential friends and maintaining amiable relations with most European police departments.[60]

Early in his career in Paris, Worth stole a valuable painting, Gainsborough's "Duchess of Devonshire." The difficulties of selling such a piece of art were immense, and Worth kept this priceless white elephant hidden for twenty-five years. By the turn of the century, however, ill health, dwindling fortunes, and fatherly concern for children residing in America forced Worth to bargain with the portrait. He wanted to return to the United States and visit his family unmolested by the police. He also wanted some guarantees that his children would be cared for after he died. There were no police chiefs to be trusted, he believed, yet he needed a man who had sufficient influence with the police to ensure his safety. In January 1901, Worth struck a bargain with William Pinkerton. He gave the painting to Pinkerton and Worth became virtually a guest of the agency while in this country. Deathly ill, Worth even accompained the Pinkerton brothers to Hot Springs, Arkansas, for a cure, but the cure did not last. Worth returned to Europe where he died in 1902. The Pinkerton agency quickly sent money and letters of encouragement to the orphaned children. One boy was even promised a job at the agency.[61] William Pinkerton also wrote a syndicated article for the McClure newspapers and later published a special pamphlet recounting "Little Adam" Worth's spectacular career.[62] It was the death of Worth that probably prompted William Pinkerton to announce an end of an era in professional criminality: "we have no great burglars or forgers in the United States today," he declared in 1902.[63]

By the turn of the century the Pinkerton agency was a national crime fighting system. Seeking out a highly mobile population of criminals was its specialty. The general lack of federal policing and the general incompetence of rural policing left Pinkerton's almost a natural monopoly of national crime fighting. The Pinkerton reputation as super-sleuths, apparently became commonly accepted in popular culture. In the 1890s, for example, Frank A. Pinkerton, a Chicago author who was not a member of the family or agency, began a long list of detective mysteries called "The Pinkerton Detective Series." In 1906, the Rotograph Company, taking advantage of the postcard mania of the period, published a picture postcard showing four puppy bloodhounds. The caption read "Pinkertons by Birth."[64] As Pinkerton's national crime fighting system grew its business goals prompted greater involvement with police chiefs. Business reasons motivated relations with professional criminals too. Some information about criminals could come only from other criminals.

Some semantic distinctions are necessary at this point. Informers were criminal friends or acquaintances who provided information on a casual basis and for informal reasons. The informer system was based upon the personal contacts and friendships cultivated by the detective, something at which William Pinkerton was masterful. Often the informer disliked a particular crook and wanted revenge for past wrongs. In many cases, they simply liked one of the Pinkerton brothers and played the sycophant. Many gentlemen burglars were turned into informers, and the practical side of Pinkerton altruism was the search for reliable informers. Informers as sources of information, consequently, went back to early days of Pinkerton history. Although distasteful, attested by the sprinkling of "stool pigeon" scandals in the late nineteenth century, the public generally accepted such a system as necessary in crime fighting, because the links between police and criminal seemed so casual. When the New York police department's informer system became public, Police Commissioner Parker defended this "common-sense" method. "I have no sympathy with mawkishness in catching crooks," Parker noted. "If a man has committed no crime, or does not intend to commit any, he has no fear of stool pigeons or detectives, or any of the machinery for the detection of crime."[65]

An informant, on the other hand, supplied information on a regular basis and was given a salary for that function. The informant was hired and sustained as a source of information. In order to carry out such tasks, informants continued to live and work in the criminal world; frequently they were simply "kept criminals." This approach to information gathering can be documented as the social composition of the burglars and thieves changed, making it a more crucial activity at the turn of the century. A new class of criminals forced the agency to adopt a new system of information gathering.

Throughout its history, Pinkerton's protected and represented upper- and upper middle-class society. Much of the time the Pinkertons specialized in apprehending the equivalent classes of the underworld, whether they were dishonest employees or professional criminals. The agency's only involvement with classism—the labor disputes of the 1880s—did not rebound to Pinkerton credit. The lower socio-economic underworld was left to the public police. But the tramp, especially during depression times, was a major problem. As early as 1878, for example, Allan Pinkerton was concerned with the growing number of tramps traveling the railroad system and credited them—along with Communists—with the strikes of 1877. Apparently, much of America agreed, as between 1876 and 1896 all but four states passed the Tramp acts forbidding tramp travel across the country. Throughout the 1890s—especially after the panic of 1893—America experienced another one of its depressions. It was at this time that Jacob S. Coxey, a Massillon, Ohio, businessman and Populist, led an "army" of unemployed on a march to Washington. Coxey's army set a precedent, and smaller and less directed armies of tramps began to roam the countryside. Such tramp armies aroused considerable fear among ruling elites, and occasionally the public police were used to suppress ruthlessly these unemployed travelers.[66] The depression lasted until 1898, but a new criminal subclass remained well into the twentieth century. Just as William Pinkerton was declaring the professional criminal extinct, the hobo burglar, or yeggsman, began his work with nitroglycerin.

These hobo burglars were the very opposite of the old-style robber, and they considerably altered the geography and style of crime in America. On the whole the yeggs avoided the large urban centers and confined their activities to the midwestern states of Minnesota, Wisconsin, South Dakota, Nebraska, Iowa, Indiana, and Illinois. Furthermore, they avoided large cities and towns and instead concentrated on those places that had minimal police protection. Consequently, they were not a considerable problem for most urban police departments. But they were certainly a challenge to the Pinkertons, who provided so much rural and small town policing service. The yeggs did not work with elaborate tools or invent new ways of breaking safes; instead they uniformly used nitroglycerin. In fact, they "prepared" their own nitro by extracting it from dynamite and carried it around with them with reckless abandon. Needless to say there were many hobo camp and crime site casualties. Very little time was wasted on painstakingly opening a safe filled with thousands of dollars. These burglars concentrated on quickly blowing the safe in a small town bank containing only a few hundred dollars and then rushing on to do it again in a neighboring town. There was no breathing spell, and the frequency of crimes increased. Between 1895 and 1900 there were only four attacks on American Bankers' Association banks. The number increased to three for the year 1900–1901 and then to twenty-five for 1901–1902. For the next nine years the number of attacks on members never fell below fifteen per year, and the fear of crime increased. The successful record of Pinkerton's was jeopardized. The situation was worse for nonmembers as the number of robberies hovered at over seventy each year. In 1904 William Pinkerton estimated that 90 percent of all bank burglaries committed since 1900 were by yeggs.[67]

These professional criminals were difficult to apprehend because of their anonymity. Yeggs did not live in cities or towns but in hobo camps along the countryside. They dressed like mechanics and railroad men, occupations many of them might have had before the depression, and disappeared into the vast army of roaming hobos. Generally they did not have police records. Frank Tillotson, the superintendent of the Pinkerton office in Kansas City, estimated that between 1901 and 1903 his men captured thirty safe blowers, only two of whom had previous police records. "This is because a new method of safe blowing has been invented in the last few years," he believed, "and every tramp in the country knows how it is done."[68]

Background information was hard to trace because of the yegg's namelessness. The old-time thief had numerous aliases and nicknames, but the genuine name was most often used. On the other hand, yeggs were simply known by colorful descriptive nicknames, and their real names were unknown even to their closest friends. "Pitts Slim" was a slender fellow from Pittsburg; the "Aged Kid" was a young man with a grey patch of hair; "Frisco Red" was a redhead from San Francisco; and "Chi Jack" was a person named John from Chicago. Others were "Michigan Red," the "Rambler," "Denver Harry," "Topeka Joe," "Meridan Joe," "Baldy," the "Frog," "Wheeling Red," "Jamesville Tommy," "D.C. (District of Columbia) Dutch," "Ohio Fatty," "Ohio Shorty," and "Oakland Sammy," to name a few.[69] In addition, there was a new language to learn. Criminal jargon was not new, but yegg terminology was different from the old criminal cant that William Pinkerton and Robert Pinkerton learned from years of experience. Blowing a safe was "snuffing a drum" or "shooting a box." The "box man" was in charge of the explosion. Nitroglycerin was called "soup," revolvers were "cannons" or "rods," and a police officer was a "bull." The prison, in which a number of them found themselves, was called the "Dump." The challenge of the new vocabulary was significant enough, at least, for William Pinkerton to study and to lecture about it before an assembled body of police chiefs in 1904. Every detective-author included chapters on criminal vocabulary in his "how-to-be-a-detective" book.[70]

The new-styled burglar was bolder and more violent. The "Missouri Kid" publicly boasted how he robbed a member bank and killed a Pinkerton detective.[71] In 1899 two chiefs of police were killed by yeggs. By 1904, two yeggsmen were executed for murder in New York, one was executed in Missouri, and three in Arkansas met similar fates. As the yegg menace increased, the American Bankers' Association advocated state legislation severely punishing burglars who used explosives. By 1907, Colorado, Kansas, Maryland, Missouri, and Nebraska responded by punishing such criminals with sentences of twenty to twenty-five years.[72] Pinkerton administrative offices increased in the period. Up to 1883, for example, Pinkerton's operated out of three offices. Three more were added by 1895, and then fifteen new ones opened by 1909, one-third of which were in the Midwest where the yeggs posed the greatest threat. In addition, pressure was put on the railroads to police the tramps. One "roadster" in 1900 confessed that in the summer there were as many bums as passengers on the trains. Most were simply unemployed men adrift, and their numbers fluctuated much like the economy. Their troublesome presence, however, may be credited as a major reason for the rise of the railroad police.[73]

The Pinkerton detectives used informers in the early 1890s to penetrate the bands of pickpockets that followed the circuses, wild west shows, and state fairs. But an informant system did not become a formal policy until Robert Pinkerton responded to the large number of yegg burglaries in the Midwest. William Pinkerton continued to rely on his personal contacts, but they were inadequate, and Robert Pinkerton pressured the Chicago office to establish a system of informants in 1902.[74] Apparently the city police forces and the post office inspectors initially developed the informant system. In New York, Robert Pinkerton got some of his early informants upon the suggestion of the police force. But Pinkerton's had one important advantage over the public police—money. Never before had relations with the New York police been as good. An arrangement evolved early in New York in which the police and the private detective worked together to secure information, and Robert Pinkerton exclaimed, "the Police are now on such friendly terms with us that we have got several very good informants from them"[75] The police detective suggested a suitable informant, Pinkerton's supplied the money, and the informant gave the information. Since the private detective had no power to arrest, the police detective and Pinkerton's apprehended the criminal together. The policeman got the reward, and Pinkerton's got the publicity and removed a menace. Naturally Robert Pinkerton was anxious to implement this system in the Midwest where the bulk of the yegg burglaries was occurring.

An examination of the Pinkerton "cipher book" suggests that the greatest use of criminal informants was in the early 1900s, when the yeggs were especially menacing. The cipher book began in 1895 and listed all clients, competitors and crooks with a code name. Clients or associates had names ending in "–wood." For example, Florenz Ziegfeld, who had some jewelry stolen, was referred to as "Maywood." Inspector Walter Abbott of the Boston police was "Teawood" and so on. The criminals had names ending in "–stone." Bank sneak Horace Hovan was "Duckstone," Adam Worth was "Jewstone," Max Shinburn was "Plowstone," and gambler Patrick Sheedy was "Prieststone." In 1895 only ten names were placed in the cipher book, but an average of fifteen names were added each year until 1902, when ninety-seven new names appeared. From that peak the number of names each year slowly decreased until after 1909, when Pinkerton's ceased to be the bankers' official detectives. The code names permitted correspondence between offices in relative secrecy. It is apparent also that a large majority of the cipher names were given to informants so that neither the police, clients, nor the crooks knew who was aiding the Pinkerton agency.[76]

Of course, the effectiveness of the informant depended upon his acceptance by the criminal class. In short, he had to be an active crook himself. Some followed the circuses and wild west shows collecting information on the road. Others remained around the few cities that acted as yegg capitals, like Toledo, Canton, Cleveland, and Pittsburgh. But most informants simply went on plying their trade and sent occasional letters to the agency. On the average, a weekly salary of twelve dollars was given to informants, except for an exceptionally gifted person. C. D. Long, an old member of the Dalton brothers' gang, had such a wealth of information about the criminals and corrupt police of Nebraska and Iowa that he was offered seventy-five dollars a month in 1908.[77]

Some of the informants were notorious burglars who were too old to work. William Forrester was sixty-one years old when he was hired as an informant. A sneak and a burglar, he had been suspected of killing Benjamin Nathan in the most notorious murder case of the 1870s. After several attempts at reformation failed, Forrester remained active as a burglar in the 1880s and 1890s. By the 1900s, however, he was old and came to be an informant. He dressed in old clothes and frequented third-class hotels in Toledo and Canton to uncover information. Forrester's past was so controversial, however, that Robert Pinkerton warned William Pinkerton to " be careful not to keep any memorandum on his person so that nothing would be found on him, if he was ever arrested."[78]

Other informants did not have such a colorful past but were still active as criminals. John C. Archer had been an insignificant member of a pickpocket and burglary gang. At the turn of the century he gave up crime and settled down with his wife, also a noted pickpocket, to manage a hotel for transients in Dayton. Large numbers of criminals congregated there.[79] Archer's reports to his Pinkerton contact, Seymour Beutler, were filled with the gossipy news of the latest yegg and pickpocket exploits.

> I don't know what connections you've got in Toldeo, but if you're interested in Yegg work throughout the country that's your town. There are now about three mobs in there, one of whom came in about three months ago $10,000 strong, and they frequent only three places, Bill Downey's on Erie St., Johnnie Henry's also Bill Herbert's place. If you've got a hot yegg kick take Toledo for it and you'll win.[80]

But Archer occasionally came out of retirement and went off on robbery sprees himself, a fact that probably eliminated any suspicion of him by other crooks.

Since Archer and other wayward informants left Pinkerton clients alone, the agency remained discreetly quiet. For example, in December 1903, the Indianapolis police picked up Archer, who was going by the name of Wilson, for suspicion of larceny. Pinkerton superintendent Irle was at the station looking over the line-up of criminals and spotted the informant. Irle remained quiet and Archer was released because of lack of evidence.[81] Again in 1910 Archer was picked up for bank burglary, and, aside from telling a superficial past history, Pinkerton's did not give any evidence.[82] So at the same time they were active among the nation's police chiefs sponsoring greater cooperation and more conclusive identification of criminals, business self-interest compelled the Pinkertons to protect many crooks from identification by not cooperating with the police.

It is difficult to determine exactly how many informants the Pinkertons had on the payrolls at any one time. A reading of the intraoffice and interoffice correspondence, however, indicates the number to be significant. As carefully as possible, the agency simply masked their informant activities in secrecy and remained aloof when other private detectives mimed them with less skill. Such a policy was dictated by the need to preserve both the long-term effectiveness of the informant and the long-term reputation of the agency. A letter about Adam Worth in 1901 points up the cautionary concerns over the informant. Robert wrote William:

> I hope you will pardon me and not think I am complaining, when I say to you that I think you write this man [Worth] too fully. He is liable to be arrested and his mail gotten hold of.
> I am aware that it is written in typewriting and signed by an initial and nothing could be proved back, but there are things said in this letter that would enable any shrewd detective to guess who the probably writer is. For instance in this letter, in speaking of Cobblestone, you speak of Ed making money and that when he makes no money, he will return. If this letter was to fall into Scotland Yard hands, would they not think that we ought to inform them of any such man being in Europe at the present time and living in London.
> Now, please don't think that I am finding fault. Perhaps it is my over caution in these matters.[83]

One of the cautions was to keep operative and informant contact, both of whom were employees, minimal. Generally informants reported to some supervisor rather than an operative. But sometimes such contact did occur and, in a revealing letter to one operative, William Pinkerton set the boundaries of appropriate behavior and also clearly indicated the strict self-interest motif of Pinkerton crime fighting. Pinkerton wrote:

> You did perfectly right in warning them [Eddie Quinn and Paddy Guerin] away from the Millard Hotel and also in your talk with Schwendler, but you did very wrong in walking around the grounds with them or to be seen in their company, and in future you must not be walking around or be seen with them because if you are caught with them or they caught afterwards it is going to be a reflection. I want to compliment you for the manner in which you picked up Schwendler, but you must not associate or be mixed up with crooked people. You have got no occasion to point these people out to the police authorities or say anything to them about anybody. We are not interfering with them as long as they do not interfere with us.[84]

As the agency moved into the early days of the twentieth century, old unresolved problems sprung up anew. Some new detective agencies, most notably that of William Burns, arose to challenge

Pinkerton hegemony. Disreputable detectives were all around, and one Chicago critic felt that

As to private detective agencies, without reference to agencies of an established local and national reputation, they are principally constituted of thieves, pickpockets, blackmailers, and porch climbers.[85]

Thomas Beet, an alleged representative of a British private investigator, condemned 90 percent of all private detectives as "rotten to the core" in his 1906 muckraking article.[86] Robert Pinkerton, with more bravado than honesty, declared that for over half a century not one of the approximate 40,000 Pinkerton employees had been convicted of a crime.[87] Presumably he was not counting the large number of informants on the payroll.

PART THREE

THE NEW CENTURY

CHAPTER 8

Pinkerton Operatives and Operations

BY THE TURN of the century, reformers were pressuring city authorities to centralize the organizational structure of police departments. Part of the Progressive agenda was to increase the power of the police chiefs, reduce the position of midlevel captains and lieutenants, and diminish the strength of rank-and-file policemen.[1] Pinkerton private police became an attractive administrative model because both the watchmen and the detectives seemed so tightly controlled. The stern standards of the founder reappeared in 1905. "The character of the operative must be above reproach and only those of strict moral principles and good habits will be permitted to enter the service." Gambling and liquor were forbidden except "as a means to accomplish an end in the detection of crime which cannot otherwise be attained."[2]

Between 1900 and 1910, the Pinkerton agency was applauded for its sophisticated managerial style. In 1893 there were eight offices. William Pinkerton had direct responsibility for five while Robert Pinkerton administered three. By 1906, however, there were twenty offices, and the Pinkerton empire was divided into administrative districts. There were the New York, Chicago, and Denver divisions. Later, the Pittsburgh division would be added, but at this time the Denver office under James McFarland came into its own.[3]

In the first decade of the twentieth century ultimate power in the Pinkerton organization resided in seven men: William Pinkerton, Robert Pinkerton, Allan Pinkerton II (Robert's son), John Cornish, Edward S. Gaylor, James McFarland, and general manager George

D. Bangs. William Pinkerton and Robert Pinkerton visited and inspected the various offices and busied themselves with public relations work. Allan Pinkerton, Jr., was serving his apprenticeship much as his father and uncle had done forty years earlier. Cornish, Gaylor, and McFarland were either division leaders or headed important offices. In terms of practical day-to-day administrative detail, general manager George D. Bangs ran the agency. His father, George H. Bangs, held the same position from 1857 to 1883, so the Bangs name and influence had as much longevity as that of Pinkerton. A professional managerial class had developed.

The typical Pinkerton office was divided into four sections. A clerical department—consisting of office boys, janitors, cashier, bookkeeper, and stenographers—kept all accounts, typed the detective reports, and assisted with all business correspondence. Morris Friedman, a clerk in the Denver office at this time, wrote the most complete administrative description and most devastating critique of the Pinkerton agency in 1907. The criminal department was composed of a rogues gallery, a card file on known criminals, and correspondence relating to case work. The Chicago and New York offices, where most of the criminal work was done, had the most complete criminal departments, and identification information went from those offices to police departments and Pinkerton branches throughout the country. The criminal departments of other offices, however, were less important.[4]

The operations department was composed of detectives. These operatives were of three kinds. A small number of special operatives were occasionally in the office. They handled unimportant cases when no regular operative was available. They were temporary operatives who came in to do one job and were released when it was over. The general operative was much more important. He was the highly publicized glamorous detective who assumed undercover roles or captured famous professional criminals. The rules of the agency required every office to have two or more general operatives on staff at all times. If they were all busy then general operatives from other offices were sent. The secret operatives were labor spies. These people were given code numbers for identification. Only the superintendent and assistant superintendent knew the secret operative's real identity. Clerical staff knew them only by their code number. Their job was to work at factories and mines in order to spy on workers.[5]

The fourth section of a Pinkerton agency was the executive department, which consisted of one superintendent and two or more assistant superintendents. These executives had to study and revise the reports of the operatives before they were typed and sent to higher Pinkerton officials and to the clients. An office of thirty operatives, for example, had five administrators. Each official was in charge of supervising five operatives. In addition, each executive had to canvass for new business each week. As much high status was given for capturing new clients as for capturing old crooks.[6]

Every afternoon the members of the executive department met to discuss the financial charges to be made to clients and to report on each operative's work performance. Then once every two weeks a summary report, called the "General Business Letter," which discussed the particular office's work (operative's work and executive's canvassing), was compiled with a financial statement and sent to division headquarters and on to George D. Bangs in New York City. Bangs then assembled an agency-wide summary for William Pinkerton and Robert Pinkerton.

The typical weekly financial statement of the Denver office, for example, read:

SALARIES:

Manager of Western Division	$ 45.00
Office Superintendent	35.00
4 Assistant Superintendents	115.00
Chief Clerk	19.00
Bookkeeper	18.00
Cashier	16.00
5 Stenographers	70.00
Office Boy	5.00
Private Janitors	4.00
30 Operatives	450.00

OTHER EXPENSES:

Office Rent	35.00
Stationary	11.00
Interagency telegrams	5.00
Telephone	2.50
Postage	10.00
TOTAL FOR WEEK	$841.00[7]

Operations were not as tidy in the Pinkerton office as suggested by organizational charts or agency spokesmen. The everyday experiences of the employees have been neglected in relating the business history of the agency and the stories of detective managers. Rank-and-file operatives generally did not write their memoirs. If an operative became famous, he moved quietly into management roles, and his fame was appropriated by the agency as a whole. But it would be remiss if some attempt was not made to see Pinkerton detective work through the eyes of the employee.

The worlds of the watchmen and the detectives were very different. Two kinds of watchmen existed: the permanent members of the Protective Patrol and the vast army of temporaries hired in response to the press of work. In ordinary times members of the Protective Patrol walked the streets and protected those businesses having contracts with Pinkerton. They worked six hours then had six hours off only to return for another round of duty. Since this type of policing was done for profit, the Pinkerton patrolman had less freedom than the police patrolman. A high premium was placed upon the captains of the Patrol, and the managing and checking of employee honesty was carried out vigorously. Many of these permanent guards had done police work before because, as one Pinkerton official declared, "there is a class of men who are constantly losing their positions on account of political changes, and I might say here we are quick to take these men in if we think they will make good men for us, and we try to get them in our employ."[8] Until the mid-1880s, however, these watchmen were pretty much confined to Chicago and New York as a supplement to official policing. They did not become a managerial problem for the agency until the decades of labor strife increased their numbers.

Another type of watchman was the "temporary," those men hired when demand exceeded the prevailing Pinkerton work force. They had little training and had considerable exposure to the public. During strike disputes the "regular" watchmen acted as leaven; they became supervisors and higher echelon professional Pinkertons amidst those men hired quickly to meet a crisis.

Edward E. Parker was one of these temporary Pinkertons. In 1886 Parker migrated to Chicago from St. Paul, Minnesota, in search of work. Within two weeks he was hired off the street by Pinkertons for $2.50 per day plus room and board. Regular watchmen undoubtedly received a higher salary.[9] Adequate information never filtered down to these temporaries; it stopped at higher levels. Characteristically, watchmen were never told of their particular job until they arrived at the work site. Parker, for example, was taken secretly to

Cheyenne, Wyoming, where a railroad strike was in progress. When Parker and 200 other watchmen arrived bewildered at the Cheyenne depot, they met a crowd that "yelled all kinds of talk at us; to lynch us; and shoot us, and everything else."[10] Parker was shaken considerably by the incident at Cheyenne. On the way to Laramie the watchmen were given guns and Parker feared for his life as he noticed the general ineptitude of the watchmen with firearms. After two uneventful weeks in Laramie, Parker returned to Chicago and complained to Pinkerton management about the general lack of preparation watchmen received for such dangerous work. He was put on the blacklist and sought work elsewhere.[11]

John W. Holway was a twenty-three year old student when he was hired for the Homestead expedition. Like Parker, Holway was kept ignorant of the particulars of the job until he was well on his way. The men were assured that the area to be protected was fenced and secured from mob violence. When shots were fired, as Holway described it, near panic and disorganization occurred. Only a small cadre were disciplined while "a good many of the men were thoroughly demoralized." Several Pinkerton watchmen aboard Holway's barge "put on life-preservers and jumped under the tables and had no control over themselves whatever."[12] When the Pinkertons surrendered and were being marched ashore, Holway attempted an escape. One hundred strikers chased him down, and, according to Holway's testimony, he was kicked and pounded with stones. For his pains and labors Holway received $15.00 per day and expenses when he returned to Chicago.[13]

John Kennedy was at Homestead, too. To him there were two responses to the violence. On one hand, a small company of 25 to 50 men were calm and sober. Kennedy believed that they "were very firm men who knew what they came there to do. They knew what their business was." Undoubtedly, they were regular Pinkertons sent to lead the watchmen. When the gunshots occurred it was these guards who placed themselves in dangerous positions and ended up guarding the guards. On the other hand, most of the men were like Kennedy himself. That is to say, they were timid and afraid because, as Kennedy declared, "we did not come [there] to fight, we only came . . . as guards." And they stoutly refused to take up arms when the regular Pinkerton guards prodded them.[14]

For Pinkerton management, however, the operatives and detectives were the agency darlings. They may not have brought in as much money for the business, but they did help create a Pinkerton mystique. The sleuth star of the nineteenth century was James McParlan. The Molly Maguire case catipulted him from shadows and shadowing to limelight. In the 1880s he was rewarded with the superintendency of the Denver office. By the turn of the century, he was division manager and a model for most upwardly mobile operatives.

McParlan's early twentieth century equivalent was Frank Dimaio. In 1888 David Hennessey had been elected chief of police in New Orleans on a reform ticket. Earlier, as a police detective, Hennessey had angered some of the Sicilian longshoremen and became embroiled in their gang wars. In 1890, as he was preparing to testify against the Provenzano gang, Hennessey was assassinated. Private detectives were hired and, to the *New York Sun,* the stunned New Orleans police seemed "disposed to hesitate in this important matter until they [heard] from Pinkerton."[15]

Frank Dimaio was selected to investigate. Dimaio's parents were Italians, and he attended school in Italy. One Pinkerton official knew of no other "man in the Agency who is his equal in regard to work among Italians." The operative was placed in jail among several Provenzano suspects and won the confidence of Emanuel Politz, who confessed the plot and associated the word "Mafia" with the killing. Later, however, the men were found innocent and released amidst charges of jury tampering, only to be lynched by an irate mob.[16] Dimaio was then put in charge of apprehending Butch Cassidy's "Wild Bunch" and traced them to Argentina before the case was closed in 1903. He returned to America and was rewarded with the general superintendency of the newly formed Pittsburgh division.[17]

Not all operatives were as stellar as Dimaio. Danger, temptation, and frustration were byproducts of detective work. Operative E. Stokes, for example, was engaged as a laborer in a construction firm to check on employee dishonesty. His leg was amputated in an elevator accident in 1906. M. B. Tobin, a longtime operative, was working the racetracks in Buffalo, New York. He started drinking, "embarrassed the Agency," and was fired. Operative W. J. Bowen, while working as a locomotive fireman in New Jersey, began furnishing false reports and was fired. Finally, W. Fliers, operating as an undercover steam fitter, simply walked off the job.[18] Such problems were so common that the ex-clerk of the Denver office felt that "the average operative is a positive trial from the day he enters the service until he resigns or is discharged. He is always doing something foolish or imprudent, and is a constant source of anxiety to the Agency."[19]

Indeed, much of the work done by an operative was mundane and even ludicrous. It simply did not lend itself to the exploits of McParlan and Dimaio. Operatives made distinctions between "real work" and "city work," the latter being dreaded. Dashiell Hammett was a Pinkerton between 1913 and 1918. In the 1920s he returned to Pinkerton's for a short time and worked on the famous Fatty Arbuckle murder case. His experiences, if they can be taken seriously, are statements on the common work done by the operative. On one occasion, for example, Hammett was hired to discharge a woman's housekeeper. On another occasion Hammett followed a man out of town. The suspect got lost and Hammett ended up directing him back to the city. As to the skills of other operatives, Hammett knew of one detective who, while looking for pickpockets at a racetrack, had his own pocket picked. Later that same operative became an official in one of the eastern offices. The cleverest and most successful Pinkerton operative Hammett ever knew was "extremely myopic."[20] If these incidences were typical of Hammett's detective career, it would be difficult to imagine them as prototypes for his detective writings. Nonetheless, one of America's most famous writers spent at least five years in one of America's most famous detective agencies. Apparently Hammett's ideal detective experiences and his real ones did not coincide.

For some operatives detective work was an extension of their personalities. Tom Horn, the notorious western gunman, was a Pinkerton operative for four years. Horn had been an army scout and Indian fighter in the 1880s, and came to the Pinkerton Denver office in 1890 with impeccable credentials.[21] For the next four years Horn roamed the Rocky Mountain area killing and arresting train robbers and cattle rustlers. He even committed a robbery in Nevada, and William Pinkerton had to come to his rescue. Another Denver operative, Charles Siringo, reported that "on one of his trips to Denver, William A. Pinkerton told me that Tom Horn was guilty of the crime, but that his people could not afford to let him go to the penitentiary while in their employ."[22] The work and the protection were good, but Horn felt too restricted by the agency. "There were a good many instructions and a good deal of talk given the operative regarding the things to do and the things that had been done," complained Horn when he resigned in 1894.[23] As a free-lance detective and hired gun for the Wyoming Cattlemen's Association, Horn's activities became so brazen that he was convicted and executed for murder in 1903. But not before he badgered the agency for all kinds of aid.

For nearly ten years after Homestead, Pinkertons avoided labor spying. The Denver office, under the leadership of McParlan and J. C. Fraser, became more active as the labor problems grew in the early years of the twentieth century. Secret operatives began to eclipse the regular operatives as they infiltrated the Colorado, Montana, and Idaho mining areas. A. H. Crane was a member of a union in Colorado City in 1902. Operatives J. H. Cummins, Philander Bailey, and George Riddell, did much the same. The unexpressed expectations were that they might duplicate the exploits of their divisional leader, McParlan. The man who came closest to McParlan's Molly Maguire episode was A. W. Gratias. Gratias had joined the Western Federation of Miners in 1902 and the following year was made chairman of the union relief committee. In 1904 Gratias was elected president of his local union and even went as a delegate to the annual convention. At all times Gratias and other operatives provided voluminous reports on union activities.[24]

For much of this period the main reader and recorder of these reports in Denver was the stenographer Morris Friedman. At first Friedman was awed by McParlan, but as time passed he became disillusioned. It came to a head in the Frank Steunenberg affair. In 1905, Steunenberg, an ex-governor of Idaho, was murdered in Caldwell, Idaho. The supposed assassin, Harry Orchard, was quickly apprehended, and McParlan thought that William Haywood, George Pettibone, and Charles Moyer—all of the Western Federation of Miners—were behind the killing. Third degree methods on Orchard soon produced enough evidence for McParlan to arrest the three labor leaders in Colorado and spirit them away to Idaho. Clarence Darrow defended the labor leaders against state prosecutor William E. Borah, and they were acquitted. Friedman was so disgusted over the incident that he left Pinkertons and wrote his book, *The Pinkerton Labor Spy* in 1907.[25]

Friedman's book, like so many muckraking books of the first decade of the century, described in detail the organization and operation of the Pinkerton business.[26] Specifically he concentrated on the Denver office, but the general implication was aimed at the entire Pinkerton empire. Even further, however, he addressed private detective work as a whole. Numerous operatives' reports were reproduced, lending documented authority to his work. Pinkerton involvement in the Cripple Creek and Telluride strikes and the Haywood trial were recounted. All of Pinkerton management were seen as a public menace masquerading as a public necessity, and the agency was equated to the Russian secret police. McParlan was accused of fabricating stories of union conspiracies to win new contracts.[27] Never before had an employee so exposed the inner workings of Pinkerton operations. The agency was stunned into silence. Never again would ex-employees find it so easy to publish their detective experiences. The next operative to try, Charles Siringo, met with considerable difficulty.

Siringo was born in Matogorda County in southwestern Texas in 1856. As a youth he was a cowboy, an identification he never abandoned. In 1877 he was a friend of Billy the Kid and Pat Garrett. Later, when he applied for work at Pinkerton's, Siringo used Garrett as a character reference. From 1883 to 1886, Siringo settled down in a small Kansas town and wrote his *A Texas Cowboy*. But much like Allan Pinkerton years before, a phrenologist convinced Siringo that he was made to be a detective. Siringo then moved to Chicago.

By chance he was in Chicago to witness the Haymarket turmoil of 1886. He was opposed to the anarchists and he joined what appeared to him then to be the chief enemy of anarchism, Pinkerton's. His first job was to watch the jury during the Haymarket trials and prevent jury tampering. Although there were good men in the Chicago office, he was shocked over the general scandalous conduct of the operatives. Two operatives, for example, went to Grant Park and struck up casual conversations with anarchists, only to inflate the talks into reports of radical plots. In addition, Siringo was introduced to the practice of overcharging his expense account. Within a year Siringo was having some misgivings and was happy to leave for a new office in the Rockies.[28]

Throughout the late nineteenth century Denver became the center of considerable detective activity. David J. Cook, for example, had drifted in and out of Denver for several years before finally opening his Rocky Mountain Detective Association in 1863. Much as Allan Pinkerton had done ten tears earlier, Cook was also a government detective in the formative years of his business. Then from 1866 to 1868 he was Denver's city marshal. In 1869 he was sheriff of Arapahoe County. For the next twenty years he combined careers as private and public policeman. In 1880 he was made chief of police. All the time his Rocky Mountain Detective Association flourished and was a major competitor to Pinkerton's. John F. Farley is another example. Farley joined Gus Thiel's St. Louis-based detective agency in 1873. By 1875 he was superintendent of Thiel's New York office. He opened and administered new Thiel offices in St. Paul (1878) and Denver (1885). In 1889, after establishing a considerable reputation, he was named chief of police in Denver.[29]

By 1888 Siringo was in the new Denver office under the superintendency of John Eams. Doc Williams, once a safe blower, and Pat Barry, the future chief of police of Portland, Oregon, accompanied Siringo to Denver. Almost immediately intraoffice conflict occurred as Eams, Barry, and Williams took a dislike to Siringo. He feared for his life every time he entered the operatives' room, and, he would write later, his best friend in Denver was "old Colt .45."[30]

In the meantime, Siringo quickly established himself as a good operative. For two months he was an undercover man in a Wyoming cowboy gang. His testimony indicted the gang. The U.S. government had him investigate the Ute Indian War. He worked as a miner in Aspen, Colorado, for two months and discovered ore thieves. For nine months in 1889 Siringo befriended a suspect and travelled throughout the Indian territory as a companion in order to get a confession. On another occasion, after eight months of strenuous camp life in New Mexico, he almost died from small pox, a disease that left his face badly pitted. These exploits led him to believe that "with all of the Agency's faults, I must confess that they do a lot of good work in running down crime for money."[31]

Siringo hated "city work" and especially disliked being near Eams and the other operatives. In 1889 Eams was caught stealing from the agency. Clients were being charged for work not done, a common practice according to Siringo. Eams, however, had not reported his manipulations to the head office, and when it was detected, the superintendent and most operatives were fired. It was at that time that McFarland was brought in and the Denver office began its climb to importance. It was at this time, also, that Tom Horn was hired, and Siringo and the gunfighter formed a strong friendship. Until the Coeur D'Alene problems occurred in 1892, Siringo remained in Denver doing the much-hated city work.[32]

Late in 1892 Siringo was assigned to the northern Idaho mine fields. As C. Leon Allison, Siringo infiltrated the mining unions and became a friend of George Pettibone. Siringo, who at first declined this assignment because of his sympathy toward the miners, became convinced that the union leaders were killers. Siringo reported all union plots and plans to the mine owners and within a year's time he became a union leader. Eventually he was found out and had to hide out in the hills, only to come into town to give testimony at the trial. John Hammond, one of the mine owners, remembered when he and Siringo

walked together down the middle of the road, each of us carrying two pistols in our coat pockets. There was a running fire of comment from miners on the sidewalk as they expressed their hatred for Siringo in no uncertain language. As he walked, Siringo kept his hands in his pockets. The outline of his guns could clearly be seen as he swayed ominously from side to side.[33]

Eighteen union leaders, including Pettibone, went to jail due to Siringo's testimony.

After the Coeur D'Alene affair, Siringo spent four years with Dimaio in search of Butch Cassidy and the Wild Bunch gang. He claimed to have traveled over 25,000 miles in search of the outlaws. Such activity made Siringo a personal favorite of William Pinkerton and Robert Pinkerton. In 1904, for example, Siringo traveled to New York and was pleasantly surprised to find his picture on Robert Pinkerton's wall. George D. Bangs wined and dined the western operative. In Chicago, William Pinkerton invited Siringo to his home to ride his favorite saddle horse. It was at this time that the San Francisco superintendency was offered, but Siringo turned it down because "I know my conscience would not allow me to act as superintendent of the Agency in a big city where so much dirty work would be expected of me. I had decided that I would rather remain a sleuth, to do as I pleased when out of sight of my superiors in office."[34]

Siringo's career with Pinkerton's ended as it had begun. After his eastern junket, Siringo was made the personal body guard to McParlan during the Haywood-Pettibone-Moyer trials in Idaho. Once again he viewed Pinkertonism and anarchism close up. Dislike for radicals and disillusionment with Pinkerton midlevel management were reaffirmed. The ambiguity that had been suggested twenty-two years earlier reappeared. In the intervening years he had avoided the problem by escape into lonely operative activities. Now, however, it seemed that those freewheeling days were over. The Wild

Bunch pretty much drew the final curtain on the western outlaws. By doing so they ended Siringo's freedom as well. He was an adventurer, and as the demand for his kind of operations declined, so did his commitment to the agency. Shortly after the Steunenberg case Siringo resigned to publish his *Pinkerton Cowboy Detective.*[35]

Siringo's book appeared shortly after Friedman's, and the agency was in no mood for public exposure. The agency tied up his book in court for two years and forced him to make substantial changes. The title, for example, was changed to *The Cowboy Detective,* and all references to Pinkerton were changed to Dickenson. Names like Tom Horn were changed to Tom Corn. Siringo became bitter. Previously he had managed to maintain his respect for William Pinkerton and Robert Pinkerton while he blamed the problems of the agency on midlevel people. Now, however, this policy of censorship convinced him that the entire agency was evil. In 1914 Siringo sent the agency another manuscript entitled *Two Evil Isms,* and asked if there were any lawful objections. Pinkerton management objected to the entire book and began a practice, which exists to this day, of controlling publication of works on the agency. Taking an independent course, Siringo published the book privately. The ex-operative was taken to court and the printing plates were confiscated and handed over to the Pinkerton agency. Only a few copies of the book survived.[36]

More than most, Charles Siringo was the best example of Pinkerton operatives and operations. He was an accurate representation of the work and the tensions in the Denver office. Although he was a "cowboy detective," the work he did was so variegated that it indicates the types of activities going on in the western division. Like Dimaio, Siringo was a top flight employee; he was an agency darling, too. But he was never an organization man. On at least three occasions he declined offers of promotion to superintendencies. Siringo was an itinerate adventurer and being a Pinkerton operative allowed him to play out his footloose life within the confines of corporate respectability.

Siringo also represents the tensions within the agency. The happiest days of his career as a Pinkerton were spent away from the office and the management. After he resigned Pinkerton's, he claimed to have joined the agency only to collect material for another book. Books did follow, but twenty years' research stretches credibility. His hatred for the agency only increased with the retelling of adventures he had experienced. Siringo was a late-nineteenth and early-twentieth-century marginal man. He was in a business he disliked to do work he loved. His ambiguity was best pointed up in *Two Evil Isms*. The cover of the book showed Uncle Sam being squeezed by a boa constrictor. The words "Pinkertonism" and "Anarchism" were printed on the reptile's sides. According to nineteenth century perceptions, Pinkerton's was the antithesis of anarchism, and one chose sides accordingly. But in the Progressive Era, new alignments and attitudes were being forged. Now two extremes were being joined: unbridled violence by radicals was matched by unbridled violence by business interests. Conflicting dichotomies were brought together to present a new enemy to democracy. Such attacks were more damaging because they came from a man who had been an operative for over two decades.

Eventually, Siringo went to California and wrote cowboy stories until his death in 1928. But before doing so, he gave one last parting shot to Pinkerton by joining its chief competitor, the William Burns Detective Agency.

CHAPTER 9

"Mushroom Agencies" in the Progressive Era

LUCRATIVE CONTRACTS with the Jewelers' Security Alliance and the American Bankers' Association, plus involvement with the International Association of Chiefs of Police, firmly reestablished Pinkerton's business position in the early years of the twentieth century. Although not forgotten, Homestead dimmed into the past. Sporadic work for various jockey clubs, railroads, and express companies contributed to the agency's growth. There were always individual clients as well. Charles Pinkham, president of Lydia E. Pinkham's Vegetable Compound industry, for example, paid Pinkerton detectives seven thousand dollars in 1900 to track down people counterfeiting and selling his patent medicine.[1] That same year the agency employed more than one thousand persons. The watchman service, or Protective Patrol, had expanded to such an extent that burglar alarm systems linked client businesses to Pinkerton headquarters.[2] The number of operatives steadily increased. In 1899 fifty-eight new detectives were hired, and another sixty-five were engaged the following year.[3] It was not uncommon for heads of foreign police systems to regard Pinkertons as America's official detective force.[4] In the first ten years of the new century, eleven offices were opened, and twelve more were added the next decade.[5] As the twentieth century began, there was little doubt about the importance of private policing in America and that the Pinkerton agency was the largest private police business in the world. The successes of such operatives as James McParlan and Frank Dimaio, and the disillusionments of such operatives as Horn and Siringo, were symptomatic of a business undergoing its own "managerial revolution." Amidst this growth during the Progressive Era, Pinkerton hegemony was challenged as never before. Competition came from numerous directions. State and federal police systems were beginning to develop. More importantly, the challenge came from within the profession as numerous private detective agencies were formed.

William Pinkerton, especially after Robert Pinkerton's death in 1907, increasingly acted as patriarch of the profession. Journalists came to Pinkerton's for news on the latest criminal threat or on a particular societal vulnerability to crime, and William Pinkerton quite readily accepted the role of elder statesman of the private detective industry.[6] By 1910 other private detectives had gained membership in the International Association of Chiefs of Police, but William Pinkerton remained the dominant figure. He continued to make speeches at every annual meeting. In 1913, for example, he addressed the question, "Do Paroles Work for Betterment?" As the Keystone Cop stereotype became particularly prevalent in popular entertainment, William Pinkerton was called upon to discuss "Moving Pictures as Factors in Education" in 1914. In 1915, 1916, and 1918, as part of his ongoing campaign for better criminal identification, he gave speeches on the history and application of fingerprinting. Finally, as the world war became a major preoccupation, he turned his attention to radicals, especially the International Workers of the World, and international crime fighting. These speeches were never carefully researched or for that matter ever thoroughly thought out. The atmosphere, more often as not, was that of cronies getting together to listen to a reminiscence. Almost always William Pinkerton prefaced his talk with excuses having to do with the "press of business."

Other Pinkerton officials attained high visibility and respectability as well. Robert Linden, superintendent of the Philadelphia Pinkerton office in the 1880s, became the head of the Philadelphia police department in the late 1890s. Linden, personally or through his protégés, continued to influence that police department well into the twentieth century.[7] After twenty-three years with Pinkerton's, George Dougherty became the deputy commissioner and chief of detectives for the New York police department in 1911. Dougherty later joined the faculty of the New York Police School for Detectives and led several crusades for the adoption of a comprehensive fingerprinting system in America.[8] Allan Pinkerton II (son of Robert Pinkerton) turned down an invitation to be the police commissioner of New York City in 1913.[9] Other members of Pinkerton management split off and either became police officials or opened their own detective agencies, creating a network of proselytizers for Pinkerton's brand of private policing. The Pinkerton family had always defended their occupation as a profession. In the early years of the century renewed efforts were called for as more and more detective agencies appeared and as sensational detectives captured the public imagination.

After President William McKinley's assassination in 1901 at the hands of an anarchist, the nation was prepared to see radicals everywhere. Old fears of radicalized labor were fanned, and a host of new detective agencies entered into the fracas between labor and management and earned the reputation as "gunmen of industry." That is not to say that Pinkerton's was totally absent from the field, but after Homestead, the agency deemphasized strike fighting. In 1902, for example, it provided 176 scabs for the Allis-Chalmers Corporation. It took a particularly ominous threat to bring Pinkerton's into strike work. Initially, however, this work was left to Archer, Baldwin-Felts, Waddell-Mahon, John Sherman, and Gus Thiel to name just a few of the more prominent agencies. So many new detective businesses appeared on the scene that, in 1912, American Federation of Labor president Samuel Gompers deplored the fact that private detectives had "never been used as extensively as in the first decade of the twentieth century." Part of Gompers concern was with the established agencies and part was due to the new type of strikebreaking agency that came into existence.[10]

Since the 1880s most detective businesses had provided strikebreakers as well as spies and guards. Jack Whitehead was the first to specialize in this activity in the early 1890s when he maintained an army of forty men solely to break strikes. The practice, however, was formalized by Jim Farley, the "King of Strikebreakers," at the turn of the century.[11] As a New York detective, Farley saw the chaos resulting when several private detective agencies provided scabs for the same strike. A centralized force of workers that could be mobilized and moved quickly by a strikebreaker general was needed, he believed. In 1895 Farley gave up any pretense of detective work and specialized in strike services. It was rumored that he earned nearly a million dollars from one strike in San Francisco. After ten years of specializing, Farley retired, noting that he had not lost any of his thirty-five strike jobs.[12] Others, like Pearl L. Bergoff, followed Farley's example. Between 1910 and 1922 Bergoff was idle only a few months a year as strikebreaking became profitable business. He charged the Erie Railroad two million dollars to smash the switchmen's walkout in the 1920s.[13] The government did nothing to restrict these activities, and the number of agencies offering extensive strikebreaking services grew to sixty by the 1930s, when a law was passed forbidding the mass transportation of scabs. In the meantime, these psuedo-detective agencies flourished by doing very little detective work.[14]

Pinkertons did get involved with labor, though not as extensively as in earlier years. A low profile was a distinct policy, since controversey, as much as possible, needed to be avoided. A few Pinkerton operatives infiltrated labor unions, and one agent was actually the chairman of the Western Federation of Miners Relief Committee in 1903. Their real or suspected presence in the ranks of labor was disconcerting enough that new exposé books soon found a printing.[15] As it had been the Mollies in an earlier time, it was now the Wobblies —the International Workers of the World—that aroused the Pinkerton agency and gave it greater exposure in the labor wars.

Beginning in 1905, with the founding of the Industrial Workers of the World, there was a considerable fear that labor in the Pacific Northwest and Rocky Mountain states would be radicalized. Based in Denver, the Wobblies, led by "Big Bill" Haywood, threatened to organize the migrant worker along anarcho-syndicalist lines. Also based in Denver was James McParlan, the Pinkerton hero of the Molly McGuire episode. When the ex-governor of Idaho, Frank Steunenberg, was assassinated in 1905, radical labor was blamed. McParlan spirited away to Idaho the three Colorado labor leaders— Haywood, George Pettibone, and Charles Moyer—and unsuccessfully tried to convict them for the murder.[16] The kidnapping was a violation of the labor leaders' legal rights, a point their attorney, Clarence Darrow, tried to make, but the trial was allowed to proceed, indicating the extent of public feeling in the Rocky Mountain area. Although these three Wobblies were released, the movement bore the brunt of persecution for the next fifteen years. Finally, during World War I, the entire force of the federal government was brought to bear, and Haywood fled the country.[17]

In a few states "company police" grew in response to strikes as well. Pennsylvania Coal and Iron Police, for example, had existed since the 1870s. Upon request from business leaders, the governor could issue special commissions conferring police power on persons employed by the various coal and iron companies. In 1901, the governor of Pennsylvania issued 570 such commissions. The following year he gave out 4,512 commissions as strikes increased in the Pennsylvania coalfields.[18] Railroad cars filled with company policemen and mounted with Gatling guns visited mining towns in order to control striker discontent. It seemed to many that the state had sold its police power to vested interests and that company police were worse than private detective agencies. America appeared to be locked into its own feudal age.[19]

Another response to the labor problems of the early twentieth century was the development of state police. Hordes of tramps, of which the yegg burglars were a part, proved the weaknesses of rural policing. Resistance to establishing a rural police, however, remained, and by the turn of the century only Texas, Massachusetts, and Arizona had state constabularies. Apparently residents of small towns feared higher taxes more than they feared criminals.[20] Besides, state police systems seemed "more nearly akin to the police forces of Europe than to the most common type of American police departments," and developments stalled in the nineteenth century.[21] Pennsylvania, with so much of its railroading and mining industry in rural counties, had considerable trouble policing labor disturbances. It was here where the Coal and Iron Police achieved considerable power at the turn of the century. By 1905 the increasing number of strikes prompted the creation of a state police under John C. Groome.

Superintendent Groome, former commander of the Philadelphia militia, disciplined his nearly two hundred troopers along strict military lines, a policy easy to implement because ninety percent of his men had seen service in the regular army or navy. Organized into troops, these policemen lived in barracks scattered throughout the state. They rode established patrols on horseback to apprehend criminals and to harrass tramps. Those troopers near industrial centers frequently maintained order during strikes. In years of severe labor trouble, such as 1916, over 50 percent of the troopers' time was spent on strike duty.[22] Organized labor quickly labeled the state troopers as the "American Cossacks" or "Black Hussars."[23] In 1920 Governor William Sproul felt the organization's function in strikes was beneficial and that "at no time since it was inaugurated has any disturbance in the state gotten beyond its control."[24]

The first two decades of the twentieth century were a golden age of private detective work. Private policing flourished as industry and commerce rapidly expanded and diversified. At a time when the public police were still characterized as lacking any business technique and efficiency, the highly competitive private police seemed more reliable.[25] Philadelphia experienced a remarkable surge, as private detective firms more than doubled between 1900 and 1908 from fourteen to thirty-seven. There were thirty-four agencies in Chicago by 1910; eight years later there were fifty-eight. In 1914, it was estimated, there were nearly 10,000 "special policemen" in Chicago. Eight hundred of them were railroad police. The stockyards, banks, factories, and department stores employed the rest.[26] New York boosters claimed they had seventy-five detective businesses in 1904; eight years later there were one hundred and fifty licensed detectives in the city.[27] "It is safe to say," one report declared, "that for every officer of the law provided by the city of New York there were at least two—possibly three—private detectives plying their vocation in this city."[28] Leonard Fuld, one of the more serious students of police administration, believed private detectives provided a valuable service on the federal level where no real detective power existed. But when the private agency comes into competition with the public police, "its influence is bad," he said, "both on the discipline of the municipal force and on the administration of justice in the community."[29]

In the nineteenth century most of the real competitive private agencies had been founded by ex-Pinkerton employees. Benjamin Franklin established an agency in Philadelphia in the late 1870s after being a member of Pinkerton management. Gus Thiel did the same in St. Louis.[30] In 1894 Charles E. Burr left Pinkerton's to organize the Pennsylvania Railroad Police. Before he arrived, the various special agents and watchmen were under a variety of administrators. Burr reorganized the 250 men along strict military lines with a hierarchy of inspectors, captains, lieutenants, and patrolmen. Within three years he had 900 men working the 2,800 miles of road. Between 1896 and 1900 they made 46,800 arrests with a 73 percent conviction rate. In 1902 Burr moved to the Baltimore and Ohio Railroad and reorganized its force.[31] By 1904 he was in Chicago to start a private agency.[32] Prior to his death in 1902, John Curtin headed one of the best known and most reliable detective businesses in San Francisco. Curtin had been a close friend of William Pinkerton since the late 1860s when he had joined the Pinkerton firm.[33]

The Pinkerton family realized they were training potential competitors, and they tired to keep most of them by offering promotions and salary increases. But the fear of a Pinkerton-trained competitor was not compelling and occasionally the agency would even help a man establish a rival business. Seymour Beutler, for example, worked twenty-six years for Pinkerton's and was considered invaluable at the racetracks. In many cases he was the key contact man between the army of informants and Pinkerton management. Rheumatism plagued Beutler, and in 1909 he asked the agency for money to start his own detective firm. Reluctant to lose a good man and create a new competitor, the Pinkerton's offered him a promotion and a transfer to warmer climates. Beutler persisted and William Pinkerton finally gave him the money to establish his own business.[34]

A few ex-Pinkertons created scandalous businesses, but most headed reputable firms and credited their training to the Pinkerton agency. After he left the New York police department and formed his own agency, George S. Dougherty remembered his Pinkerton days fondly. "There never was a cleaner institution in the world," he recalled. "They have always been the soul of honor and teach their employees accordingly."[35] Competition then was not the issue, especially if it came from a network of friends who shared the Pinkerton philosophy.

The private detective industry also provided a field of entrepreneurship for policemen cut off from their public careers by retirement, dismissal, politics, or desire for profit. In the nineteenth century, ex-Secret Service men like Ichabod Nettleship, James J. Brooks, Andrew Drummond, and L. A. Newcome formed their own private agencies after retiring from government service.[36] The major thrust of their businesses was detection, an art they learned on the federal level. The nineteenth-century city police departments were more patrol-oriented than detective-oriented, and the number of detective agencies established by ex-city policemen was small. By the turn of the century, however, detection had become a significant factor in the city police department. In 1907 John Hayes opened a detective office after twenty-seven years with the Kansas City, Missouri, police. The following year William McLaughlin retired from the New York police and opened the United States Detective Agency.[37] Richard E. Engright, a New York police commissioner for eight years and editor of *Police Stories* magazine, founded a private agency with ex-police inspector Samuel Belton.[38] John W. Bishop had been chief deputy sheriff in Miami before forming the Bishop and Pearce Detective Agency.[39] The number of city detectives forming private detective businesses increased to such an extent that one observer felt that "the first resource of the superannuated or discharged police detective [was] to start an agency."[40]

Most of these agencies were based upon the ex-policeman's reputation and retirement checks, neither of which were very large. Many were historic reminders of the Cyrus Bradley detective model of the mid-nineteenth century. Often they were confined to one city and heated competition existed among them. Anthony F. Vachris, formerly a police lieutenant in New York City, complained that his detectives frequently were beaten by another private detective, Adam Cross, who was also a former police inspector.[41] Pinkerton's increasingly felt that it had lost control of its profession. It no longer functioned as the informal training school of future owners of private agencies. Clearly, the danger was that as the public police modernized, some of its old disreputable elements would move into the private police field. As the number of these small agencies increased, the New York district attorney, Arthur Train, saw that they had "all the faults of the police without any of their virtues."[42]

Reminiscent of the Allan Pinkerton and Cyrus Bradley days, a polarization developed between the larger, more established agencies and the newer, local based businesses. Arthur Train, obviously a friend of the Pinkerton agency, believed that

> the national detective agency, with its thousands of employees ... is a powerful organization, highly centralized, and having an immense sinking fund of special knowledge and past experience. ... This accumulated fund of information is the heritage of an honest and long established industry. It is seventy-five percent of its capital. It is entirely beyond the reach of the mushroom agency, which in consequence has to accept less desirable retainers involving no such requirements, or go to the wall.[43]

The tensions between the older concerns and these "mushroom agencies" festered early during the Progressive Era. In 1904, one private detective, Lawrence H. St. Clair, was convicted for his annoying shadowing. Several larger agencies hailed the decision as a means by which the smaller disreputable detective business would be forced out of the profession. "It will mean protection to us rather than otherwise," declared the head of a large agency.

Now we know where we are at, and that we always have been well within the law in our work. But it will prove a hard knock for many of the smaller so-called dectective agencies which spring up like mushrooms everywhere, and which, besides doing bungling work, take up work of a character that has tended to bring the calling of the private detective into general disrepute.[44]

The next year a highly respected Cleveland detective, Jake Mintz, lamented that "the detective business is not what it used to be years ago. It is deteriorating every year and something ought to be done to make it respectable again. There are so many fake agencies springing up daily that it is difficult for a legitimate concern to make a living."[45]

The growing professionalism of the public police on both the local and state levels and the Pinkerton monopoly of many contracts compelled many new agencies to rely upon showmanship and theatrics to win clients.[46] The Pinkerton agency had done the same thing in its formative period, but by the twentieth century it viewed such activities as unbecoming and as detrimental to the profession. William Pinkerton felt that the cheap "yellow-back" magazines, the works of men like Conan Doyle, and the budding motion picture industry distorted the image of the private detective.[47] He ridiculed the use of disguises so popular in the penny sleuth stories and felt there was no mystery surrounding the detective business because "we work along the same lines that a business man builds up a great business."[48] As early as 1896 William Pinkerton cultivated this non-glamorous image of his profession. An interviewer concluded that "No, Mr. Pinkerton is not a graduate of any of the weirdly wonderful schools of detection with which dramatists and novelists have made us so pleasantly familiar."[49] Four years later a Chicago reporter, searching for America's Sherlock Holmes, agreed, because "commonsense is the chief stock in trade of William A. Pinkerton."[50] Methodical efficiency took precedence over any form of theatrics. As head of the profession, Pinkerton's became as businesslike and as conservative as their clients.

As the number of agencies grew a competitive battle occurred between the old-style detective, represented by Pinkerton's, and the new upstarts. Beginning at the close of the first decade of the twentieth century, these competitive forces confronted the agency with its first major threat in fifty years. The most famous and, for Pinkerton's, the most troublesome of these "upstart" agencies was that of

William Burns. His conduct on one hand was a powerful reminder of their father's early career patterns with all of its popular appeal, and, on the other hand, it reaffirmed notions of how inappropriate such activities were for the twentieth century.

William J. Burns was born in Baltimore in 1858 and was raised in Zanesville, Ohio. He moved to Columbus in 1873, where his father opened a tailor shop and then later became police commissioner. Burns worked a while as a tailor, but his father's police work fascinated him. In 1888 he started his own detective business working as an out-of-state agent for the Furlong Detective Agency of St. Louis. He entered the Secret Service in 1891 and was occupied with exposing counterfeiting until loaned to the Interior Department in 1903.[51] It was from that point that his career started its meteoric rise.

Several land speculators had been defrauding the government out of hundreds of thousands of acres in the Pacific Northwest at a time when President Theodore Roosevelt was publicizing conservation. Government prosecutor Frank Heney borrowed Burns from the Secret Service and went to Oregon to investigate rumors of corruption. They uncovered a scandal that rivaled the Crédit Mobilier of an earlier time. The U.S. Land Office was found to be corrupt, as were U.S. Senator John Mitchell and Congressman John Williamson of Oregon. Over one hundred indictments were secured before Burns left the state in the summer of 1906.[52]

Heney and Burns did not return to Washington immediately. Instead they answered the call of a wealthy young reformer in California, Rudolph Spreckels, to come to the Bay Area. San Francisco had been in the clutches of the Union-Labor party's political machine since 1901. A good-government crusade began after the earthquake when it was learned that Mayor Eugene Schmitz and boss Abe Ruef sold favors to the utilities, transit, and construction companies of the Bay Area. Within two years of his arrival, Burns gathered enough evidence to convict both Schmitz and Ruef and force the resignation of eighteen city officials.[53]

The "star of the secret service," as Burns then became known, had a dramatic flair that captured wide attention, especially from journalists like Lincoln Steffens. The detective's exploits on the Pacific Coast were publicized in six major magazine articles during 1907 and 1908, and Pinkerton's labeled him a "newspaper detective." Burns turned this publicity to profit by resigning government service and joining William Sheridan's Detective Agency in September 1909. Six months later he reorganized it into William J. Burns' National Detective Agency and dominated the country's newspapers for the next decade. This is not to say that the Pinkertons were eclipsed by Burns. William Pinkerton continued to have a strong voice in the International Association of Chiefs of Police and even tried to counter some of Burns' growing notoriety in 1911 by writing several articles for a friendly Chicago newspaper. The Pinkerton name remained synonymous with detective work, but Burns was a true threat—a condition that was quickly seen in 1909 when his new agency took over the very profitable American Bankers' Association contract.[54]

After a compatible ten years, the Pinkerton-banker partnership began to weaken by 1905. The main issue was economic. Ill feelings first erupted over the Pinkerton policy of pursuing criminals until they were imprisoned. Generally the bankers agreed with that policy, but when the leaders of the Wild Bunch—Butch Cassidy and Harry Longbough—fled to Argentina, the thrifty businessmen dropped the matter. Pinkerton's angrily pursued the case at their own expense until the bandits were killed by Argentine police in 1911.[55]

Tensions increased further in 1907 when the bankers decided to extend their protective services to cover crimes committed by non-professional criminals. Previously such cases were handled by Pinkerton's on an individual contract. In one blow the expansion of the protective features of the association increased Pinkerton's work load and decreased its potential profit. To insure themselves of some stability, the Pinkertons demanded a five year contract in 1908, but instead they received one for three years. That same year the number of members in the association reached 10,000, and the bankers, thinking that the expense of protection leveled off at that number, desired a reduction in membership assessment. Pinkerton management refused to cut the fees, and the following year the association instituted other economic features. A new protective committee was established in 1909 under the supervision of L. W. Gammon, a sixteen-year veteran of the Secret Service. Gammon angered Pinkerton's by requiring a strict reckoning of the agency's expense accounts. Furthermore, he demanded that all publicity for the apprehension of criminals go to the protective committee rather than to Pinkerton's. In addition, Gammon attacked as old fashioned the idea of watching only the professional thief. Instead, aggressive measures were needed to cut down on crimes by the casual, inexperienced criminals as well.[56]

For years the bankers had no choice but to retain Pinkerton's. Very few agencies could meet the requirements of such national crime fighting. Gammon and Burns, however, had known each other in Washington, and when the enterprising private detective offered to work for a lower fee, the change occurred in the winter of 1909. It was a major crisis in administration for both Burns and Pinkerton's. The former, whose agency was only three months old, had to begin protecting over 10,000 banks. The resourceful detective spent several months hastily building his organization to such an extent that by 1916 he could provide additional protective services for the National Retail Dry Goods Association, the Railway Ticket Protective Bureau, and various hotels and stores. Also, in 1915 he started guarding industrial plants.[57] Such rapid overnight growth contributed to his image as a "mushroom agency." William Pinkerton appeared glad to be free of Gammon's meddling, but the shift was a financial shock, and he immediately set up the Pinkerton Bank and Bankers' Protection unit to rival the American Bankers' Association.[58] He traveled throughout the country soliciting banks for his protective service, only to be accused by Burns of a guerilla war of misrepresentation and vituperation.[59]

Burns not only took the coveted banking contract, but in the first five years of his agency's existence he handled several spectacular cases. On October 1, 1910, the *Los Angeles Times* building was dynamited and twenty persons killed. The Los Angeles mayor hired Burns, who was investigating a similar bombing in the Midwest. Convinced there was a connection between the Illinois and Los Angeles bombings, Burns suspected John J. McNamara, leader of the International Association of Bridge and Structural Iron Workers in Indianapolis. After a six month investigation, McNamara and his brother were arrested. Labor leaders hired Clarence Darrow, but the McNamaras confessed and were convicted. After Pinkerton's dismal failures to convict three labor radicals in Idaho, the Burns' successes seemed a godsend, and he was called "the only detective of genius ... this country has produced."[60]

A second important case occurred in April 1913 when thirteen-year-old Mary Phagan was murdered in Atlanta. The victim's employer, Leo Frank, hired Pinkerton detectives to find the killer. In an outburst of anti-Semitism, however, most Atlantans suspected Frank. Investigations by Pinkerton's proceeded slowly, and the *Atlanta Constitution* raised a public fund to hire Burns in May. Before Burns could start his investigation, however, public opinion was inflamed by agitators like Congressman Tom Watson, and Frank was convicted of murder. Convinced that Georgia had its own Dreyfus affair, Frank's lawyers got financial support from northern Jews to rehire Burns in February 1914. After a year of suggestive headline revelations Burns presented enough evidence to convince the governor and the sentence of death was commuted. Many Georgians disagreed with that decision, and on August 16, 1915, Leo Frank was kidnapped from jail, with little opposition, spirited away to Mary Phagan's hometown of Marietta, and lynched.[61]

The "old-school" detectives, like the Pinkertons, resented the brass band techniques of Burns and claimed that they were simply attempts to gain notoriety.[62] Indeed, Burns did court publicity, and he conducted his press conferences with the fervor of a religious exhorter.[63] After William Pinkerton's and Arthur Conan Doyle's friendship ended over the rendition of some Pinkerton exploits in fictional form, Burns rushed to pose for a family picture with the famous author. Burns hoped to appear as America's Sherlock Holmes.

Much of the Pinkerton resentment was due to jealousy, too, as many newspapers across the country began favoring Burns. For example, William Pinkerton believed that the *Chicago Tribune* only printed the Pinkerton name in connection with scandalous cases while Burns received flowery praise.[64] On the other hand, Burns' notoriety was interpreted as an openness very rare among detective agencies. At a time when most people felt that the only prerequisite for a common detective was that he be a common liar, Burns seemed to be as incorruptible as a saint.[65] In fact, Burns made his position quite clear when he declared that with the exception of himself, all private detectives were crooked.[66] While Burns appeared to be open, the Pinkertons were busy avoiding and repressing adverse publicity, such as Charles Siringo's book.[67]

There seemed more fundamental differences between Burns and the Pinkertons than showmanship or publicity. The Pinkerton brothers were on record as declaring the country's greatest enemies to be strikers and anarchists, which endeared them to the business interests. The Oregon and San Francisco incidents proved that

Burns regarded the rich criminal as abhorently as he did the poor thief, and he declared the nation's enemy to be municipal corruption and commercial depravity—a notion that placed him among the reformers of the Progressive Era.[68] Furthermore, Burns set himself apart from all private detectives by announcing he would never accept strike work, a position he later abandoned.[69] At the same time, he gladdened the hearts of union-haters by virtually destroying organized labor in southern California when the McNamaras were indicted. Then, when Pinkerton's seemed to weaken under local pressures in Atlanta, Burns showed remarkable courage by risking his personal safety in the Leo Frank incident.

The two agencies, furthermore, differed on the use of "modern" detective devices. Historically, the professional criminal was more adroit at wiretapping than the police. On several occasions the Western Union lines between race tracks and city poolrooms were spliced to the advantage of the swindler.[70] Some business enterprises got an edge by listening in on the phone calls of competitors. This practice became so flagrant among newspaper publishers that Illinois and California declared it illegal in the early 1900s.[71]

When the police started wiretapping in the mid-1890s, there were only an estimated 300,000 telephones in the entire country. The technique was infrequently used until the second decade of the twentieth century, when it became common practice. One New York policeman boasted that he tapped thousands of telephone wires between 1908 and 1916.[72] For decades private detectives had been centers of public concern over spying. Now the issue of privacy seemed all the more relevant, and Pinkerton's exercised caution and refused to become involved with wiretapping.

At first, Americans were ambivalent over the wiretapping issue. This new kind of spying, which really resembled activities of traditional police states, was permissible if applied to criminals. The New York police, for example, had been criticized in 1916 for using such methods to collect evidence against Catholic priests who publicly disapproved of some of the mayor's policies.[73] In the same year, Burns was hired to work with the New York police in planting listening devices in the offices of Seymour and Seymour, lawyers suspected of selling to the Germans some stolen secret documents concerning J. P. Morgan's munitions dealings.[74] Pinkerton's, hired by Morgan, was the first to discover the eavesdropping and, hoping to discredit their rivals, they notified the district attorney. A congressional investigation followed, and Pinkerton's disavowed the use of such devices to intrude on privacy. The investigating committee agreed that such items were an infringement of a citizen's rights and recommended that Burns be prosecuted.[75] Neither the constitutionality nor the propriety of wiretapping had been established as yet, and instead Burns was convicted of illegal entry. The Allied Trade Council of New York, not satisfied with the one hundred dollar fine Burns received, pressured for severer sanctions. More investigations followed, but the public and politicians lost interest and the charges were set aside in 1921.[76]

Since New Yorkers seemed not to care about wiretapping in criminal matters, the technique became a mainstay for both private and public detectives. Soon, however, it was discovered that the tap was used frequently for disreputable reasons. In 1917, for example, a New York policeman admitted tapping a hotel line to get divorce evidence for a private detective. Organized labor, of course, assumed that all its telephones were bugged. During World War I there was considerable fear of foreign spies obtaining vital information from wiretaps.[77] As those incidences and fears increased, the New York legislature tried to forbid such activity in 1918, but the governor vetoed the bill. Ten years later the United States Supreme Court, in *Olmstead* v. *United States,* upheld evidence obtained by wiretapping as long as the premises had not been entered or violated. Private detectives increasingly used such techniques, and a new specialization developed within the profession, with Burns rather than William Pinkerton being in the forefront.[78] If the "eye" had been an appropriate symbol of nineteenth-century criminal detection, the "ear" became equally meaningful beginning in the second decade of the twentieth century.

William Burns was the most visible private detective of the second decade; he was also the most controversial. Rapid business expansion had its dangers, and Burns admitted that occasionally his agency had been careless in selecting operatives, which led to some embarrassing mishaps.[79] Within his first year as representative of the American Bankers' Association, Burns was sued for making a false arrest. For the first time in its history, the association had to disclaim any responsibility for the mistakes of its detectives.[80] Then the case that catapulated Burns to fame, the Oregon land frauds of 1905, was turned against him. In 1911 President Taft's attorney general, George Wickersham, accused Burns of investigating prospective jurors during the Oregon trials and seeing to it that the jury box was filled with prejudiced people. By 1911 Burns challenged the police establishment. The International Association of Chiefs of Police had been on record for sometime favoring the regulation or prohibition of handguns. One bill to require handgun registration in Ohio, said the head of the Toledo police, was stymied when the "Burns Detective Agency came there and raised so much hell with the legislature that we couldn't get any further."[81] In 1915 the International Association of Chiefs of Police dropped Burns from its rolls, and then quickly dispelled widespread rumors that the reason was for the detective's unprofessional activities in Georgia during the Leo Frank case.[82] A few months later a Denver military board of inquiry accused Burns and the United Mine Workers with trying to prevent the recruitment of the Colorado state militia.[83]

One of Burns' more costly blunders occurred over the capture of the "Holiday Crook" who victimized bankers and merchants during the Christmas seasons between 1908 and 1918. The American Bankers' Association and the Jewelers' Security Alliance brought the rival detective agencies into the case. Nothing happened except the annual posting of warning circulars at each holiday, until January 1917 when Burns' detectives arrested Alexander McCauley in St. Louis. Eyewitnesses, handwriting experts, and even Pinkerton officials in St. Louis thought McCauley guilty, and he was extradited to New York.[84] The "Holiday Crook" resumed his activities late in 1917, however, and McCauley was released. Immediately he hired Pinkerton's to investigate Burns. In a short time Pinkerton's captured the real swindler, Lawrence Farrell, and McCauley sued the American Bankers' Association, the National Retail Dry Goods Association, and Burns for $100,000.[85] With a mixture of personal glee and professional chagrin, Pinkerton's thereafter kept a file on the "startling methods" used by Burns.[86]

Burns, then, represented all that people felt to be good and bad about detective work in the second decade of the century. At the same time that he stood out as America's greatest detective, he also seemed to be a clownish opportunist. His connection with the Justice Department's Bureau of Investigation complicated the picture even more.

For years the Pinkertons had pressured for a strong national detective service. Various government departments, such as the post office and treasury, had had detective inspectors for some time. But when the Justice Department was established in 1870 there was a consistent effort to forestall the creation of any official spy system. Instead, the yearly appropriation for crime fighting was used to hire private detectives. This practice continued until the Homestead turmoils of 1892, when Congress forbade the use of detectives from any source outside the government. Thereafter, the attorney generals merely borrowed Secret Service agents from the Treasury Department.[87] As early as 1901 Robert Pinkerton attacked the politically-ridden, inefficient Secret Service and implied that President McKinley's assassination could have been prevented. America was too soft on criminals, he maintained, and the war against the anarchist could best be done by a strong, well-disciplined body of detectives such as those found in Europe.[88] But it was that kind of police that was most feared. Such a police system, said an oft-quoted Chicago newspaper in 1904, was "absolutely contradictory to the democratic principles of government."[89]

Congressional resistance to a national detective force was strong, especially after Burns, working as a Secret Service agent, exposed the corruption of a U.S. senator and congressman in 1906. Already tensions existed between Theodore Roosevelt and Capitol Hill over certain reform measures, and rumors that the president wanted to investigate the entire Congress engendered further opposition. Most congressmen held all detectives in contempt, and in 1908 the Congress denied Attorney General Charles Joseph Bonaparte's request to use part of his appropriation to create a small permanent detective force in the Justice Department. Furthermore, they forbade the use of Secret Service agents by other departments. This latter ploy actually made the creation of a detective bureau inevitable. Prevented from using either private detectives or Secret Service men, Roosevelt and Bonaparte simply created their own Bureau of Investigation on July 1, 1908.[90] The institution was formalized under the next attorney general, George Wickersham.

For the next ten years the services of the Bureau of Investigation were broadened. The Mann Act of 1910 empowered the government to apprehend white slavers. Burglaries from railroad cars in interstate commerce became a federal crime in 1913. Violations of the neutrality, perjury, libel, and lottery laws came under the bureau's jurisdiction in the second decade of the twentieth century. William Pinkerton welcomed these developments, and at a meeting of the International Chiefs of Police in 1919, he called for even further centralization of the government's detective system under competent detective managers to wage war on anarchists and bolshevists.[91]

Of course, William Pinkerton felt that he, or at least a Pinkerton-type detective, should be that detective manager. But even here Burns won the move and almost ruined the game. In 1920, a bomb explosion on Wall Street killed twenty-nine persons, and Burns set out to duplicate his Los Angeles exploits of ten years earlier. Although the assassin was never found, the Burns agency seemed aggressive by pursuing a suspect as far as eastern Europe. The Justice Department's Bureau of Investigation, headed by William Flynn, did nothing. Flynn's position was undermined further in 1921 when the new president, Warren G. Harding, began appointing "Ohio friends" to high governmental positions. Harry M. Daugherty, an old Ohio acquaintance of Burns, was made attorney general, and rumors were rife that the private detective would be made the director of the Bureau of Investigation. There was much resistance to such an idea. The Central Trades and Labor Council of Greater New York wrote the president urging him to find another man for the position. But most of these criticisms and caveats never reached the president, and Burns was made head of the national detective bureau on August 18, 1921.[92]

The Justice Department was as riddled with politics as was the rest of the government during the Harding era. The political affiliation of each agent was determined with an eye to future promotion or dismissal. Most newly appointed agents had been private detectives.[93] One example of the type of agents Burns appointed was the ex-private detective Gaston Means. Means had been tried in 1916 for being an agent of Germany paid to embarrass British commerce. In 1917 he was accused of the murder of a rich widow in North Carolina, and, after acquittal, he was proven to have falsified her will in order to obtain money. Nevertheless, he was a friend of Burns, and after his appointment to the bureau in 1921 he worked with Jesse Smith, the notorious "mystery man," to investigate people and matters of interest to Daugherty. When the Teapot Dome scandal surfaced, Senator Burton Wheeler of Montana led the fight to remove Daugherty. In turn Wheeler was investigated by Means in an attempt to discredit the senator. In subsequent disclosures Means confessed that he headed a group of agents that spied on all congressional enemies of Daugherty. Smith committed suicide, President Harding died, and Secretary of Interior Albert Fall was indicted. It was widely agreed that under the Daugherty-Burns-Means rule, the Department of Justice reached its lowest level of morale, morals, and efficiency. On March 28, 1924, President Coolidge demanded Daugherty's resignation and appointed Harlan Fiske Stone as attorney general. Two months later Burns was replaced by J. Edgar Hoover.

The activities of William Burns aroused the excitement and ambitions of many private detectives. The Pinkertons had exhibited similar flamboyancy in the 1860s and 1870s, but little was done to curtail or regulate the private detective in those days of business freedom. Burns, on the other hand, stirred fears and angers at a time when government regulations were in vogue. It was difficult to be a nineteenth century private detective in the twentieth century, though Burns' successes indicated that the public and politicians still could be fascinated with such characters. But in the twentieth century, at least, more positive actions were taken to control the private detective.

Burns, of course, was not soley responsible for the trend toward restraining private detectives. The rise of numerous "mushroom" detective agencies, the years of near monopoly or "detective trust" contolled by Pinkerton's, and the conspicuous career of Burns, however, did hasten that trend. In 1913 some people wanted all the books of detective agencies open to government inspection.[94] In 1915 California passed a "Spotters Bill." It gave the conductor an opportunity to face his accuser. Other states soon followed California's example.[95] Fearful that the private agencies would be mistaken for the new government detective bureaus, others tried to eliminate the words "secret service" or "United States" from business names.[96] More important was the desire for stricter licensing regulations. Between 1898 and 1910 five states created detective licensing laws; eight more followed from 1913 to 1925. Significantly, Georgia did so during the Leo Frank uproar in 1913. Other states, like New York and Massachusetts, strengthened their laws by increasing the license fee and reducing the licensing period.[97] Many agencies continued to operate illegally. In 1915 Deputy State Controller William Boardman arrested eight unlicensed detectives and determined that several hundred more operated without licenses in New York.[98] Even some private detectives saw the need for regulation. James H. McQueeny of McQueeny's Investigating Agency in Chicago thought the only solution to be stricter license laws. Perhaps in a near classic statement McQueeny pleaded, "Give us a State Law; then protect the honest licensed agency."[99]

By the 1920s private detectives themselves viewed the changes in their profession with alarm. Disillusioned and disgusted, one ex-private detective, Stephen Doyle, petitioned President Woodrow Wilson to abolish all private detectives as a menace to society.[100] Other private detectives, however, were less pessimistic and sought to clean up their vocation by establishing standards of conduct through professional societies. In March 1921, the International Secret Service Association was organized in Chicago by a number of agency leaders. Its main purpose was to elevate the profession and eliminate the larger number of existing "bogus detectives," a long-time goal of the Pinkerton agency.[101] A similar organization, the World Association of Detectives, was founded in 1925.

For over half a century the Pinkerton family had been in quest of professionalism. For them, however, that meant proper public recognition and respect for private policing and detection in America. To accomplish this goal the Pinkertons established models of appropriate private detective work, avoided disreputable detectives, and linked up with the respectable elements of society. Throughout the Progessive Era, affiliations were much stronger with the public police than with private police. Increasingly, the Pinkerton organization was cautious and conservative, and embarrassment over the "mushroom agencies" was stronger than desire to associate with other private detective businesses. Pinkerton's did not assume leadership roles, or for that matter ever join any of the new private detective professional organizations. It would seem that the pioneers of the profession were being out distanced by changes in that profession.

EPILOGUE

Private Detection
to Private Security

WILLIAM BURNS did not slip into obscurity after his tenure at the Bureau of Investigation. In 1927, Henry Sinclair, the oil tycoon involved in the Teapot Dome scandal, asked Burns to keep his jury under surveillance to guard against tampering. When Sinclair was acquitted, the judge in a fit of fury fined the detective one thousand dollars. Burns reacted with some harsh remarks and was cited with contempt of court. Later, when the case was being appealed, the Supreme Court denounced the Burns agency for contaminating the processes of justice.[1] Thereafter, his two sons, Raymond Burns and Sherman Burns, took over the agency and instilled a more cautious style into their business. When their father died in 1932, the William Burns International Detective Agency was the second largest detective business in America, and it made a concerted effort to specialize in guard services.

Rapid changes came to both private and public policing after World War I. Beginnings of these changes were evident earlier. When Robert Pinkerton died in 1907, for example, his son, Allan Pinkerton II, took over the New York office. The young Harvard business school graduate had little toleration for the informant system created by his father and uncle. William Pinkerton was busy trying to sell the idea of a National Bureau of Criminal Identification to members of the police establishment, and Allan Pinkerton II simply began dismantling the system.[2] On one level this was a tactic to protect the agency from any unfavorable publicity, as numerous exposés were attacking the private detective system. On another level this was the beginning of policy changes. Slowly, detection and crime fighting were becoming less important than security and property protection. As long as William Pinkerton lived, however, this was more of an indicator of future development than a statement of current-day practice.

The plans of Allan Pinkerton II were interrupted by the war. He served on General Pershing's staff as chief of the provost marshal's criminal investigating unit and received gas wounds from which he never fully recovered. Consequently, the 1920s were a twilight time for the agency as William's activity steadily decreased and Allan could never fully reestablish his leadership. Management was left to mid-level people until 1930, when Allan died. His son, Robert Allan Pinkerton, then reluctantly left a career as a Wall Street broker to become the fourth and last generation of family leadership in the business. Robert Allan did not appreciate crime detection, and before the decade was gone, Pinkerton's ceased to be a detective agency and became a security police. The area this was most clearly seen was in labor relations.

Labor contracts were an important source of income for private detectives throughout the first two decades of the century. Labor violence, however, was infrequent during the 1920s. Between 1916 and 1921 there had been one hundred violent episodes. Between 1926 and 1931 there were only eighteen. Nonetheless, the number of private detective agencies offering strike services continued to grow, and by 1929 it was estimated that two hundred thousand labor spies existed.[3] Industrial and business leaders, no doubt, could claim that the presence of such spies accounted for so few problems in the 1920s. The 1930s, in contrast, was a more turbulent period that ushered in a new federal government policy towards organized labor.

Franklin D. Roosevelt's "New Deal" for labor was enacted with the passage of Section 7(a) of the National Industrial Recovery Act in 1933. The National Labor Relations Act reinstated and reinforced this policy of guaranteeing labor the right to collective bargaining. The union was a legal entity in the industrial world. Detective agencies prior to 1933 acted in a wonderland of public ambiguity and governmental inaction. The next five years was a period of adjustment when business and detective leaders tested this legislation by continuing their old practices. The Senate Committee on Education and Labor, with its important subcommittee on Civil Liberties, chaired by Robert M. LaFollette, Jr., carefully investigated detective practices and called them to account.[4]

Throughout the last two-thirds of the decade, the LaFollette committee carried out extensive studies of private police. The nation's five largest detective agencies were selected for thorough investigation. The Pinkerton National Detective Agency, William Burns International Detective Agency, the National Corporation Service, the Railway Audit and Inspection Company, and the Corporations Auxiliary Company were subpoenaed. It was quickly evident that the Burns and Pinkerton agencies had carried over their previous differences and had taken somewhat divergent paths when it came to labor.[5]

Both agencies had arrived at similar conclusions regarding strikebreaking—specifically of providing substitute workers or scabs. It was too risky and was left to others like the Railway Audit and Inspection Company. The Burns people submitted records indicating a few scabs had been supplied during the Hudson Automobile strikes in Pittsburgh in 1935. The figures, however, revealed no substantial income derived from breaking strikes. Robert Allan Pinkerton's General Order No. 132, dated December 2, 1935, declared that

This agency does not furnish its employes [sic] to any client for the exclusive purpose of providing workmen to take the place of client's striking employees, nor to physically protect employes [sic] at work or on the highways to and from work during a strike, nor to ride trucks, taxicabs or other vehicles on the highways for protection purposes while a labor strike is in progress.

Pinkerton's, therefore, not only disavowed strikebreaking but in their timidity did not want to even protect property during a strike. The committee concluded that fear of incurring notoriety restricted Pinkerton's.[6]

The Burns agency took up the slack and provided industrial guards. Between 1933 and 1936 Burns made $329,368 from furnishing guards. In 1936 alone Burns made $155,908 on its guard service, an increase of about 266 percent over the previous year. In the 1930s the Burns agency expected at least a 100 percent profit on their watchmen services.[7] Pinkerton's also supplied data on their patrol. Income from their guards, other than those rendered under strike conditions, was good: 1934, $362,056; 1935, $387,002; and 1936, $230,978. But patrol revenue, in relation to strikes, steadily decreased. Strike work earned Pinkerton's $79,708 in 1934; $8,125 in 1935 with the issuing of General Order No. 132; and $814 in 1936. LaFollette's committee concluded that

The rules and orders of the Pinkerton organization considered together with these income figures, indicate that at least for the period under examination the Pinkerton agency was not anxious to secure strike business. It apparently preferred to place emphasis on its undercover work, which, being secret, created less antagonism, and to leave the business of strike breaking to the other agencies in the field.[8]

Industrial espionage, or undercover spying, was so common that the LaFollette committee began studying that activity as well. Labor spying, it was discovered, actually came from three sources: first, employers' associations provided spy services to their employer members; second, many corporations provided their own spy systems; and third, private detectives spied for profit. Pinkerton's was the largest detective agency involved with union spying. Most of the agencies, including Pinkerton's, tried to destroy their records before being subpoenaed, but enough evidence remained to piece together a picture of intrigue. The investigation of industrial espionage pretty much became and exposé of the Pinkerton agency resembling that of Homestead, some forty years earlier.[9]

By 1935 Pinkerton's had twenty-seven offices and grossed over $2 million annually. There were 300 clients for whom Pinkerton's did industrial work, the largest in the 1930s being General Motors. Between 1933 and 1935 the agency had 1,228 operatives, or "ops" as they were known in the business, in practically every union in the country. Five were in the United Mine Workers, nine in the United Rubber Workers, and seventeen in the United Textile Workers. Fifty-two members of the United Auto Workers were Pinkerton spies who reported on unionization in General Motors. Most were Pinkerton employees, but numerous spies were union members "roped" or connived into giving information. One spy was even the national vice president of one union. At least one hundred Pinkerton operatives held positions of importance in various unions. Other members of the "spy trust"—William Burns International Detective Agency, Corporations Auxiliary Company, National Corporation Service, and Railway Audit and Inspection Company—came no where near Pinkerton's in spying. Corporations Auxiliary Company called it "human engineering." While revenue from guarding declined, the general income of the agency increased from $1.4 million in 1933, to $2.1 million in 1934, and then to $2.3 million in 1935. Most of this increase, felt the committee, could be attributed to spying.[10]

The techniques and rationale of such spying had not changed in the previous sixty years. Even some of the code references were familiar. "Datewood," for example, was the designation for the superintendent of the Cleveland office. "Pegwood" was a Pinkerton official in Detroit. Justifications for spying harkened to earlier days as well. Infiltration by radicals and Communists was the threat; prevention of sabotage was the goal. The same had been said in the 1880s and 1890s. Upon examination, however, superintendent Joseph Littlejohn admitted never finding any Communists. Labor spying, as it turned out, was merely an excuse to wreck unions. Furthermore, the various agencies acted contemptuously toward the committee. One Pinkerton, Sam Brady, had been a spy for thirty years. At the time of the investigations he was superintendent of the Cincinnati office. To the astonishment of the committee, Brady tried to use influential friends to obtain the job of investigating the private police system for the LaFollette committee. Such activity was thought to be "typical of the brazen effrontry of the espionage agencies in their contempt for the Government and their anxiety to preserve their business."[11]

The LaFollette committee condemned industrial espionage as un-American. Private detective agencies, especially the Pinkerton agency, were examined carefully under uncomplimentary limelight. Always sensitive to notoriety, the agency cringed. When the committee made its report and the Senate passed a resolution declaring industrial espionage contrary to public policy, a change of Pinkerton policy occurred. In April 1937 another general order, number 105, appeared. "Recent years have brought extensive changes in the field of employer-employee relations," it declared. The American government and the American people had changed their feelings about labor during the Depression. The supplying of names of union members or sympathizers, the reporting of events transpiring at union meetings, and a number of other union related investigations had to be stopped. "It is the purpose of this order, therefore, to completely divorce the Agency from this type of work."[12] Pinkerton management had given up much that had been the substance of its existence. Strikebreaking, the guarding of property during a strike, and union spying—activities over sixty years old in the agency—ended. At the same time challenges were coming to another service rooted deep in Pinkerton history—crime detection.

Developments in local, state, and federal public policing affected Pinkerton's in the 1920s and 1930s. Nineteenth century successes for Pinkerton's were due to the weaknesses of the city police structure, technology, and orientation and to the absences of state and federal police systems. The "professionalization" of the urban police, beginning in the Progressive Era, was an attempt to break down all the old nineteenth century restraints and refashion a modern police based upon middle-class ideals of efficiency and effectiveness. A new mission was in the making as well. Society, as a whole, began to expect more from its police. New energies were to be devoted to crime fighting.[13]

Reforms did not come all at once, but they were well underway by the late 1920s. Technological advances were the first to be implemented. The Bertillion and fingerprinting systems of criminal identification were employed. The Sacco-Vanzetti case in Boston and the St. Valentine Day's massacre in Chicago, due to the work of Calvin Goddard, gave criminalistics wide publication. Crime labs increased in number throughout the 1930s. At a time when old-fashioned "third degree" roughhouse techniques were being called into question, the lie detector machine was invented. Better communication systems developed after the invention of the radio. Automobiles and motorcycles—more appropriate symbols of the Roaring Twenties than flappers and flasks—made city policemen more efficient crime fighters.[14]

Critics, like Raymond Fosdick and Bruce Smith, and practitioners, like August Vollmer and Orlando Wilson, instigated a managerial revolution in policing. Police administration, at the expense of precinct captains, was centralized. Police chiefs were given more power, longer tenure, and greater freedom from political interference. Because politics was so firmly entrenched this was a more arduous than a technological reform. Chicago, for example, moved rapidly when it came to new techniques and technology. The police, however, were thoroughly politicized. A Citizens Police Committee finally appointed Bruce Smith, of the National Institute of Public Administration, to study Chicago police problems. Due to that study, newly elected mayor Anton Cermak appointed a reform-minded police commissioner in 1931, ending a thirty year battle between civic reformers and police leadership.[15]

Police education became an important element of reform. In the nineteenth century police training was based on the apprenticeship system—one learned the job on the streets. Some police academies appeared at the turn of the century and grew rapidly in the 1920s. Police work was increasingly complex and formal training was needed. August Vollmer's police education ideas at Berkeley evolved into the "college cop" movement. Here were the origins of academic criminal justice.[16] Vollmer became the main leader of the professional police movement. When asked in 1930 to discuss police progress in the past twenty-five years, his answers were predictable. He highlighted better police training, more complete record keeping, more adequate communications, and modern investigative procedures. The modern cop, according to Vollmer and the "professionalizers," was to be a crime fighter.[17]

Much of earlier policing had been preventive or patrol oriented. Detection was minimized because society wanted it that way. Changes occurred in the 1920s and 1930s. Difficulties in enforcement of prohibition laws and unrestrained rule of gangs in many cities publicized police problems. In several cities, crime commissions and citizen watchdog groups arose to study the police and crime in their areas. A National Crime Commission (the Wickersham Commission) published two reports on America's police.[18] Some states, after the introduction of the interstate compact idea in 1921, began creating agreements to allow officers to cross state lines in pursuit of fugitives.[19] In short, public expectation of what the police could do and should do had changed. The city police, as Pinkerton's had done earlier, placed greater emphasis on their crime-fighting image.

The state police grew at this time as well. The Texas and Massachusetts state police were the leaders in the nineteenth century, and Pennsylvania organized a state police in the twentieth century. Few states, however, were eager to finance a full-time police force to handle occasional strikes, as in Pennsylvania. By 1917, however, the automobile had made its impact. The need to regulate rural highways (and handle a new deviant class, the traffic law violator), and pursue highly mobile criminals forced a change. New York established its state constabulary in 1917, and in the next twelve years eighteen other states did the same. Most created highway patrols, but some statewide agencies with the broader police powers appeared. California's state police, for example, had its own Bureau of Criminal Identification with over nine thousand fingerprints on file by 1918.[20] Rural law and order, once a lucrative option for Pinkerton's, fell to the state police by the 1920s. The most dramatic development in policing at this time was on the federal level. Throughout the nineteenth century federal policing was minimal. Postal inspectors in the post office and secret servicemen in the Treasury Department did limited policing. Even in its first phase of development (1908–1924) the Bureau of Investigation was relatively inactive until the world war aroused fears about radicals and Communists. J. Edgar Hoover, who assumed directorship in 1924, obtained the identification records of Leavenworth prison and the International Association of Chiefs of Police, providing a base 'for the massive investigative files he later accumulated. But,by and large,his empire building would come in the next decade.

Franklin D. Roosevelt's election had a great impact on the Federal Bureau of Investigation, as it was becoming known. Greater commitments of government involvement in the ordinary lives of citizens occured, something unheard of for years. Time was ripe for a government police to do what a private police had done during the nineteenth century. A sensational crime broadened federal police power in 1932 as well. The baby of a national hero, Charles Lindbergh, was kidnapped and murdered. Kidnapping became a federal crime shortly after. A group of modern outlaws appeared. Instead of riding horses and carrying Colt revolvers, they came driving automobiles and firing Thompson submachine guns. Pretty Boy Floyd, Bonnie and Clyde, and John Dillinger menaced the Midwest. Bank robbery became a federal offense in 1934 and Hoover labeled these new outlaws "public enemies." Splashy and dramatic as they were, these public enemies were easily caught or killed. Much like Pinkerton's had done earlier, by carefully selecting out who the public enemies were, Hoover could more easily become the public hero.

Throughout the 1930s Hoover placed himself in such a position so as to be regarded as America's leading expert on crime. He formed linkages between the local police departments and the Federal Bureau of Investigation. Police statistics, for example, were sent to the bureau where they were interpreted and portrayed as a Uniform Crime Report in 1930 so Hoover could tell the country about its crime problems. In 1932 a crime laboratory was established in the bureau to aid investigation. Upon request, local police could tap into that expertise. In 1935 a National Police Academy was created and many local police officials attended. Numerous articles appeared between 1932 and 1935 calling attention to bank robbery, auto theft, fraud, freight car robbery, and the white slave traffic. By 1940 Hoover was the country's leading law enforcement officer.[21]

Much of what Hoover had done for the public and the police, however, had been done earlier by Allan Pinkerton and his two sons. With some exaggeration, Murray Kempton believed that Allan Pinkerton had invented most of the devices used by Hoover. The director of the Federal Bureau of Investigation "found the tablets already engraved; no further exercise was demanded of him except some tracing at the edges." Hoover must be given more credit than that, but a comparison of the two detective administrators indicates that Hoover may well have been the twentieth century "son of Pinkerton."[22]

Many traditional Pinkerton activities were gone by 1940. Most labor work was against agency policy. Crime detection was being done by others. Small scale detection was available for accounting firms and insurance companies. The Jewelers Security Alliance still retained Pinkerton's. Most activity, however, had shifted to guarding property. Significantly, in 1964 the agency got the largest private security contract in history, the guarding of the New York world's fair. Pinkerton's had gone from being thief-takers to being caretakers. Soon, even the designation "detective agency" would fall from the letterhead.

But, almost as if a swan's song, a series of Pinkerton detective stories began to appear. Throughout the 1940s and into the early 1950s *True Detective Magazine* published over sixty Pinkerton stories, and *Master Detective Mysteries* magazine retold thirteen. Lloyd Wendt, at the *Chicago Tribune,* ran eighteen Pinkerton stories in 1947. Justin Gilbert's "Solved by the Pinkertons" series appeared for several months in 1951 in the *New York Daily Mirror.* James Horan, in 1951, 1962, and 1968, wrote his "Pinkerton Detective Dynasty" books. Pinkerton's, it would appear, was being rediscovered. These stories, most of them set in the nineteenth and early twentieth centuries, were nostalgic restatements of what the Pinkerton private detective had been, as opposed to what he had become. Commitments to security services rather than detection now made these old stories and images dearer because their reality was gone.

Bibliography

It is a rare organization that is insensitive to its own past. Present day profits, of course, are of upmost concern, but in time, all businesses ponder their own history. Generally, these are not intellectual exercises, and the records are carefully screened and sifted to present the proper picture. Many such "company histories" are chronicles lacking any unifying theme, historical perspective, or critical analysis. History, in short, becomes a public relations technique. Businesses are record keeping, record analyzing enterprises, and information is abundant. Some businesses, like Pinkerton's, have archives so that visitors may view the artifacts of an illustrious past.

The Pinkerton archives in New York is rich in materials. Over one hundred binders, bound according to the criminal case or criminal character, are available. These materials, plus those manuscripts at the Library of Congress and the Chicago Historical Society, are the major resources for this book. They constitute a major part of other books as well, especially the information I call "defensible data." This trace-and-chase material makes up the popular histories of Richard Rowan (*The Pinkertons: A Detective Dynasty,* 1931) and James D. Horan, (*The Pinkertons: The Detective Dynasty that Made History,* 1968). The *True Detective Magazine* literature mentioned in the epilogue was based on this readily available material.

Another set of information in the Pinkerton archives I call "managerial data." In Pinkerton's it ranks from the mysterious to the mundane. The operatives' reports to the supervisor and clients are filled with the day-to-day activities of the detective. Unlike the "defensible data," these reports are not meant for the scholar's eyes. In fact, much of the work of the private detective is secret. In 1924 a London private detective, Herbert Marshall, touched on this when he drew distinctions between the public and private detective

> Most of my work has never before been made public and I think that this is where the chief difference between the police and the private detective lies. The work of the former is the detection of criminals, the bringing of them to justice, and thus to public notice, while in most cases the object of the latter is so to unravel twisted skins that certain individuals may resume the even tenor of their life without the public even knowing that it was disturbed.

Such secrecy might protect the innocent and the guilty, but it hampers the historian. Some of the operatives' reports are in the Pinkerton archives, but most are tucked away in the various collections of the client company. The Burlington Railroad manuscripts at Chicago's Newberry Library is one example.

The more mundane of this "managerial data" are the correspondences between Pinkerton and his two sons, between the Pinkerton family and subordinates, and among the various supervisors. Most interesting were the letters between Robert Pinkerton and William Pinkerton. These letters and directives were sandwiched into the case binders and overlooked by those interested in the crime story.

MANUSCRIPT MATERIAL

Ann Arbor, Michigan. Michigan Historical Collections. James Frederick Joy Papers.
Austin, Texas. University of Texas Library. William Gilmore Beymer Papers.
Brunswick, New Jersey. Rutgers University Library. John Emley Papers.
Chicago, Illinois. Chicago Historical Society. Allan Pinkerton Papers.
Chicago, Illinois. Newberry Library. Chicago Burlington and Quincey Railroad Papers.
Chicago, Illinois. University of Chicago Library. Ebenezer Lane Papers.
Columbia, Missouri. State Historical Society of Missouri. Scott Carey Papers.
Newark, New Jersey. New Jersey Historical Society. Ichobod C. Nettleship Papers.
New York, New York. Pinkerton's Incorporated Archives. Pinkerton National Detective Agency Papers.
Philadelphia, Pennsylvania. Historical Society of Pennsylvania. Samuel Morse Felton Papers.
Seattle, Washington. University of Washington Library. Luke S. May Papers.
Washington, D.C. Library of Congress. George Brinton McClellan Papers.
Washington, D.C. Library of Congress. Pinkerton National Detective Agency Papers.

NEWSPAPERS

Chicago Daily Democrat, 1852–1861.
Chicago Daily Inter-Ocean, 1887–1904.
Chicago Daily News, 1884–1900.
Chicago Eagle, 1897.
Chicago Mail, 1887.
Chicago Record-Herald, 1905–1911.
Chicago Times, 1855–1890.
Chicago Tribune, 1853–1890.
New York Inter-Ocean, 1903.
New York Sun, 1895.
New York Times, 1861–1926.
New York Tribune, 1857–1866.
New York World, 1875–1896.

CONTEMPORARY CITY DIRECTORIES AND HISTORIES

Biographical History With Portraits of Prominent Men of the Great West. Chicago: Manhattan Publishing Co., 1894.

Boyd's Philadelphia City Directory. Philadelphia: C. E. Howe, 1908.

Chicago City Directory and Business Advertiser. Chicago: Robert Fergus, 1855.

Colbert, Elias. *Colbert's Chicago: Historical and Statistical Sketch of the Garden City from the Beginning until Now with Full Statistical Tables.* Chicago: P. T. Sherlock, 1868.

Directory of Chicago for the Year 1858. Chicago: D. B. Cooke and Co., 1858.

Edwards, Richard, comp. *Chicago Census Reports and Statistical Review.* Chicago: Richard Edwards, 1857.

Flinn, John J. *Chicago, The Marvelous City of the West, a History: An Encyclopedia and a Guide.* Chicago: National Book and Picture Co., 1893.

Gager's Chicago City Directory. Chicago: John Gager, 1857.

Gopsill's Philadelphia City Directory. Philadelphia: James Gopsill's Sons, 1880, 1888, and 1900.

King, Moses, ed. *King's Handbook of New York City.* Boston: Moses King, 1893.

Lakeside Business Directory and Yearbook of the City of Chicago. Chicago: Williams, Donnelley and Co., 1874–1914.

McElrey's Philadelphia City Directory for 1860. Philadelphia: E. C. and J. Biddle and Co., 1860.

Trow's General Directory of the Boroughs of Manhattan and Bronx. New York: Trow Director, Printing and Book Binding, 1880–1910.

Trow's New York City Directory for the Year Ending May 1, 1856. New York: John F. Trow, 1855.

Wood, David Ward, ed. *Chicago and Its Distinguished Citizens; Or the Progress of Forty Years.* Chicago: Milton George and Co., 1881.

PROCEEDINGS, REPORTS, AND DOCUMENTS

American Bankers' Association. *Proceedings of the American Bankers' Association Annual Convention.* New York, 1893–1910.

Commission of Inquiry. Interchurch World Movement of North America. *Public Opinion and the Steel Strike, Supplementary Reports of the Investigators.* New York: Harcourt, Brace and Co., 1921.

International Association of Chiefs of Police. *Proceedings of the International Association of Chiefs of Police Annual Convention.* n.p., 1906–1910.

National Association of Chiefs of Police of the United States and Canada. *Proceedings of the National Association of Chiefs of Police Annual Convention.* n.p., 1893–1906.

National Prison Association of the United States. *Proceedings of the National Prison Association's Annual Congress.* New York, 1888–1910.

New York. State Legislature. Senate. *Minutes and Testimony of the Joint Legislative Committee Appointed to Investigate the Public Service Commissions.* S. Doc. 32, 139th sess., (Albany 1916).

New York Society for the Suppression of Vice. *Annual Report.* New York: 1874/75–1899/1900.

Report of the Trial of Frederick P. Hill, Late Conductor of the Philadelphia and Reading Railroad on a Charge of Embezzling the Funds of that Co. in His Capacity as a Conductor. Chicago: George H. Fergus, 1864.

Report of the Trial of John Van Daniker, on a Charge of Embezzlement, in His Capacity as Conductor on the Philadelphia and Erie Railroad. Philadelphia: H. G. Leisenning, 1867.

Report of the Trial of Oscar Caldwell, Late Conductor on the Chicago and Burlington Railroad Line, for Embezzlement. Chicago: Daily Democratic Press, 1855.

U.S. Congress. House. Committee on Labor. *Peonage in Western Pennsylvania.* H. R. 90, 62d Cong., 1st sess., 1911.

————. *Employment of Pinkerton Detectives.* H. R. 2447, 52d Cong., 2d sess., 1893.

U.S. Congress. Senate. Committee on Education and Labor. *Violations of Free Speech and Rights of Labor.* S. Rept. 6, 76th Cong., 1st sess., 1939.

————. *Investigation in Relation to the Employment for Private Purposes of Armed Bodies of Men, or Detectives, in Connection with Differences Between Workmen and Employers.* S. Rept. 1280, 52d Cong., 2d sess., 1893.

MEMOIRS, REMINISCENCES, AND
CONTEMPORARY OBSERVATIONS

Alcorn, E. M. *The Shadow, Explaining Method and Purpose of Shop Spy-system; Also Criminal Mysteries Uncovered by Former Private Detectives.* (Syracuse, N.Y.: H. Baumler, 1925).

Altgeld, John P. *Live Questions.* Chicago: George S. Bowen and Son, 1899.

Baker, LaFayette C. *History of the United States Secret Service.* Philadelphia: LaFayette C. Baker, 1867.

Bryce, James. *The American Commonwealth.* 2 vols. London: Macmillan and Co., 1906.

Buchanan, Joseph R. *The Story of a Labor Agitator.* New York: Outlook, 1903.

Burham, George P. *Memoirs of the United States Secret Service.* Boston: Laban Heath, 1872.

Burns, William John. *The Masked War: The Story of a Peril that Threatened the United States by the Man Who Uncovered the Dynamite Conspirators and Sent Them to Jail.* New York: George H. Daron, 1913.

Byrnes, Thomas. *1886: Professional Criminals of America.* New York: Chelsa House Publishers, 1969.

Clendenen, Rufus H. *Clendenen's Detective Manual: How to Become a Successful Detective.* Charleston, W.Va.: Rufus H. Clendenen, 1922.

Costello, A. E. *Our Police Protectors: History of the New York Police.* New York: A. E. Costello, 1885.

Crapsey, Edward. *The Nether Side of New York; or the Vice, Crime and Poverty of the Great Metropolis.* New York: Sheldon and Co., 1872.

Curon, L. O. *Chicago: Satan's Sanctum.* Chicago: C. E. Phillips and Co., 1899.

[Dennis, Ernest Douglas]. *Secrets the Professional Detective Must Know.* (Batavia, Ohio: Commercial Press, 1921).

Dorey, John Joseph. *The Business Man's Private Investigator.* n.p.: John Joseph Dorey, 1923.

Dougherty, George. *The Criminal as a Human Being.* New York: D. Appleton and Co., 1924.

Drummond, Andrew L. *True Detective Stories.* New York: G. W. Dillingham, 1908–09.

Dunbar, Robin. *The Detective Business.* Chicago: Charles H. Kerr and Co., 1909.

Farley, Phil. *Criminals of America; or Tales of the Lives of Theives. Enabling Everyone to be His Own Detective.* New York: Phil Farley, 1876.

Flinn, John Joseph. *History of the Chicago Police, from the Settlement of the Community to the Present Time, under Authority of the Mayor and Superintendent of the Force.* Chicago: Police Book Fund, 1887.

— Furlong, Thomas. *Fifty Years a Detective.* St. Louis, Mo: C. E. Barnett, 1912.

Gerard, James W. *London and New York: Their Crime and Police.* New York: William C. Bryant and Co., 1853.

Grannan's Pocket Gallery of Noted Criminals of the Present Day Containing Portraits of Noted and Dangerous Criminals, Pickpockets, Burglars, Bank Sneaks, Safe Blowers and All-Round Thieves. Cincinnati: Grannan Detective Bureau, 1890.

Hapgood, Hutchins, ed. *The Autobiography of a Thief.* New York: Fox, Duffieldand Co., 1903.

Holbrook, J. *Ten Years Among the Mail Bags: or Notes From the Diary of a Special Agent of the Post Office Department.* Philadelphia: H. Cowperthwait, 1855.

Horn, Tom. *Life of Tom Horn: Government Scout and Interpreter, Written by Himself, Together with His Letters and Statements by His Friends.* Norman: University of Oklahoma Press, 1964.

Hunter, Robert. *Violence and the Labor Movement.* New York: Macmillan, 1914.

[Ludwig, C. T.] *The Successful Detective.* Kansas City, Mo.: C. T. Ludwig Detective Training Correspondence School, 1913.

McCabe, James D., Jr. *Lights and Shadows of New York Life; or The Sights and Sensations of the Great City.* Philadelphia: National Publishing, 1872.

McNutt, George W. *My Twenty-Three Years Experience as a Detective,* n.p.: George W. McNutt, 1923.

McWatters, George S. *Knots Untied: or Ways and By-Ways in the Hidden Life of American Detectives.* Hartford, Conn.: J. B. Burr and Hyde, 1871.

Marks, Harry H. *Small Change; or Lights and Shades of New York.* New York: Standard Publishing, 1882.

— Marshall, Herbert. *Memories of a Private Detective.* London: Hutchinson and Co., 1924.

Martin, Edward Winslow. *The Secrets of the Great City: A Work Descriptive of the Virtues and the Vices, the Mysteries, Miseries and Crime of New York City.* Philadelphia: National Publishing, 1868.

Newcome, A. *Capture of the Paddy Ryan Gang of Burglars.* New York: Newcome and Traver's Detective Agency and Bureau of Inquiry and Investigation, 1887.

Parkhurst, Charles Henry. *My Forty Years in New York.* New York: Macmillan, 1923.

Pinkerton, Allan. *Bank Robbers and the Detectives.* New York: G. W. Dillingham, 1882.

———. *Bucholz and the Detectives.* New York: G. W. Dillingham, 1880.

———. *Claude Melnotte as a Detective and Other Stories.* Chicago: W. B. Keen, Cooke and Co., 1875.

———. *The Detective and the Somnabulist.* Chicago: W. B. Keen, Cooke and Co., 1875.

———. *A Double Life and the Detectives.* New York: G. W. Dillingham, 1884.

———. *The Expressman and the Detectives.* Chicago: W. B. Keen, Cooke and Co., 1875.

———. *General Principles of Pinkerton's National Police Agency.* Chicago: Church, Goodman and Donnelley, 1869.

———. *The Gypsies and the Detectives.* New York: G. W. Dillingham, 1879.

———. *History and Evidence of the Passage of Abrabam Lincoln from Harrisburgh, Pa. to Washington, D.C. on the 22d and 23d of February, 1861.* Chicago, 1868.

———. *Mississippi Outlaws and the Detectives.* New York: G. W. Carleton and Co., 1879.

———. *The Model Town and the Detectives.* New York: G. W. Dillingham, 1876.

———. *The Molly Maguires and the Detectives.* New York: G. W. Dillingham, 1877.

———. *Professional Thieves and the Detectives.* New York: G. W. Carleton and Co., 1880.

———. *The Rail-Road Forger and the Detectives.* New York: G. W. Dillingham, 1881.

———. *Special Rules and Instructions to be Observed in Testing Conductors, Designed for the Operatives of the National Police Agency.* Chicago: George H. Fergus, 1864.

———. *The Spiritualists and the Detectives.* New York: G. W. Carleton and Co., 1877.

———. *The Spy of the Rebellion, Being a True History of the Spy System of the United States Army during the Late Rebellion.* New York: G. W. Dillingham, 1888.

———. *Strikers, Communists, Tramps and Detectives.* New York: G. W. Carleton and Co., 1878.

———. *Thirty Years a Detective.* New York: G. W. Dillingham, 1884.

Ray, Clarence Everly. *The Railroad Spotter: An Expose of the Methods Employed by Detective Agencies and Bonding Companies.* [St. Paul: Virtue Printing, 1916].

Savage, Edward H. *A Chronological History of the Boston Watch and Police, from 1631 to 1865; Together with the Recollections of a Boston Police Officer; or, Boston by Daylight and Gaslight, from the Diary of an Officer Fifteen Years in the Service.* Boston: Edward H. Savage, 1865.

Scott, A. W., Col. *Life Experiences of a Detective,* n.p.: 1878.

Scott, Wellington. *Seventeen Years in the Underworld.* New York: Abingdon Press, 1916.

Shaw, Alonzo B. *Trails in Shadow Land: Stories of a Detective.* Columbus, Ohio: Hann and Adair, 1910.

Siringo, Charles A. *A Cowboy Detective: A True Story of Twenty-Two Years with a World-Famous Detective Agency.* Chicago: W. B. Conkey, 1912.

Smith, Matthew Hale. *Sunshine and Shadow in New York.* Hartford, Conn.: J. B. Burr and Co., 1868.

Speer, Victor, ed. *Memoirs of a Great Detective: Incidents in the Life of John Wilson Murry.* New York: Baker and Taylor, 1904–1905.

Stead, W. T. *Satan's Invisible World Displayed; or Despairing Democracy.* New York: R. F. Fenno and Co., 1897.

Stimson, A. L. *History of the Express Companies, and the Origin of American Railroads, Together with some Reminiscences of the Latter Days of the Mail Coach and Baggage Wagon Business in the United States.* New York: n.p., 1858.

Tucker, T. W. *Waifs from the Way-Bills of an Old Expressman.* Boston: Lee and Shepard, 1872.

Vidocq, Eugene Francois. *Memoirs of Vidocq: The Principal Agent of the French Police.* Philadelphia: T. B. Peterson and Brothers, 1859.

Wagar, LeRoy Herbert. *Confessions of a Spotter.* [St. Louis, Missouri: Wilson Printing, 1918].

Walling, George W. *Recollections of a New York Chief of Police.* New York: Caxton Book Concern, 1887.

Warran, John H., Jr. *Thirty Years' Battle with Crime, or the Crying Shame of New York as Seen under the Broad Glare of an Old Detective's Lantern.* Poughkeepsie, N.Y.: J. J. White, 1875.

Warren, Lewis L. *Industry, Society and the Human Element: A Few True Detective Stories.* Boston: Sherman Detective Agency, 1917.

Wheeler, Martin P. *Judas Exposed; or, The Spotter Nuisance: An Anti-secret Book Devoted to the Interests of Railroad Men.* Chicago: Utility Book and Novelty, 1889.

White, Phil H. *How to Become a Detective in All its Branches.* New York: Phil H. White, 1915.

Whitley, H. C. *In It.* Cambridge, Mass.: Riverside Press, 1894.

Whitlock, Brand. *On the Enforcement of Law in Cities.* Indianapolis: Bobbs-Merrill [1913].

Willard, Josiah Flynt. *Notes of an Itinerant Policeman.* Boston: L. C. Page and Co., 1900.

————. *The World of Graft.* New York: McClure, Phillips and Co., 1901.

Wooldridge, Clifton R. *Twenty Years a Detective in the Wickedest City in the World.* n.p.: 1908.

SECONDARY SOURCES

Aaron, Daniel, ed. *America in Crisis: Fourteen Crucial Episodes in American History.* New York: Alfred A. Knopf, 1952.

Adams, Graham. *Age of Industrial Violence, 1910–15: The Activities and Findings of the United States Commission on Industrial Relations.* New York: Columbia University Press, 1966.

Armitage, Gilbert. *The History of the Bow Street Runners, 1729–1829.* London: Wishart and Co., 1932.

Auerbach, Jerold S. *Labor and Liberty: The LaFollette Committee and the New Deal.* New York: Bobbs-Merrill, 1966.

Barton, George. *The True Stories of Celebrated Crimes: Adventures of the World's Greatest Detectives.* New York: McKinlay Stone and Mackenzie, 1909.

Bellamy, John. *Crime and Public Order in England in the Later Middle Ages.* London: Routeledge and Kegan Paul, 1973.

Bernstein, Irving. *The Lean Years: Workers in an Unbalanced Society.* Boston: Houghton Mifflin, 1960.

Blake, Nelson Manfred. *The Road to Reno: A History of Divorce in the United States.* New York: Macmillan, 1962.

Boyer, Paul S. *Purity in Print: The Vice-Society Movement and Book Censorship in America.* New York: Scribner's [1968].

Bradley, Hugh. *Such Was Saratoga.* New York: Doubleday, Doran and Co., 1940.

Bruce, Robert V. *1877: Year of Violence.* Chicago: Quadrangle Books, 1970.

Caesar, Gene. *Incredible Detective: The Biography of William J. Burns.* Englewood Cliffs, N.J.: Prentice-Hall, 1968.

Chandler, Alfred D., Jr. *The Visible Hand: The Managerial Revolution in American Business.* Cambridge, Mass.: Harvard University Press, 1977.

Chapman, Samuel G., and St. Johnston, T. Eric. *The Police Heritage in England and America: A Developmental Survey.* East Lansing: Michigan State University Press, 1962.

Clayton, Tom. *The Protectors: The Inside Story of Britain's Private Security Forces.* London: Oldbourne, 1967.

Cochran, Thomas. *Railroad Leaders, 1845–1890.* Cambridge, Mass.: Harvard University Press, 1953.

Cook, Adrian. *The Armies of the Streets: The New York City Draft Riots of 1863.* Lexington: University of Kentucky Press, 1974.

Cook, Frederick Francis. *Bygone Days in Chicago: Recollections of the "Garden City" of the Sixties.* Chicago: A. C. McClurg, and Co., 1910.

Cummings, Homer, and McFarland, Carl. *Federal Justice: Chapters in the History of Justice and the Federal Executive.* New York: Macmillan Company, 1937.

Dash, Samuel, Schwartz, Richard, and Knowlton Robert E. *The Eavesdroppers.* New Brunswick, N.J.: Rutgers University Press, 1959.

DeLa Torre, Lillian, comp. *Villainy Detected; Being a Collection of the Most Sensational True Crimes and the Most Notorious Real Criminals that Blotted the Name of Britain in the Years 1660 to 1880.* New York: D. Appleton-Century, 1947.

Denniston, Elinore. *America's Silent Investigators: The Story of the Postal Inspectors Who Protect the United States Mail.* New York: Dobb, Mead and Co., 1964.

de Polnay, Peter. *Napoleon's Police.* London: W. H. Allen, 1870.

Derthick, Martha. *The National Guard in Politics.* Cambridge, Mass.: Harvard University Press, 1965.

Dewhurst, Henry Stephen. *The Railroad Police.* Springfield, Ill.: Charles C. Thomas, 1955.

Dinnerstein, Leonard. *The Leo Frank Case.* New York: Columbia University Press, 1968.

Doyle, Stephen A. *Startling Disclosures of the Private Detective Agency.* Rockford, Ill: Labor News, 1920.

Dubofsky, Melvyn. *We Shall Be All: A History of the Industrial Workers of the World.* Chicago: Quadrangle Books, 1969.

[Duggan, Tom]. *The History of the Jewelers' Security Alliance of the United States, 1883–1958.* New York: Jewelers' Security Alliance, 1958.

Dupuy, R. Ernest. *The National Guard: A Compact History.* New York: Hawthorn Books, 1971.

Ezell, John Samuel. *Fortune's Merry Wheel.* Cambridge, Mass.: Harvard University Press, 1960.

Fehrenbacher, Don E. *Chicago Giant: A Biography of "Long John" Wentworth.* Madison, Wisc.: American History Research Center, 1957.

Fine, Sidney. *Laissez Faire and the General-Welfare State: A Study of Conflict in American Thought, 1865–1901.* Ann Arbor: University of Michigan Press, 1956.

Fink, Arthur Emil. *Causes of Crime: Biological Theories in the United States, 1800–1915.* Philadelphia: University of Pennsylvania, 1938.

Fite, Emerson David. *Social and Industrial Conditions in the North During the Civil War.* New York: Macmillan, 1910.

Fogelson, Robert M. *Big-City Police.* Cambridge, Mass.: Harvard University Press, 1977.

Fosdick, Raymond B. *American Police System.* New York: Century, 1920.

Friedman, Morris. *The Pinkerton Labor Spy* New York: Wilshire Book Co., 1907.

Fuld, Leonhard Felix. *Police Administration: A Critical Study of Police Organizations in the United States and Abroad.* New York: G. P. Putnams' Sons, 1910.

Ginger, Ray. *Altegeld's America: The Lincoln Idea Versus Changing Realities.* New York: Funk and Wagnalls, 1958.

Grover, David H. *Debaters and Dynamiters: The Story of the Haywood Trial.* Corvallis: Oregon State University Press, 1964.

Guillot, Ellen E. *Social Factors in Crime: As Explained by American Writers of the Civil War and Post Civil War Period.* Philadelphia: University of Pennsylvania, 1943.

Harlow, Alvin F. *Old Waybills: The Romance of the Express Companies.* New York: D. Appleton-Century, 1934.

Haskins, George Lee. *Law and Authority in Early Massachusetts: A Study in Tradition and Design.* New York: Macmillan, 1960.

Hatch, Alden. *American Express: A Century of Service, 1850–1950.* Garden City, N.Y.: Doubleday and Co., 1950.

Haycraft, Howard. *Murder for Pleasure: The Life and Times of the Detective Story.* New York: Biblo and Tannen, 1968.

Haydon, Arthur L. *The Riders of the Plains: A Record of the Royal Northwest Mounted Police of Canada, 1873–1910.* Toronto: Copp-Clark, 1910.

Hobsbaum, Eric. *Bandits.* London: George Weidenfeld and Nicoloson, 1969.

Hollon, W. Eugene. *Frontier Violence: Another Look.* New York: Oxford University Press, 1974.

Horan, James David. *Desperate Men: Revelations from the Sealed Pinkerton Files.* Garden City, N.Y.: Doubleday and Co., 1962.

———. *The Pinkertons: The Detective Dynasty that Made History.* New York: Crown [1968].

Horan, James David, and Swiggett, Howard. *The Pinkerton Story.* New York: Putnam's [1951].

Howson, Gerald. *Thief-Taker General: The Rise and Fall of Jonathan Wild.* New York: St. Martin's, 1970.

Huberman, Leo. *The Labor Spy Racket.* New York: Modern Age Books, 1937.

Hurst, J. Willard. *Law and the Conditions of Freedom in the Nineteenth Century United States.* Madison: University of Wisconsin Press, 1967.

Johnson, David R. *Policing the Urban Underworld: The Impact of Crime on the Development of the American Police, 1800–1887.* Philadelphia: Temple University Press, 1979.

Kirkland, Edward Chase. *Dream and Thought in the Business Community, 1860–1900.* Chicago: Quadrangle Books, 1964.

Lane, Roger. *Policing the City: Boston, 1822–1885.* Cambridge, Mass.: Harvard University Press, 1967.

————. *Violent Death in the City: Suicide, Accident, and Murder in Nineteenth-Century Philadelphia.* Cambridge, Mass.: Harvard University Press, 1979.

Lavine, Sigmund A. *Allan Pinkerton: America's First Private Eye.* New York: Dodd, Mead and Co., 1963.

Levinson, Edward. *I Break Strikes! The Technique of Pearl L. Bergoff.* New York: Robert M. McBride and Co., 1935.

Lowenthal, Max. *The Federal Bureau of Investigation.* New York: William Sloane Associates, 1950.

McAdoo, William. *Guarding a Great City.* New York: Harper and Brothers, 1906.

McCague, James. *The Second Rebellion: The Story of the New York City Draft Riots of 1863.* New York: Dial Press, 1968.

McKelvey, Blake. *American Prisons: A Study in American Social History Prior to 1915.* Chicago: University of Chicago Press, 1936.

McMurry, Donald, L. *The Great Burlington Strike of 1888: A Case History in Labor Relations.* Cambridge, Mass.: Harvard University Press, 1956.

Mather, F. C. *Public Order in the Age of the Chartists.* New York: Augustus M. Kelley, 1967.

Mayo, Katherine. *Justice to All. The Story of the Pennsylvania State Police.* Boston: Houghton Mifflin, 1920.

Miller, Wilbur. *Cops and Bobbies: Police Authority in New York and London, 1830–1870.* Chicago: University of Chicago Press, 1977.

Millspaugh, Arthur Chester. *Crime Control by the National Government.* Washington: Brookings Institution, 1937.

Mitchell, C. Ainsworth. *Science and the Criminal.* Boston: Little, Brown and Co., 1911.

Monas, Sidney. *The Third Section: Police and Society in Russia Under Nicholas I.* Cambridge, Mass.: Harvard University Press, 1961.

Monroe, David Geeting. *State and Provincial Police.* Evanston, Ill.: International Association of Chiefs of Police and the Northwestern University Traffic Institute, 1941.

Mosse, George L., ed. *Police Forces in History.* Beverly Hills, Calif.: Sage Publications, 1975.

Olander, Victor A. *The State Constabulary Bill. A Statement by Victor A. Olander, Secretary-Treasurer Illinois State Foundation of Labor.* n.p.: Illinois State Federation of Labor, 1921.

O'Neill, William L. *Divorce in the Progressive Era*. New Haven, Conn.: Yale University Press, 1967.

Overstreet, Harry and Bonaro. *The F.B.I. in Our Open Society*. New York: W. W. Norton and Co., 1969.

Packard, Vance. *The Naked Society*. New York: David McKay, 1964.

Payne, Howard D. *The Police State of Louis Napoleon Bonaparte, 1851–1860*. Seattle: University of Washington Press, 1966.

Peterson, Virgil W. *Barbarians in Our Midst: A History of Chicago Crime and Politics*. Boston: Little, Brown and Co., 1952.

Pierce, Bessie Louise. *A History of Chicago*. Vol. 1: *The Beginning of a City, 1673–1848*. New York: Alfred A. Knopf, 1937.

———. *A History of Chicago*. Vol. 2: *From Town to City, 1848–1871*. New York: Alfred A. Knopf, 1940.

———, ed. *As Others See Chicago: Impressions of Visitors, 1673–1933*. Chicago: University of Chicago Press, 1933.

Pivar, David J. *Purity Crusade: Sexual Morality and Social Control, 1868–1900*. Westport, Conn.: Greenwood Press [1973].

Pringle, Patrick. *Hue and Cry: The Story of Henry and John Fielding and Their Bow Street Runners*. New York: William Morrow and Co., 1955.

———. *The Thief-Takers*. London: Museum Press, 1958.

Radzinowicz, Leon. *A History of English Criminal Law and Its Administration From 1750: The Clash Between Private Initiative and Public Interest in the Enforcement of the Law*. London: Stevens and Sons, 1956.

Richards, Leonard. *Gentlemen of Property and Standing: Anti-Abolition Mobs in Jacksonian America*. New York: Oxford University Press, 1970.

Richardson, James F. *The New York Police: Colonial Times to 1901*. New York: Oxford University Press, 1970.

Riker, William H. *Soldiers of the States: The Role of the National Guard in American Democracy*. Washington: Public Affairs Press, 1957.

Robinson, Louis Newton. *History and Organization of Criminal Statistics in the United States*. New York: Houghton Mifflin, 1911.

Rothman, David. *The Discovery of the Asylum: Social Order and Disorder in the New Republic*. Boston: Little, Brown and Co., 1971.

Rowan, Richard Wilmer. *The Pinkertons: A Detective Dynasty*. Boston: Little, Brown and Co., 1931.

Samaha, Joel. *Law and Order in Historical Perspective: The Case of Elizabethan Essex*. New York: Academic Press [1973].

Schneider, John C. *Detroit and the Problem of Order, 1830–1880: A Geography of Crime, Riot, and Policing*. Lincoln: University of Nebraska Press, 1980.

Schneider, Wilbert M. *The American Bankers' Association: Its Past and Present*. Washington: Public Affairs Press, 1956.

Schwoerer, Lois G. *"No Standing Armies!" The Anti-Army Ideology in Seventeenth Century England*. Baltimore: Johns Hopkins University Press [1975].

Shalloo, Jeremiah Patrick. *Private Police: With Special Reference to Pennsylvania*. Philadelphia: American Academy of Political and Social Science, 1933.

Shannon, Fred Albert. *The Organization and Administration of the Union Army, 1861–1865*. 2 vols. Cleveland: Arthur H. Clark, 1928.

Smith, Bruce. *Police Systems in the United States*. New York: Harper and Row, 1960.
——. *Rural Crime Control*. New York: Columbia University's Institute of Public Administration, 1933.
——. *The State Police: Organization and Administration*. New York: Macmillan, 1925.
Sprogle, Howard O. *The Philadelphia Police: Past and Present*. Philadelphia: Howard O. Sprogle, 1887.
Squire, P. S. *The Third Department: The Establishment and Practices of the Political Police in the Russia of Nicholas I*. Cambridge: Cambridge University Press, 1968.
Stead, Philip John. *The Police of Paris*. London: Staples Press, 1957.
——, ed. *Pioneers in Policing*. Montclair, N.J.: Patterson Smith, 1977.
Taylor, George Rogers. *The Transportation Revolution, 1815–1860*. New York: Holt, Rinehart and Winston, 1951.
Thorwald, Jurgen. *The Century of the Detective*. New York: Harcourt, Brace and World, 1964.
Tobias, J. J. *Crime and Industrial Society in the Nineteenth Century*. London: B. T. Batsford, 1967.
Walker, Samuel. *A Critical History of Police Reform: The Emergence of Professionalism*. Lexington, Mass.: Lexington Books, 1977.
Ware, Norman J. *The Labor Movement in the United States, 1860–1895: A Study in Democracy*. New York: D. Appleton and Co., 1929.
Warrum, Henry. *Peace Officers and Detectives: The Law of Sheriffs, Constables, Marshals, Municipal Police and Detectives*. Greenfield, Ind.: William Mitchell, 1895.
Weiss, Harry B., and Weiss, Grace M. *An Introduction to Crime and Punishment in Colonial New Jersey*. Trenton, N.J.: Past Times Press, 1960.
Westley, William. *Violence and the Police: A Sociological Study of Law, Custom and Morality*. Cambridge, Mass.: MIT Press, 1970.
Wiebe, Robert H. *The Search for Order, 1877–1920*. New York: Hill and Wang, 1967.
Wiley, Bell Irvin. *The Life of Billy Yank: The Common Soldier of the Union*. New York: Bobbs-Merrill, 1951.
Williams, Allan. *The Police of Paris, 1718–1789*. Baton Rouge: Louisiana State University Press, 1979.
Williams, Jack Kenny. *Vogues in Villainy: Crime and Retribution in Ante-Bellum South Carolina*. Columbia: University of South Carolina Press, 1959.
Wood, James Playsted. *Scotland Yard*. New York: Hawthorn Books, 1970.
Woodward, C. Vann. *Tom Watson: Agrarian Rebel*. New York: Oxford University Press, 1963.
Yellen, Samuel. *American Labor Struggles*. New York: Harcourt, Brace and Co., 1936.
Zierold, Norman. *Little Charley Ross: America's First Kidnapping for Ransom*. Boston: Little Brown and Co., 1967.

ARTICLES

Ansley, Norma. "The United States Secret Sevice: An Administrative History." *Journal of Criminal Law, Criminology and Police Science* 47 (May–June 1956), pp. 93–109.

Beet, Thomas. "Methods of American Private Detective Agencies." *Appleton's Magazine* 8 (July–December 1906), pp. 439–45.

Bourke, Charles Francis. "The Pinkertons." *Leslie's Monthly Magazine* 60 (May 1905), pp. 36–45; (June 1905), pp. 205–14.

Braun, Michael A., and Lee, David J. "Private Police Forces: Legal Powers and Limitations." *University of Chicago Law Review* 38 (Spring 1971), pp. 555–82.

Brown, Calvin B. "San Francisco Regeneration." *American Review of Reviews* 36 (August 1907), pp. 195–201.

Brown, Henry S. "Punishing the Land-Looters." *Outlook* 85 (23 February 1907), pp. 427–39.

"Burns—Star of the Secret Service." *Overland Monthly* 51 (January 1908), pp. 58–60.

Conover, Milton. "State Police." *American Political Science Review* 15 (February 1920), pp. 82–93.

———. "State Police Developments, 1921–24." *American Political Science Review* 18 (November 1924), pp. 773–81.

Cooley, Verna. "Illinois and the Underground Railroad to Canada." *Transactions of the Illinois State Historical Society*, no. 23 (May 1917), pp. 76–98.

Corcoran, Margaret M. "State Police in the United States: A Bibliography." *Journal of Criminal Law and Criminology* 14 (February 1924), pp. 544–55.

Craige, John H. "The Professional Strike-Breaker." *Colliers Weekly* 46 (3 December 1910), pp. 20, 31–32.

———. "The Violent Art of Strike-Breaking." *Colliers Weekly* 46 (7 January 1911), pp. 22, 29.

Curtis, George Ticknor. "The Homestead Strike: A Constitutional View." *North American Review* 155 (September 1892), pp. 364–70.

Ferguson, David. "The 'Shadow' in High Finance." *Everybody's Magazine* 41 (March 1907), pp. 336–43.

"Gompers Speaks for Labor." *McClures' Magazine* 38 (February 1912), pp. 371–76.

Gutman, Herbert B. "The Braidwood Lockout of 1874." *Journal of the Illinois State Historical Society* 53 (1960), pp. 5–28.

Haller, Mark. "Police Reform in Chicago, 1905–1935." Harland Hahn, ed. *Police in Urban Society.* Beverly Hills, Calif.: Sage Publications, 1971, pp. 39–56.

Hammett, Dashiell. "From the Memoirs of a Private Detective." *Smart Set* 70 (March 1923), pp. 88–90.

Hastings, W. G. "The Development of Law as Illustrated by the Decisions Relating to the Police Power of the State." *American Philosophical Society Proceedings* 39 (September 1900), pp. 359–554.

Henderson, Charles Richmond. "Rural Police." *Annals of the American Academy of Political and Social Science* 40 (March 1912), pp. 228–33.

"History of William J. Burns." *Nation* 125 (23 November 1927), p. 561.

Hogg, J. Bernard. "Public Reaction to Pinkertonism and the Labor Question." *Pennsylvania History* 2 (July 1944), pp. 171–99.

Hoover, J. Edgar. "The United States Bureau of Investigation in Relation to Law Enforcement." *Journal of Criminal Law, Criminology and Police Science* 23 (1932–1933), p. 439.

Inglis, William. "For the Kingdom of California." *Harper's Weekly* 52 (23 May 1908), pp. 10–12.

Johnson, Bruce C. "Taking Care of Labor: The Police in American Politics." *Theory and Society* 3 (1976), pp. 89–117.

Kempton, Murry. "Son of Pinkerton." *New York Review of Books* 17 (20 May 1971), pp. 22–25.

Langeluttig, Albert. "Federal Police." *Annals of the American Academy of Political and Social Science* 146 (November 1929), pp. 41–54.

Lewis, Lloyd. "Lincoln and Pinkerton." *Journal of the Illinois State Historical Society* 41 (December 1948), pp. 367–82.

Lubove, Roy. "Progressives and the Prostitute." *Historian* 24 (1962) pp. 308–30.

McLellan, Howard. "The Shadow Business." *North American Review* 230 (July 1930), pp. 29–35.

McQuiston, F. B. "The Strike Breakers." *Independent* 53 (17 October 1901), pp. 245–56.

Meloney, William Brown. "Strikebreaking as a Profession." *Public Opinion* 38 (25 March 1905), pp. 440–41.

Moss, Frank. "National Danger from Police Corruption." *North American Review* 173 (October 1901), pp. 470–80.

Oates, William C. "The Homestead Strike: A Congressional View." *North American Review* 155 (September 1892), pp. 355–64.

Pinkerton, Allan. "The Character and Duties of a Detective Police Force." *Proceedings of the Annual Congress of the National Prison Association of the United States: Selected Articles.* New York: Arno, 1971. pp. 241–46.

Pinkerton, Robert A. "Detective Surveillance of Anarchists." *North American Review* 173 (November 1901), pp. 607–17.

———. "Forgery as a Profession." *North American Review* 158 (April 1894), pp. 454–63.

Pinkerton, William A. "Highwaymen of the Railroad." *North American Review* 157 (November 1893), pp. 530–40.

"Pinkerton's Men." *Nation* 44 (27 January 1887), p. 70.

Powderly, T. V. "The Homestead Strike: A Knight of Labor's View." *North American Review* 155 (September 1892), pp. 370–75.

"The Private Armies of Capital." *Literary Digest* 48 (4 April 1914), pp. 743–44.

"The Question of State Police." *New Republic* 6 (1 April 1916), pp. 230–31.

"Report of Her Majesty's Commissioners Appointed to Inquire Into the Alleged Disturbances in Hyde Park, With Minutes of Evidence, 1856." *Quarterly Review* 99 (June–September 1856), pp. 160–200.

Scott, Leroy. "Strikebreaking as a New Occupation." *World's Work* 10 (May 1905), pp. 6199–204.

Sofchalk, Donald G. "The Chicago Memorial Day Incident: An Episode of Mass Action." *Labor History* 6 (Winter 1965), pp. 3–43.

Steffens, Lincoln. "William J. Burns, Intriguer." *American Magazine* 65 (April 1908), pp. 614–25.

———. "The Taming of the West: Discovery of the Land Fraud System. A Detective Story." *American Magazine* 64 (May–October 1907), pp. 489–505.

"Strike-Policing." *New Republic* 6 (15 April 1916), pp. 281–82.

Sullivan, Daniel W. "Recent Legal Decisions Regulating the Business of Private Detectives." *American Federationists* 32 (December 1925), pp. 1189–92.

Train, Arthur. "The Private Detective's Work." *Colliers Weekly* 48 (18 November 1911), pp. 37–39.

Vollmer, August. "Police Progress in the Past Twenty-Five Years." *Journal of Criminal Law and Criminology* 24 (May 1933), 161–175.

Warren, Samuel D., and Brandeis, Louis D. "The Right to Privacy." *Harvard Law Review* 4, (December 1890), pp. 193–200.

Wigmore, John H. "State Cooperation for Crime-Repression." *Journal of Criminal Law and Criminology* 28 (1937–1938), pp. 327–334.

Wilson, Frank. "American First Editions: Allan Pinkerton, 1819–1884." *Publishers Weekly* 130 (28 November 1936), pp. 2135–36.

UNPUBLISHED MATERIALS

Holmes, Joseph J. "The National Guard of Pennsylvania: Policeman of Industry, 1865–1905." Ph.D. Dissertation, University of Connecticut, 1971.

Ketcham, George Austin. "Municipal Police Reform. A Comparative Study of Law Enforcement in Cincinnati, Chicago, New Orleans, New York and St. Louis, 1844–1877." Ph.D. Dissertation, University of Missouri, 1967.

Myers, Howard Barton. "The Policing of Labor Disputes in Chicago: A Case Study." Ph.D. Dissertation, University of Chicago, 1929.

Notes

PREFACE

1. U.S., Congress, Senate, *Investigation of Labor Troubles at Homestead,* 52nd Cong., 2d sess., 1893, Report No. 1200, po. 12, 51.

INTRODUCTION

1. G. T. Crook, ed., *The Complete Newgate Calendar* (5 vols., London: Navarre Society Limited, 1972), 3:30.

2. *Applebee's Journal,* May 29, 1725, quoted in William Robert Irwin, *The Making of Jonathan Wild: A Study of the Literary Method of Henry Fielding* (Hamden, Conn.: Archon Books, 1966), p. 11.

3. Patrick Pringle, *The Thief Takers* (London: Museum Press, 1958), pp. 9, 216–17. Gerald Howson, *Thief-Taker General: The Rise and Fall of Jonathan Wild* (New York: St. Martin's Press, 1970), pp. 34–36.

4. Joseph Cox, "Thief Takers, alias Thief-Makers," *Villainy Detected, Being a Collection of the Most Sensational True Crimes and the Most Notorious Real Criminals that Blotted the Name of Britain in the Years 1660 to 1800* (New York: D. Appleton-Century, 1947), pp. 154–74.

5. Gilbert Armitage, *The History of the Bow Street Runners, 1729–1829* (London: Wishart and Co., 1932), p. 58.

6. Leon Radzinowicz, *A History of English Criminal Law and Its Administration from 1750.* Vol. III: *Cross-Currents in the Movement for the Reform of the Police* (London: Stevens and Sons, 1956), p. 12.

7. Quoted in Hargrave L. Adam, *The Police Encyclopedia* (8 vols., London: Waverly Book Co., n.d.), 1:125.

8. Armitage, *History of the Bow Street Runners,* pp. 47, 61, 64, 129, 266–67; also "Report of Her Magesty's Commissioners Appointed to Inquire into the Alleged Disturbances in Hyde Park with Minutes of Evidence," *Quarterly Review* 99 (June–September 1856), p. 174.

9. Radzinowicz, *History of English Criminal Law,* 3:65, 89; Romilly quote, ibid., 3:108.

10. Ibid., pp. 109, 154.

11. J. L. Lyman, "The Metropolitan Police Act of 1829: An Analysis of Certain Events Influencing the Passage and Character of the Metropolitan Police Act in England," *Journal of Crimial Law, Criminology and Police Science* 55 (1964), p. 151.

12. Radzinowicz, *History of English Criminal Law,* III, 3:354, 358, 362.

13. John Stuart Mill, "Representative Government" in *Utilitarianism, Liberty and Representative Government,* ed. A. D. Lindsay (New York: Dutton, 1950), p. 347.

14. Letter is quoted in W. L. Melville Lee, *A History of Police in England* (London: Methuen and Co., 1901–1905), p. 243.

15. For the best discussion of the formative years of the London Metropolitan Police, see Wilber R. Miller, *Cops and Bobbies: Police Authority in New York and London, 1830–1870* (Chicago: University of Chicago Press, 1977), pp. 12, 13, 15, 25, 27.

16. Georges Lefebvre, *The Coming of the French Revolution*, trans. R. R. Palmer (Princeton, N.J.: Princeton University Press, 1971), pp. 18, 113–14; Alan Williams, "The Police and the Administration of Eighteenth-Century Paris," *Journal of Urban History* IV (February 1978), pp. 159, 165, 169, 178.

17. Howard C. Payne, *The Police State of Louis Napoleon Bonaparte, 1851–1860* (Seattle: University of Washington Press, 1966), pp. 3–33.

18. Nils Forssell, *Fouché: The Man Napoleon Feared* (London: George Allen and Unwin, 1928), pp. 138, 140–41, 148–70; Hubert Cole, *Fouché: The Unprincipled Patriot* (New York: McCall Publishing, 1971), pp. 115, 120, 140, 157.

19. Eugene Francois Vidocq, *Memoires of Vidocq: The Principal Agent of the French Police*, trans. unknown (Philadelphia: T. D. Peterson, 1859), pp. 215, 315, 337, 340, 352, 437; A. C. Murch, *The Development of the Detective Novel* (New York: Greenwood Press, 1958), pp. 41–45.

20. Radzinowicz, *History of English Criminal Law*, 3:347.

21. Frederick Oughton, *Ten Guineas a Day: A Portrait of the Private Detective* (London: John Long, 1961), pp. 36–44.

22. Carl Bridenbaugh, *Cities in the Wilderness: The First Century of Urban Life in America, 1625–1742* (New York: Ronald Press, 1938), pp. 64–67; Carl Bridenbaugh, *Cities in Revolt: Urban Life in America, 1743–1776* (New York: Capricorn Books, 1964), pp. 108–10.

23. Charles N. Glaab, ed., *The American City: A Documentary History* (Homewood, Ill.: Dorsey Press, 1963), pp. 65–69, 78–79.

24. George Austin Ketcham, "Municipal Police Reform, a Comparative Study of Law Enforcement in Cincinnati, Chicago, New Orleans, New York, and St. Louis, 1844–1877" (Ph.D. dissertation, University of Missouri, 1967), pp. 40, 60–63, 76.

25. Richard Wade, "Violence in the Cities: An Historical View," *University of Chicago Center for Policy Study*, ed. Charles U. Daly (Chicago: *Papers from a Conference Held by the University of Chicago Center for Policy Studies* 1969), pp. 9–11. Leonard L. Richards, *"Gentlemen of Property and Standing": Anti-Abolition Mobs in Jacksonian America* (New York: Oxford University Press, 1970), pp. 95–96, 112, 118, 126.

26. Roger Lane, *Policing the City: Boston 1822–1885* (Cambridge, Mass.: Harvard University Press, 1967), pp. 98, 100, 117; James F. Richardson, *The New York Police: Colonial Times to 1901* (New York: Oxford University Press, 1970), p. 49; Raymond B. Fosdick, *American Police Systems* (New York: Century Co., 1926), pp. 58–67; A. E. Costello, *Our Police Protectors: History of the New York Police* (New York: A. E. Costello, 1885), p. 402.

27. For a sample of attitudes towards city detective police, see *New York Times*, 3 April, 9 August 1866, 16 July 1875; *Chicago Tribune*, 21 April 1887.

28. *New York Tribune*, 5 February 1857.

29. J. W. Gerard, *London and New York: Their Crime and Police* (New York: William C. Bryant and Co., 1853).

30. Allan Nevens and Milton Halsey Thomas, eds., *The Diary of George*

Templeton Strong, Vol. II: *The Turbulent Fifties, 1850–1859* (New York: Macmillan, 1952), p. 99.

31. *Philadelphia Public Leader,* 29 September 1848.

32. Lane, *Policing the City,* pp. 83–84.

33. Ibid.

34. David R. Johnson, *Policing the Urban Underworld: The Impact of Crime on the Development of the American Police, 1800–1887* (Philadelphia: Temple University Press, 1979), pp. 12–40.

35. David J. Rothman, *The Discovery of the Asylum: Social Order and Disorder in the New Republic* (Boston: Little, Brown and Co., 1971), pp. 237, 254.

36. *The National Era,* 1 (12 August 1847), p. 3.

1. CHICAGO GENESIS

1. For the case and testimony, see *Report of the Trial of Oscar Caldwell, Late Conductor on the Chicago Burlington Railroad Line, For Embezzlement* (Chicago: Daily Democratic Press, 1855).

2. Jerome Hall, *Theft, Law and Society,* pp. 34–37, 66. See also Joel Prentiss Bishop, *Commentaries on the Criminal Law,* (Boston: Little, Brown and Company, 1859), 2:222–23, 233. For a theoretical study, see Donald R. Cressey, *Other People's Money: A Study in the Social Psychology of Embezzlement* (Glencoe, Ill.: Free Press, 1953).

3. *Phrenological Description of Allan Pinkerton, Esq. made by Professor O. S. Fowler, Tremont House, Chicago, December 14, 1865* (Chicago: Lakeside Publishing and Printing, 1874), p. 10; Allan Pinkerton to Robert Pinkerton, 28 December 1874, Pinkerton National Detective Agency Papers (Library of Congress, Washington).

4. Quoted in Bessie Louise Pierce, ed., *As Others See Chicago: Impressions of Visitors, 1673–1933* (Chicago: University of Chicago Press, 1933), p. 123; *Chicago Weekly Times,* 13 September 1855.

5. Allan Pinkerton to [name illegible], 6 October 1861, Allan Pinkerton Letterbook 1861, Part I Pinkerton Papers (Library of Congress).

6. Ray Boston, *British Chartist in America, 1839–1900* (Manchester, Eng.: Manchester University Press, 1971), pp. 6, 9, 13, 15, 22, 26, 29–30, 73, 86.

7. *The Past and Present of Kane County, Illinois* (Chicago: William Le-Baron, Jr., and Co., 1878), pp. 229–30.

8. James D. Horan, *The Pinkertons: The Detective Dynasty that Made History* (New York: Crown Publishers, 1967), p. 14.

9. Allan Pinkerton, *Professional Thieves and the Detective* (New York: G. W. Carleton and Co., 1880), pp. 20, 24–25.

10. Ibid., p. 54.

11. *Past and Present of Kane County, Illinois,* p. 254. Leonard Richards, *Gentlemen of Property and Standing: Anti-Abolition Mobs in Jacksonon America* (New York: Oxford University Press, 1970) places this in national perspective.

12. Bessie Louise Pierce, *A History of Chicago.* Vol. 2: *From Town to City, 1848–1871* (New York: Alfred A. Knopf, 1940), p. 198; Verna Cooley, "Illinois and the Underground Railroad to Canada," *Illinois State Historical Society, Transactions* 23 (May 1917), pp. 81, 86–87.

13. *Chicago Daily Times,* 1 September 1857; Oswald Garrison Villard, *John Brown, 1800–1859* (Boston: Houghton Mifflin Co., 1910), p. 390; Jules Abels, *Man on Fire: John Brown and the Course of Liberty* (New York: Macmillan Co., 1971), p. 230.

14. *Chicago Daily Tribune,* 16 December 1853.

15. *Chicago Daily Democratic Press,* 9 February 1852; *Chicago Tribune,* 24 October 1880.

16. *Chicago Daily Democratic Press,* 9 September 1853 and *Daily Chicago Tribune,* 9 September 1853.

17. Elenore Denniston, *America's Silent Investigators: The Story of the Postal Inspectors Who Protect the United States Mail* (New York: Dobb, Mead and Co., 1964), p. 30; Arthur Chester Millspaugh, *Crime Control by the National Government* (Washington: Brookings Institution, 1937), p. 63.

18. *Chicago Daily Democratic Press,* 17 March, 2 July 1855; *Chicago Times,* 17 March 1855; *Chicago Weekly Times,* 19 July 1855; *Chicago Daily Tribune,* 17 March 1855.

19. *Chicago Daily Democratic Press,* 13 April 1855; *Chicago Weekly Times,* 19 April 1855.

20. Alfred D. Chandler, Jr., *The Visible Hand: The Managerial Revolution in American Business* (Cambridge, Mass.: Harvard University Press, 1977), pp. 7, 79, 80, 87, 109.

21. R. B. Mason, "Report of the Chief Engineer," *Report and Accompanying Documents of the Illinois Central Railroad Company,* 19 March 1856, p. 27, Annual Reports Box, Illinois Central Papers (Newberry Library, Chicago, Ill.); for an overview, see Carlton Jonathan Corliss, *Trails to Rails: A Story of Transportation Progress in Illinois* [Chicago, 1934].

22. *The Railroads, History and Commerce of Chicago: Chicago and Her Railroads,* 31 January 1854, pp. 3, 7, 12, 13; *Fourth Annual Review of the Commerce of Chicago for 1855,* p. 5, Illinois Central Papers.

23. R. B. Mason to William P. Bewall, 6 August 1854, Mason's Outletter Bundle, Illinois Central Papers.

24. *Chicago Daily Democratic Press,* 28 July, 18 and 28 September 1855; *Chicago Weekly Times,* 20 September 1855.

25. Benjamin F. Johnson to J. N. Perking, 7 October 1856, Johnson's Outletter Book, December 1853-December 1856, Illinois Central Papers.

26. The railroads were the Illinois Central, the Michigan Central, the Michigan Southern and Northern Indiana, the Chicago and Galena Union, the Chicago and Rock Island, and the Chicago Burlington and Quincey. See contract between Pinkerton and the Illinois Central Railroad, 1 February 1855, Illinois Central Papers.

27. *Chicago Daily Democratic Press,* 4 October 1854.

28. Ibid., 12 April 1855.

29. "Report to the Shareholders," *Illinois Central Annual Reports, 1858,* Illinois Central Papers.

30. Johnson to Perkins, 17 September 1855, Illinois Central Papers; Johnson to William H. Osborn, 19 and 27 November 1855, ibid.

31. David R. Johnson, *Policing the Urban Underworld: The Impact of Crime on the Development of the American Police, 1800–1887* (Philadelphia: Temple University Press, 1979), pp. 59–60.

32. John J. Flinn, *History of the Chicago Police* (Chicago: Police Book Fund, 1887), pp. 66–67, 71–78; *Chicago Daily Democratic Press,* 23 April 1855.

33. Flinn, *History of the Chicago Police,* p. 79.

34. *Illinois State Register,* 9 February 1857.

35. Ibid.; *Journal of the House of Representatives of the Twentieth General Assembly of the State of Illinois,* 5 January 1857 (Springfield: Lanphier and Walker, 1857), pp. 408, 446, 482.

36. *Daily Democrat,* 11 March 1857.

37. Ibid., 16, 25 June 1857; Don E. Fehrenbacker, *Chicago Giant: A Biography of "Long John" Wentworth* (Madison, Wisc: American History Research Center, 1957), pp. 143, 145.

38. *Chicago Daily Tribune,* 24 June 1857.

39. *Daily Democrat,* 25 June 1857.

40. Ibid., 30 June 1857.

41. Ibid., 26 June 1857.

42. *Chicago Tribune,* 6 October 1858.

43. *Daily Democrat,* 12 December 1859; *Chicago Daily Times,* 25 October and 26 November 1859.

44. Henry Warrum, *Peace Officers and Detectives: The Law of Sheriffs, Constables, Marshals, Municipal Police and Detectives* (Greenfield, Ind.: William Mitchell Printing Co., 1895), pp. 84, 85, 86.

45. Johnson, *Policing the Urban Underworld,* p. 29.

46. *Chicago Daily Times,* 25 October 1859.

47. *Daily Democrat,* 26 June 1857.

48. Ibid., 15 October 1860; Pinkerton, *Professional Thieves and the Detective,* p. 113.

49. Flinn, *History of the Chicago Police,* pp. 80, 88, 93, 95.

50. *Daily Democrat,* 5 March 1861.

51. *Observer,* 14 November 1896.

2. LESSONS OF WAR

1. A. L. Stimson, *History of the Express Companies: And the Origin of American Railroads, Together with Some Reminiscences of the Latter Days of the Mail Coach and Baggage Wagon Business in the United States* (New York: n.p., 1858), pp. 129–30.

2. Ibid., pp. 32, 36, 38, 42–43, 68. For links between the express industry and the development of the mail service, see Wayne E. Fuller, *The American Mail: Enlarger of the Common Life* (Chicago: University of Chicago Press, 1972), pp. 162–63.

3. Stimson, *History of the Express Companies,* pp. 97–98, 104, 106, 116.

4. Ibid., pp. 155–56.

5. Ibid., pp. 161, 184, 194, 201; Bessie Louise Pierce, *A History of Chicago.* Vol. 1: *From Town to City, 1848–1871* (New York: Alfred A. Knopf, 1937), p. 63.

6. Stimson, *History of the Express Companies,* p. 208.

7. Ibid., pp. 266–67; T. W. Tucker, *Waifs from the Way-Bills of an Old Expressman* (Boston: Lee and Shepard, 1872), pp. 73–74.

8. Stimson, *History of the Express Companies,* p. 128; Pinkerton, *The Expressman and the Detective,* pp. 30, 205.

9. *Montgomery, Alabama Daily Confederation,* 22 June 1860.

10. New York Office Journal, 1865–1866, pp. 9, 42, 88–90, Pinkerton National Detective Agency Papers (Library of Congress, Washington).

11. Ibid., p. 7.

12. Edward Waldo Emerson and Waldo Emerson Forbes, eds., *Journals of Ralph Waldo Emerson with Annotations.* Vol. X: *1864–1876* (Boston, Houghton Mifflin, 1914), p. 33.

13. *Chicago Times,* 1 September 1882.

14. Autobiographical Document written by Samuel Morse Felton, 17 January 1866, Samuel Morse Felton Collection (Chicago Historical Society, Chicago).

15. Allan Pinkerton, *History and Evidence of the Passage of Abraham Lincoln From Harrisburg, Pa., to Washington, D.C., on the 22nd and 23rd of February, 1861* (Chicago, 1868), p. 10.

16. Allan Pinkerton to Felton, 19 March 1861, Samuel M. Felton Collection (Historical Society of Pennsylvania, Philadelphia).

17. John Joseph Flinn, *History of the Chicago Police* (Chicago: Police Book Fund, 1887), pp. 92, 114.

18. Allan Pinkerton, *The Spy of the Rebellion* (New York: G. W. Dillingham, 1888), pp. 46, 54–56, 62, 68.

19. Ibid., pp. 84–85, 88, 92.

20. *New York Times,* 31 October 1867; George W. Walling, *Recollections of a New York Chief of Police* (New York: Caxton Book Concern, 1887), pp. 68–74.

21. T. Harry Williams, ed., *Abraham Lincoln: Selected Speeches, Messages, and Letters* (New York: Holt, Rinehart and Winston, 1964), p. 137.

22. Pinkerton, *The Spy of the Rebellion,* pp. 95–97.

23. *Richmond Daily Dispatch,* 6 March 1861.

24. *New York Daily Tribune,* 25 February 1861; *New York Times,* 25, 26, and 27 February 1861.

25. *Chicago Tribune,* 28 February 1861.

26. *Chicago Democrat,* 5 March 1861; see also file no. 3 in Pinkerton National Detective Agency Papers (Pinkerton's Incorporated Archives, New York).

27. *Chicago Post,* 30 March 1861; *Chicago Democrat,* 9 March 1861; Don E. Fehrenbacher, *Chicago Giant: A Biography of "Long John" Wentworth* (Madison, Wisc: American History Research Center, 1957), p. 188. Subsequently many agreed with John Wentworth. See Ward H. Lamen, *The Life of Abraham Lincoln: From His Birth to His Inauguration as President* (Boston, 1872), p. 514; Edward Stanley Lanes, "Allan Pinkerton and the Baltimore 'Assassination' Plot Against Lincoln," *Maryland Historical Magazine,* 24 (March 1950), pp. 12–13.

28. U.S., Congress, House, *Alleged Hostile Organization Against the Government Within the District of Columbia,* Reports of Committees of the House of Representatives, no. 79, vol. 2, sess. 1105, 36th Cong., 2d sess., 1861, p. 2.

29. Pinkerton to William H. Hernden, 23 August 1866, Pinkerton Papers (Chicago Historical Society).

30. Fred Albert Shannon, *The Organization and Administration of the Union Army, 1861–1865* (Cleveland: Arthur H. Clark, 1928), 2:57–59, 62, 64; Robert James, "Fortunes of War," *Harpers's Monthly Magazine,* 29 (July 1864), p. 228.

31. Eugene Converse Murdock, *Patriotism Limited, 1862–1865: The Civil War Draft and the Bounty System* (Kent, Ohio: Kent State University Press, 1967), pp. 19, 81, 208.

32. Shannon, *Organization and Administration of the Union Army,* II, p. 71.

33. George Burnham, *Members of the United States Secret Service* (Boston: Laban Heath, 1872), p. 27; LaFayette C. Baker, *History of the United States Secret Service* (Philadelphia: LaFayette C. Baker, 1867), pp. 45–46, 72; Winfield Scott to Abraham Lincoln, 4 April 1861, in David C. Means, *The Lincoln Papers,* 2 vols. (New York: Doubleday and Co., 1948), 2:526.

34. H. J. Eckenrode and Bryan Conrad, *George B. McClellan: The Man Who Saved the Union* (Chapel Hill: University of North Carolina Press, 1941), pp. 2, 4, 10, 13, 15.

35. Allan Pinkerton to Lincoln, 21 April 1861, and N. B. Judd to Lincoln, 21 April 1861, Allan Pinkerton Papers (Chicago Historical Society).

36. George S. Bryan, *The Spy in America* (Philadelphia: J. B. Lippincott, 1943), p. 123.

37. Allan Pinkerton to George McClellan, 22 July 1861, and McClellan to E. J. Allen, 25 July 1861, McClellan Papers (Library of Congress, Washington).

38. Allan Pinkerton to Lincoln, 21 April 1861, Pinkerton Papers (Chicago Historical Society); Pinkerton, *Spy of the Rebellion,* p. 156.

39. Allan Pinkerton to Thomas Scott, 21 August 1861, Binder 76, Pinkerton Papers (Pinkerton's Archives).

40. Allen to Col. H. F. Clarke, 12 March 1862; ibid.

41. Allan Pinkerton to Abraham Lincoln, 19 July 1861, Pinkerton Papers (Chicago Historical Society).

42. Allen to Capt. W. W. Averell, 29 August 1861, Binder 76, Pinkerton Papers (Pinkerton's Archives).

43. Rose Greenhow, *My Imprisonment and the First Year of Abolition Rule at Washington* (London: Richard Bentley, 1863), p. 40; *New York Times,* 26 August 1861, 25 and 28 September 1861, 5 November 1861, 2 June 1862; Pinkerton, *Spy of the Rebellion,* pp. 250–70.

44. Allen to McClellan, 3 July 1861, Pinkerton Papers (Chicago Historical Society).

45. Pinkerton, *Spy of the Rebellion,* pp. 158, 210–11, 485–501. Allan Pinkerton never forgave Price Lewis for exposing Timothy Webster. Lewis joined a New York private detective to form Lewis and Scott Detective Agency. When Scott died, Lewis became an insurance investigator and a subpoena server for a lawyer. Since he was a British subject, he never received a war pension and in 1911 committed suicide. William Inglis, "A Republic's Graditude," *Harper's Weekly,* 30 December 1911, p. 24.

46. Allen to McClellan, 15 November 1861, McClellan Papers.

47. George B. McClellan, "Complete Report of the Organization and Campaigns of the Army of the Potomac, Campaign Document, November 3, 1864," *Handbook of the Democracy for 1863–64,* p. 70.

48. Lloyd Lewis, "Lincoln and Pinkerton," *Journal of the Illinois State Historical Society,* 31 (December 1948), p. 373.

49. Nearly a century later, an inhouse "agency history" felt it had to apologize for the inadequacy of the founder as a wartime spy. "Agency History," *Eye of Pinkerton's National Detective Agency,* 3 (December 1954), p. 14.

50. Jacob Dolson Cox, *Military Reminiscences of the Civil War,* 2 vols. (New York: Charles Scribner's Sons, 1900), I, pp. 250–51; Bruce Catton, *Mr. Lincoln's Army* (New York: Doubleday and Co., 1951), pp. 122, 124.

51. R. J. Athinson to McClellan, 7 July 1863, Binder 76, Pinkerton Papers (Pinkerton's Archives); Allan Pinkerton's *Day Book, 1860–62,* ibid.

52. Allan Pinkerton to Robert Pinkerton, 28 April 1883, Pinkerton Papers (Library of Congress).

53. Allan Pinkerton to Felton, 22 December 1865, Felton Collection.

54. "Announcement of Sentence," *Report of the Trial of Frederick P. Hill, Late Conductor of the Philadelphia and Reading Railroad, On a Charge of Embezzling the Funds of That Company in His Capacity as a Conductor* (Chicago: George H. Fergus, 1864), p. 59.

55. Allan Pinkerton, *Tests on Passenger Conductors Made by the National Police Agency* (Chicago: George H. Fergus, 1867), pp. 9, 14; *Report of the Trial of Frederick P. Hill,* p. 60.

56. *Report of the Trial of John Van Daniker, on a Charge of Embezzlement, in His Capacity as Conductor on the Philadelphia and Erie Railroad* (Philadelphia: H. G. Leisenning, 1867).

57. Allan Pinkerton, *Tests on Passenger Conductors Made by the National Police Agency* (Chicago: Beach and Bernard, 1870).

58. George H. Bangs to Allan Pinkerton, 20 April 1871, Pinkerton Papers (Library of Congress).

59. Alfred D. Chandler, Jr., *The Visible Hand: The Managerial Revolution in American Business* (Cambridge, Mass.: Harvard University Press, 1977), pp. 97–98.

60. H. Wilson, comp., *Trow's New York City Director for the Year Ending May 1, 1856* (New York: John F. Trow, 1855), pp. 77, 374, 795; *Directory for the City of New York for 1870–1871,* pp. 46, 62, 77, 142, 152, 208, 279, 347, 450, 495, 514, 593, 615, 627, 638, 653, 696, 708, 813, 814, 856, 965, 1029, 1056, 1092, 1168, 1243, 1263, 1331.

61. New York Office Journal, 1865–1866, pp. 9, 42, 88–90, Pinkerton Papers (Library of Congress).

62. *Chicago Western Democrat,* 22 January 1859; *Chicago Daily Times,* 25 October 1859; *Chicago Tribune,* 30 April 1864.

63. Flinn, *History of the Chicago Police,* pp. 93, 96, 103, 114–115; *The Lakeside Business Directory* (Chicago: William, Donnelly and Co., 1874), pp. 1250–1356.

64. See New York Office Journal, 1865–1866, p. 26, Pinkerton Papers (Library of Congress); David Ward Wood, ed., *Chicago and Its Distinguished Citizens; Or the Progress of Forty Years* (Chicago: Milton George and Co., 1881), pp. 566–70; Elias Colbert, *Colbert's Chicago: Historical and Statistical Sketch of the Garden City from the Beginning until Now* (Chicago: P. T. Sherlock, 1868), p. 91.

65. Benson J. Lossing, *Pictorial History of the Civil War in the United States of America,* 3 vols. (Philadelphia: George W. Childs, 1866), I, pp. 278–79.

66. *New York Times,* 31 October 1867; Allan Pinkerton to Felton, 31 October 1867, Felton Collection.

67. Allan Pinkerton to Bangs, 31 December 1868, Pinkerton Papers (Library of Congress).

68. Allan Pinkerton to Felton, 10 November 1867, Felton Collection;

Bangs to Allan Pinkerton, 7, 14, and 28 February, 2 March 1869, Pinkerton Papers (Library of Congress).

69. Bell Irving Wiley, *The Life of Billy Yank: The Common Soldier of the Union* (New York: Bobbs-Merrill, 1951), pp. 254–55.

70. *New York Times,* 14 December 1864, 4 January 1866.

71. A. H. Guernsey, "Robbery as a Science," *Harper's New Monthly Magazine* 27 (May 1863), pp. 738, 940–43; *New York Times,* 30 January, 11 February, 4, 18 July, 11, 12 August 1866; *New York Herald Tribune,* 13, 14 August 1866.

72. *New York Times,* 8 April, 12 August 1866, 12 February 1869; *New York Herald Tribune,* 13 August 1866.

73. Edward Crapsey, *The Nether Side of New York; Or the Vice, Crime and Poverty of the Great Metropolis* (New York: Sheldon and Co., 1872), pp. 10, 51; *New York Times,* 12 February 1869.

74. Bangs to Allan Pinkerton, 7 February 1869, Pinkerton Papers (Library of Congress).

75. Bangs to Allan Pinkerton, 14 and 28 February, 6 March 1869, ibid.

76. Bangs to Allan Pinkerton, 14 February 1868, ibid.

77. Alexander B. Callow, Jr., *The Tweed Ring* (New York: Oxford University Press, 1975), p. 147.

78. Bangs to William Pinkerton, 26 September 1869, Pinkerton Papers (Library of Congress); James F. Richardson, *The New York Police: Colonial Times to 1901* (New York: Oxford University Press, 1970), pp. 162–63.

79. "Pinkerton Men," *New York World,* 19 September 1875.

80. Allan Pinkerton, *Claude Melnotte as a Detective* and *Other Stories* (Chicago: W. B. Keen, Cooke and Co., 1875), pp. 251–52. Chief of the New York Police, George Walling, also demonstrated the impact of the war on a policeman's thinking. He wrote: "To draw a simile from army organization, the main force of the police is the infantry; the detectives, the cavalry and the scouts." Walling, *Recollections of a New York Chief of Police,* p. 517.

81. For an example of these coded letters see Bangs to Allan Pinkerton, 24 December 1872, Pinkerton Papers (Pinkerton's Archives).

82. Allan Pinkerton to Salmon P. Chase, 13 September 1870, Salmon P. Chase Papers (Library of Congress, Washington).

3. PINKERTON AND THE PINKERTON MEN

1. As will be shown in a subsequent chapter, the Pinkerton business would not be free of arbitrary actions of subordinates. That was one of the problems in the labor wars of the 1880s.

2. Information gleaned from testimony given in the Caldwell case. See *Report of the Trial of Oscar Caldwell* (Chicago: Daily Democratic Press, 1855).

3. Allan Pinkerton to Robert Pinkerton, 26 May 1875, Pinkerton National Detective Agency Papers (Library of Congress, Washington).

4. Allan Pinkerton, *The Expressman and the Detective* (Chicago: W. B. Keen, Cooke and Co., 1875), p. 85; *New York Times,* 15 September 1883; *Chicago Daily Democratic Press,* 7 March 1855.

5. New York Office Journal, 1865–1866, pp. 51, 78, 87, Pinkerton Papers (Library of Congress).

6. For data on background of operatives, see testimony in *Report of the Trial of John Van Daniker, on a Charge of Embezzlement, in His Capacity as Conductor on the Philadelphia & Erie Railroad* (Philadelphia: H. G. Leisenning, 1867). See also *Report of the Trial of Frederick P. Hill, Late Conductor of the Philadelphia and Reading Railroad on a Charge of Embezzling the Funds of that Co. in His Capacity as a Conductor* (Chicago: George H. Fergus, 1864).

7. George H. Bangs to Allan Pinkerton, 30 May 1872, Pinkerton Papers (Library of Congress).

8. Ibid., 27 May 1872.

9. *Report of the Trial of John Van Daniker.* pp. 18, 20, 31.

10. George H. Bangs to Allan Pinkerton, 31 May 1872, Pinkerton Papers (Library of Congress).

11. John Flinn, *History of the Chicago Police* (New York: Arno Press 1973), pp. 391, 392, 426.

12. Howard O. Sprogle, *The Philadelphia Police: Past and Present* (New York: Arno Press, 1971), pp. 286–287.

13. George P. Burnham, *Memories of the United States Secret Service* (Boston: Laban Heath, 1872), pp. 122–124.

14. New York Office Journal, 1865–1866, pp. 95–97, Pinkerton Papers (Library of Congress); *New York Times,* 14 May 1865.

15. *New York World,* 19 September 1875.

16. Allan Pinkerton, *Special Rules and Instruction to be Observed in Testing Conductors, Designed for the Operatives of the National Police Agency* (Chicago: George H. Fergus, 1864).

17. Bangs to Allan Pinkerton, 9 January 1873, Pinkerton Papers (Library of Congress).

18. Allan Pinkerton, *General Principles of Pinkerton's National Police Agency* (Chicago: George H. Fergus, 1867), p. 6.

19. Ibid., p. 11.

20. Ibid., p. 8.

21. For the public police, see William A. Westley, *Violence and the Police: A Sociological Study of Law, Custom, and Morality* (Cambridge, Mass.: MIT Press, 1970), pp. 8–11, 25–30.

22. "Pinkerton Men," *New York World,* 19 September 1875.

23. Joseph R. Gusfield, *Symbolic Crusade: Status Politics and the American Temperance Movement* (Urbana: University of Illinois Press, 1966), pp. 32–35.

24. Allan Pinkerton to Robert Pinkerton, 23 December 1874, Pinkerton Papers (Library of Congress).

25. Ibid., 25 July 1874.

26. *Chicago Mail,* 5 April 1887.

27. Bangs to W. E. Thayer, 23 August 1869; and Bangs to Allan Pinkerton, 17 October 1869, Pinkerton Papers (Library of Congress).

28. Bangs to Allan Pinkerton, 3 April, 9 August, 23 October 1869, ibid.

29. Allan Pinkerton to Robert Pinkerton, 20 November 1872, ibid.

30. Allan Pinkerton to Benjamin Franklin, 4 September 1875, Pinkerton Papers (Library of Congress).

31. Allan Pinkerton to Bangs, 2 September 1875, ibid.

32. Bangs to Allan Pinkerton, 23 December 1870, ibid.

33. Bangs to Allan Pinkerton, 23 December 1870; Allan Pinkerton to William Pinkerton, 28 January 1873, ibid.

34. Allan Pinkerton to Bangs, 2 October 1873, 1 November 1874; Allan Pinkerton to William Pinkerton, 22 October 1873; Allan Pinkerton to A. P. Charles, 1 November 1874, ibid.

35. Allan Pinkerton to Bangs, 18 May 1874, ibid.

36. Allan Pinkerton, *Claude Melnotte as a Detective and Other Stories* (Chicago: W. B. Keen, Cooke and Co., 1875), p. 15.

37. Allan Pinkerton to Robert Pinkerton, 26 May 1875, Pinkerton Papers (Library of Congress).

38. Allan Pinkerton to William Pinkerton, 18 August 1869; Bangs to George Smith, 29 December 1870; Bangs to Allan Pinkerton, 13 March 1872, ibid.

39. Bangs to Allan Pinkerton, 13 December 1870, ibid.

40. Allan Pinkerton to William Pinkerton, 7 November 1872, ibid.

41. Bangs to Allan Pinkerton, 2 December 1872, ibid.

42. Bangs to Frank Warner, 8 December 1872, ibid.

43. Bangs to Allan Pinkerton, 15 December 1872, ibid.

44. For the information on Gus Thiel's activities, see Martin P. Wheeler, *Judas Exposed; or The Spotter Nuisance; an anti-secret book devoted to the interests of railroadmen* (Chicago: Utility Book and Novelty Co., 1889), pp. 27–28, 30–31, 129, 135. Wheeler thinly disguises the Thiel agency by calling it Zeal's, but the connection is obvious.

45. Bangs to Allan Pinkerton, 23 December 1870, Pinkerton Papers (Library of Congress).

46. Allan Pinkerton to Robert Pinkerton, 28 December 1874, ibid.

47. Bangs to Franklin, 5 January 1873; Allan Pinkerton to Bangs, 8 June 1874, ibid. Norman Zierold, *Little Charley Ross: America's First Kidnapping for Ransom* (Boston: Little, Brown and Co., 1967), pp. 11–13, 30, 131–32, 160, 286.

48. *New York Times,* 14 November 1871.

49. Allan Pinkerton to Salmon P. Chase, 3 February 1872, Allan Pinkerton Papers (Chicago Historical Society).

50. Allan Pinkerton to George Julian Harney, 5 September 1872, Pinkerton Papers (Library of Congress).

51. *New York World,* 19 September 1875.

52. Allan Pinkerton to William Pinkerton, 7 November 1872, Pinkerton Papers (Library of Congress).

53. Allan Pinkerton to Robert Pinkerton, 28 December 1874, ibid.

54. *Chicago Tribune,* 12 August 1882.

4. PRIVATE DETECTIVES AND PUBLIC IMAGES

1. "Our Detective Police," *Chambers Journal of Popular Literature, Science, and Art,* Fifth Series, I (May 31, 1884), pp. 338–339.

2. "Methods of Detectives," *Chicago Daily News,* 16 February 1884 (evening issue); Wilber R. Miller, *Cops and Bobbies: Police Authority in New York and London, 1830–1870* (Chicago: University of Chicago Press, 1977), p. 103.

3. L. C. Baker, *History of the United States Secret Service* (Philadelphia: L. C. Baker, 1867), pp. 34–35.

4. *Report of the Trial of John Van Daniker, on a Charge of Embezzlement in His Capacity as Conductor on the Philadelphia and Erie Railroad* (Philadelphia: H. G. Leisenrigh, 1867), p. 63.

5. Matthew Hale Smith, *Sunshine and Shadow in New York* (Hartford: J. B. Burr and Co., 1868), pp. 161–62.

6. George H. Bangs to Allan Pinkerton, 13 May 1872, Pinkerton National Detective Agency Papers (Library of Congress, Washington).

7. *New York Times,* 5 December 1878.

8. T. D. Woolsey, "Nature and Sphere of Police Power," *Journal of Social Science* 3 (1871), p. 114.

9. *New York Times,* 25 June, 30 September 1870.

10. Ibid., 20 March, 5 May 1882, 16 January 1885.

11. Ibid., 5 December 1878.

12. *New York Daily Tribune,* 31 December 1874.

13. *New York Times,* 25 July 1875.

14. Allan Pinkerton, *The Rail-Road Forger and the Detectives* (New York: G. W. Dillingham, 1881), p. 42.

15. Allan Pinkerton, *Professional Thieves and the Detectives* (New York: G. W. Carleton and Co., 1880), p. 309.

16. *The Lakeside Annual Directory of the City of Chicago, 1885,* pp. 1590.

17. "Methods of Detectives," *Chicago Daily News,* 16 February 1884 (evening issue).

18. Miller, *Cops and Bobbies,* pp. 48, 103.

19. *New York Times,* 19, 22, 23, and 28 May 1869 had a series of editorials and letters condemning the "social and commercial espionage" of private detectives.

20. Edward Crapsey, *The Nether side of New York; or The Vice, Crime and Poverty of the Great Metropolis* (New York: Shelden and Co., 1872), pp. 61–62. Also, James D. McCabe, Jr., *Lights and Shadows of New York Life; or The Sights and Sensations of the Great City* (Philadelphia: National Publishing, 1872), pp. 364–71.

21. Britton A. Hill, *Liberty and Law; or Outlines of a New System for the Organization and Administration of Federative Government* (St. Louis: G. I. Jones and Co., 1880), p. 311.

22. *New York Times,* 5 and 24 August 1869; George P. Burnham, *Memoirs of the United States Secret Service* (Boston: Laban Heath, 1872), pp. 132–146; H. C. Whitley, *In It* (Cambridge, Mass.: Riverside Press, 1894), p. 307.

23. Allan Pinkerton to Bangs, 31 December 1868 and 25 August 1872, Pinkerton Papers (Library of Congress).

24. Allan Pinkerton, *Professional Thieves and the Detectives* (New York: G. W. Carleton and Co., 1880), p. 113.

25. *Chicago Daily Democrat,* 20 November 1860. Also, ibid., 9, 10, 22, and 23 November 1860, 5 March 1861.

26. Nelson Manfred Blake, *The Road to Reno: A History of Divorce in the United States* (New York: Macmillan, 1962), pp. 134–35.

27. Ibid., pp. 9, 12, 23, 63.

28. Smith, *Sunshine and Shadow,* p. 162.

29. *New York Times,* 19 March 1873.

30. Ibid., 8 March 1880, 7 July 1887.

31. A. Parlette Lloyd, *A Treatise on the Laws of Divorce* (Boston: Houghton Mifflin and Co., 1887), p. 186. *New York Times,* 30 September 1880.

32. *New York Times,* 5 June 1873.

33. Ibid., 13 and 14 November 1873. The same type of thing occurred six years later. See ibid., 30 July, 28 September, 10 October 1879.

34. Ibid., 22 July, 19 December 1868; Charles Francis Bourke, "The Pinkertons," *Leslie's Monthly Magazine* 60 (May–June 1905), pp. 38–42; William Pinkerton, "Highwaymen of the Railroad," *North American Review* 157 (November 1893), p. 530.

35. "Train Robbery-Merchant's Union Express Company, Hudson River Railroad, May 4, 1868—$100,000," vol. 3, Binder 3, Pinkerton National Detective Agency Papers (Pinkerton's Incorporated Archives, New York); "Brief on the Train Robbery, Merchant's Union Express Co.," Binder 6, ibid.; *Nashville Republican Banner,* 20 December 1871; *Nashville Union and American,* 20 December 1871; Allan Pinkerton, *Mississippi Outlaws and the Detectives* (New York: G. W. Carleton and Co., 1879), pp. 10, 12–13, 39–40, 88–89, 101, 108, 120.

36. Either Pinkerton's was behind the Indiana lynchings or thought them a good idea. In 1875, Allan Pinkerton wrote Bangs suggesting the formation of a vigilance committee to assassinate Molly Maguires as that used in Seymour. Allan Pinkerton to Bangs, 25 August 1875, Pinkerton Papers (Library of Congress).

37. Allan Pinkerton to Bangs, 12 April 1874, ibid. *Chicago Tribune,* 22 March 1874.

38. *Chicago Tribune,* 2 February 1875.

39. Allan Pinkerton to Mr. Woodward, 27 January 1875, Pinkerton Papers (Library of Congress).

40. See William A. Settle, Jr., *Jesse James Was His Name* (Columbia: University of Missouri Press, 1966), pp. 77–78, 80.

41. *Kansas City Times,* 5 May 1875. Also see Eric Hobsbaum, *Bandits* (London: George Weidenfeld S. Nicolson, 1969), pp. 36, 38, 42, 43, 83.

42. *Chicago Tribune,* 2 February 1875. See also Frank Triplett, *History, Romance and Philosophy of Great American Crimes and Criminals* (New York: N. D. Thompson and Co., 1884), p. 602.

43. Allan Pinkerton to Robert Pinkerton, 20 February 1876, Pinkerton Papers (Library of Congress). *New York Times,* 7 November 1875.

44. See Jacques Barzun, "Detection and the Literary Art," and Robert A. W. Lourdes, "The Contributions of Edgar Allan Poe," in *The Mystery Writers Art,* ed. Francis M. Nevins, Jr. (Bowling Green, Ohio: Bowling Green University Popular Press, 1970).

45. Quoted in Frank Luther Mott, *A History of American Magazines, 1850–1865* (Cambridge, Mass.: Harvard University Press, 1938), p. 326. See also ibid., p. 187.

46. Ibid., pp. 328–29; 331.

47. For Erastus Beadle's dime-novel empire, see Albert Johannsen's *The House of Beadle and Adams and its Dime and Nickel Novels: The Story of a Vanished Literature* (Norman: University of Oklahoma Press, 1950).

48. Edward Pearson, *Dime Novels, or Following an Old Trail in Popular Literature* (Port Washington, N.Y.: Kennikat Press, 1978), pp. 138–140, 152; Mary Noel, *Villains Galore: The Heyday of the Popular Story Weekly* (New York: Macmillan, 1954), pp. 124, 165–166.

49. He was not alone in such attitudes. See W. H. Bishop, "Story-Paper Literature," *Atlantic Monthly* 44 (1879), pp. 383–93; Anthony Comstock, *Traps for the Young* (New York: Funk and Wagnalls, 1883).

50. "Methods of Detectives," *Chicago Daily News,* 16 February 1884 (evening issue).

51. Bangs to Allan Pinkerton, 20 April 1871, Pinkerton Papers (Library of Congress).

52. R. B. Marcey, "Detective Pinkerton," *Harper's New Monthly Magazine* 47 (October 1873), pp. 720–27.

53. *Chicago Times,* 12 October 1873.

54. *New York Times,* 14 November 1871.

55. They were, *Strange Stories of a Detective, Experiences of a French Detective, Leaves from the Notebook of a New York Detective, Autobiography of a London Detective,* and *Diary of a Detective Police Officer. Publishers' Trade-List Annual* (New York: Office of the Publishers' Weekly, 1875).

56. "Publisher's Note," in Allan Pinkerton, *Claude Melnotte as a Detective* (Chicago: W. B. Keen, Cooke and Co., 1875); Allan Pinkerton to Robert Pinkerton, 1 October, 20 December 1874, Pinkerton Papers (Library of Congress).

57. *Chicago Daily Tribune,* 10 October 1874.

58. Allan Pinkerton, *Model Town and the Detective* (New York: G. W. Dillingham, 1876), p. 24; Allan Pinkerton, *The Rail-Road Forger and the Detectives* (New York: G. W. Dillingham, 1881), p. 359; Allan Pinkerton, *The Spy of the Rebellion* (New York: G. W. Dillingham, 1888), p. xxiv.

59. Pinkerton, *Claude Melnotte as a Detective,* pp. 250–51.

60. Allan Pinkerton, *Strikers, Communists, Tramps and Detectives* (New York: G. W. Carleton and Co., 1878), p. 15.

61. Ibid., pp. 86, 88.

62. Ibid., pp. 95–134.

63. Allan Pinkerton, *Bankers, Their Vaults, and the Burglars* (Chicago: Fergus Printing, 1873), pp. 3, 4, 16.

64. Allan Pinkerton, *The Expressman and the Detectives* (Chicago: W. B. Keen, Cooke and Co., 1875), p. 261.

65. Allan Pinkerton, *Thirty Years a Detective* (New York: G. W. Dillingham, 1878), p. 13.

66. Luther Mills, "In Memory of Allan Pinkerton," 3 July 1884, Allan Pinkerton Papers (Chicago Historical Society, Chicago); *New York Times,* 2 July 1884.

5. KNIGHTS OF LABOR VS. KNIGHTS OF CAPITALISM

1. Allan Pinkerton to Robert Pinkerton, 19 January 1877, 2 May 1877, 10, 14 June 1877, Pinkerton National Detective Agency Papers (Library of Conress, Washington).

2. *Chicago Tribune,* 22 October 1878.

3. Allan Pinkerton to Robert Pinkerton, 20 July 1878, Pinkerton Papers (Library of Congress).

4. Allan Pinkerton to Robert Pinkerton, 15 May 1879, 26 April 1883, 28 April 1883, 3 May 1883, ibid.

5. Ibid.

6. *Chicago Times,* 12 May 1887, 7 March 1889; *Chicago Tribune,* 7, 8, March 1889.

7. William Pinkerton, "Highwaymen of the Railroad," *North American Review* 157 (November 1893) p. 539.

8. *New York Times,* 9 July 1873, 16 November 1873, 2 June 1874; *Railroad Gazette,* 12 July 1873, p. 281; 25 January 1878, p. 43.

9. *Railroad Gazette,* 25 January 1878, p. 46, 19 April 1878, p. 201, 5 July 1878, p. 338, 12 July 1878, p. 352, 19 July 1878, p. 362, 26 July 1878, p. 374, 16 August 1878, p. 406, 30 August 1878, p. 423, 8 November 1878, p. 539.

10. Alfred D. Chandler, Jr., *The Visible Hand: The Managerial Revolution in American Business* (Cambridge, Mass.: Harvard University Press, 1977), pp. 159–71.

11. R. J. Bayer, "An Army for Defense," *Traffic World* 44 (26 October 1929), p. 1046.

12. James McParlan to Allan Pinkerton, 10 October 1873, Vol. I, Binder 14, Pinkerton National Detective Agency Papers (Pinkerton's Incorporated Archives, New York).

13. Allan Pinkerton, *The Molly Maguires and the Detectives* (New York: G. W. Dillingham, 1905), pp. 459–73, 476–77, 503; *New York Times,* 14 May 1876, 10 February 1878, 21 and 22 June 1877, 26 and 29 March 1878, 12 June, 20 December 1878. Also see Wayne G. Broehl, Jr. *The Molly Maguires,* (Cambridge, Mass.: Harvard University Press, 1964), pp. 131–238.

14. *New York Times,* 13 February 1877.

15. For the *Irish World* and *Labor Standard* quotes, see Anthony Bimba, *The Molly Maguires* (New York: International Publishers, 1932), pp. 10, 15, 121. Anthony Bimba felt this was the first major class battle in American labor history. Ibid., p. 17.

16. Also, Terence V. Powderly, *Thirty Years of Labor, 1859–1889* (New York: Augustus M. Kelley, 1967), p. 133.

17. John T. Morse, Jr., "The Molly Maguire Trials," *American Law Review* 11 (January 1877), pp. 233, 235.

18. Allan Pinkerton, *Strikers, Communists, Tramps and Detectives* (New York: G. W. Carleton and Co., 1878), p. 124, 387. See also Robert Bruce, *1877: Year of Violence* (Indianapolis: Bobbs Merrill, 1959) for the best account of the strikes.

19. Thomas Scott, "The Recent Strikes," *North American Review,* 125 (September 1877), pp. 352, 358; "The Rioters and the Regular Army," *Nation* 25 (9 August 1877) pp. 85–86.

20. Martha Derthick, *The National Guard in Politics* (Cambridge, Mass: Harvard University Press, 1965), pp. 16, 18, 20; R. Ernest Dupuy, *The National Guard: A Compact History* (New York: Hawthorn Books, Inc., 1971), p. 76; William H. Riker, *Soldiers of The States: The Role of the National Guard in American Democracy* (Washington, D.C.: Public Affairs Press, 1957), pp. 46–47, 51, 55.

21. *National Guard Association Convention, Proceedings, 1881* (n.p., n.d.), pp. 13–14.

22. "Strikes and Lockouts," *Sixteenth Annual Report of the Commissioner of Labor, 1901* (Washington: Government Printing Office, 1901), pp. 803–806.

23. Herbert G. Gutman "The Braidwood Lockout of 1874," *Journal of the Illinois State Historical Society* 53 (1960) pp. 17, 19–20.

24. U.S., Congress, Senate, *Investigation of Labor Troubles at Homestead,* S. Rept. 1280, 52d Cong., 2d sess., 1893, p. 242.

25. See reports for 24, 26, and 30 October, 5 and 27 November 1888 in *Pinkerton Reports of the Annual Convention of the Brotherhood of Locomo-*

tive Engineers at Richmond, Virginia, Burlington Papers (Newberry Library, Chicago).

26. *New York Times,* 9 May 1889.

27. *Investigations of Labor Troubles at Homestead,* p. 49.

28. Ibid., p. 63; *Chicago Herald,* 7 November 1886; Pinkerton Patrol Time Book, 1884–1885, Pinkerton Papers (Pinkerton Archives).

29. *New York Times,* 11 October 1887.

30. Norman J. Ware, *The Labor Movement in the United States, 1860–1895: A Study in Democracy* (New York: D. Appleton and Co., 1929), p. 359; John Altgeld, *Live Questions* (Chicago: George S. Bowen and Son, 1899), pp. 385–87, 391.

31. *New York Times,* 17 July 1887.

32. Harry J. Carman, Henry David, and Paul N. Guthrie, eds., *The Path I Trod: The Autobiography of Terence V. Powderly* (New York: Columbia University Press, 1940), p. 149, 154. For development of the Knights of Labor elsewhere see Melten Alonza McLawrin, *The Knights of Labor in the South* (Westport, Conn.: Greenwood Press, 1978), pp. 52–79.

33. *Chicago Times,* 3 February 1887; *Chicago Tribune,* 22 April 1887; *Journal of the House of Representatives of the Thirty-Sixth General Assembly of the State of Illinois* (Springfield, Illinois: State Printing Office, 1889), pp. 137, 349, 350.

34. "Pinkerton's Men," *Nation* 44 (27 January 1887), p. 70.

35. H. Ledyard to A. Osborne, February 23, 1889, quoted in Thomas Cochran, *Railroad Leaders, 1845–1890* (Cambridge, Mass.: Harvard University Press, 1953), p. 181.

36. William Pinkerton to H. B. Stone, 15, 29 March; 2 April 1888, Burlington Papers (Newberry Library, Chicago).

37. Donald L. McMurry, *The Great Burlington Strike of 1888: A Case History in Labor-Relations* (Cambridge, Mass.: Harvard University Press, 1956), pp. 192–204, 287.

38. *Lakeside Annual Directory of the City of Chicago, 1881* (Chicago: Chicago Directory Co.) p. 1379; *Lakeside Annual Directory of the City of Chicago, 1885,* p. 1591; *Lakeside Annual Directory of the City of Chicago, 1892,* pp. 1743–47; *Chicago Business Directory, 1889,* pp. 473–474; Moses King, *King's Handbook of New York City* (Boston: Moses King, 1893), p. 528; William H. Boyd, *Boyd's Philadelphia City Business Directory for 1881* (Philadelphia: C. E. Howe. [1881]), p. 229; Boyd, *Boyd's Philadelphia City Business Directory for 1893,* p. 943.

39. *Investigation of Labor Troubles at Homestead,* pp. 24–34; *Joliet Signal,* 24 June 1887; *New York Times,* 31 May 1886.

40. *Investigation of Labor Troubles at Homestead,* pp. 81, 84. Also Veteran's Police Patrol Broadside, "To the Public," 4 May 1886 (Chicago Historical Society, Chicago).

41. *New York Times,* 31 May 1886.

42. U.S., Congress, *Congressional Record,* 52d. Cong., 1st sess., 1893, 23:4223, 4225, pt. 5.

43. U. S., Congress, House, *Employment of Pinkerton Detectives,* 52nd Cong., 2nd sess., 1893, p. 196.

44. S. G. Spaeth, *Weep Some More My Lady* (Garden City, N.Y.: Doubleday, Page & Co., 1927), p. 235.

45. *New York Times,* 7 July 1892.

46. U.S., Congress, House, *Congressional Record,* 52d Cong., 1st sess., 1893, 22:7007, pt. 7. For Watson's anti-detective views, see Thomas Watson, *The People's Party Campaign Book* (Washington: National Watchman [1892]).

47. *Employment of Pinkerton Detectives,* p. 215; *Investigation of Labor Troubles at Homestead,* pp. 16, 64, 91–92, 140; *New York Times,* 19 November 1892.

48. *Investigation of Labor Troubles at Homestead,* pp. 121–125.

49. Ibid., p. 129.

50. Ibid., pp. 47–60.

51. Ibid., p. xv; *Employment of Pinkerton Detectives,* pp. xv, xxiv.

52. *Investigation of Labor Troubles at Homestead,* p. 227.

53. "Strikes and Lockouts," *Sixteenth Annual Report of the Commissioner of Labor,* 1901, (Washington: Government Printing Office, 1901), pp. 992–1033; *Chicago Tribune,* 17 June 1893; Henry Warrum, *Peace Officers and Detectives: The Law of Sheriffs, Constables, Marshals, Municipal Police and Detectives* (Greenfield, Ind.: William Mitchell, 1895), pp. 106, 108–9, 112–13.

54. William Oates, "The Homestead Strike: A Congressional View," *North American Review* 155 (September 1892) pp. 355–64; George Ticknor Curtis, "A Constitutional View," ibid., pp. 364–70; T. V. Powderly, "A Knight of Labor's View," ibid., pp. 370–75; Z. S. Holbrook, *The Lessons of the Homestead Troubles: Address Before the Sunset Club, November 17, 1892* (Chicago: Knight, Leonard and Co., 1892), p. 3; J. Bernard Hogg, "Public Reaction to Pinkertonism and the Labor Question," *Pennsylvania History* 2 (July 1944), p. 199.

55. Quoted in Ray Boston, *British Chartist in America, 1839–1900* ([Manchester, Eng.]: Manchester University Press. [1971]), p. 78. See also *Open Court* VI (1892), p. 3316.

6. PROFESSIONAL CRIMINALS AND CRIME PREVENTION

1. *New York Times,* 9, 10, and 12 August 1882.

2. Ibid., 11 March 1903.

3. Ibid., 20 July 1887, 17 April 1888.

4. Ibid., 13 March 1877, 12 February 1895; Anthony Comstock, "Bookmakers and Poolselling," *Independent* 44 (5 May 1892), pp. 3–5.

5. Timebook of the Pinkerton Preventive Patrol, 1891–1897, New York Office, Pinkerton National Detective Agency Papers (Pinkerton's Incorporated Archives, New York).

6. *New York Times,* 17 April 1888.

7. Ibid., 21 May 1891.

8. Ibid., 15 September 1891.

9. Ibid., 16, 17, and 18 September 1891, 3 July 1892.

10. Report of Superintendent Beutler, 20 April 1901, Binder 69, Pinkerton Papers (Pinkerton's Archives).

11. *Chicago Sunday Record-Herald,* 24 September 1905.

12. Ibid.

13. Edwin H. Sutherland, ed., *The Professional Thief, by a Professional Thief* (Chicago: University of Chicago Press, 1967), pp. 123, 128.

14. *New York Times,* 13 March 1873.

15. Tom Duggan, *The History of the Jewelers' Security Alliance of the United States, 1883–1950* (New York: The Alliance, 1958), pp. 5, 20–22, 35; *New York World,* 11 May 1891.

16. Ibid.

17. John C. Schneider, *Detroit and the Problem of Order, 1830–1880: A Geography of Crime, Riot, and Policing* (Lincoln, Nebr: University of Nebraska Press, 1980), pp. 98, 103, 127, 130.

18. John Jay Knox, *A History of Banking in the United States* (New York, 1903), pp. 295–303, 312; Paul B. Trescott, *Financing American Enterprise: The Story of Commercial Banking* (New York: Harper and Row, 1963), pp. 90–92, 145, 148; Ray B. Westerfield, *Historical Survey of Branch Banking in the United States* (New York: American Economists Council for the Study of Branch Banking, 1939), p. 11.

19. David R. Johnson, *Policing the Urban Underworld: The Impact of Crime on the Development of the American Police, 1800–1887* (Philadelphia: Temple University Press, 1979), p. 57.

20. [Max Shinburn], "Safe Burglary: Its Beginnings and Progress," Binder 12, pp. 2, 12 Pinkerton Papers (Pinkerton Archives). For identification of authorship see "Maximilian Shoenbeen, alias Max Shinburn, etc. and his Career," Binder 5, ibid.

21. William Pinkerton, "The Professional Sneak Thief," *Proceedings of the International Association of Chiefs of Police, 1906,* pp. 32, 36.

22. Shinburn "Safe Burglary", p. 8.

23. *New York World,* 2 September 1888.

24. Ibid., 26 December 1886.

25. W. Espey Albig, "The Origin of the American Bankers' Association," *Banking* 35 (September 1942), pp. 172–76; *Proceedings of the American Bankers' Association, 1893* (New York: American Banker's Association), p.70.

26. *Bankers' Magazine* 44 (August 1889), pp. 92–98.

27. Ibid., 46 (December 1891), p. 440.

28. *Proceedings of the American Bankers' Association, 1894,* p. 10.

29. Robert A. Pinkerton, "Forgery as a Profession," *North American Review,* p. 58 (April 1894), pp. 454–63.

30. *Proceedings of the American Bankers' Association, 1894,* p. 19.

31. Robert A. Pinkerton to President of American Bankers' Association, 5 October 1894, Binder 1, Vol. 3, Pinkerton Papers (Pinkerton Archives).

32. *Proceedings of the American Bankers' Association, 1894,* p. 9.

33. *American Banker,* 15 July 1896.

34. *Proceedings of the American Bankers' Association, 1896,* pp. 15, 19.

35. *Chicago Eagle,* 16 October 1897.

36. Josiah Flynt, *The World of Graft* (New York: McClure, Phillips and Co., 1901), p. 47.

37. *Seattle Post,* 14 December 1902.

38. Flynt, *World of Graft,* pp. 32–33, 182–83.

39. *Report and Proceedings of the Senate Committee Appointed to Investigate the Police Department of the City of New York,* 5 vols. (Albany, 1895), 5:5670–71.

40. William Pinkerton to Robert Pinkerton, 14 July 1906, Binder 113, Pinkerton Papers (Pinkerton Archives).

41. "The Pinkertons," *Detective* (March 1887).

42. Charles E. Felton, "Police Organization and Administration" *Proceedings of the National Prison Association, 1888* (New York: National Press Association), pp. 4, 11–12, 20. And "The Police Force of Cities—A Protest Against Political Intermedelling, and a Plea for Greater Preventive Effort," *Proceedings of the National Prison Association, 1890,* p. 131.

43. Roger Lane, *Policing the City: Boston, 1822–1885* (Cambridge, Mass.: Harvard University Press, 1967), p. 66.

44. This process was called "getting a spot" on a criminal and gave rise to one of the first slang references of private detectives as "spotters."

45. *New York Times,* 20 December 1893; "International Association of Chiefs of Police: Its History and Its Purpose," *Police Chief* 33 (October 1966), p. 189; Brian S. Boyd, "The Founding of the I.A.C.P., 1893," ibid., 38 (May 1971), pp. 16–17.

46. R. W. McClaughry and John Bonfield, "Police Protection at the World's Fair," *North American Review* (1893) pp. 710, 716.

47. *National Association of Chiefs of Police, Proceedings, 1893,* pp. 5–7, 15; Ibid., *1895,* pp. 9–11, 32; Ibid., *1896,* pp. 18–19, 32.

48. *National Association of Chiefs of Police, Proceedings, 1895,* p. 11; Ibid, *1896,* pp. 18–19, 32; Ibid, *1897,* pp. 17, 20, 37. *Detective* 20 (January 1905) p. 2.

49. *National Association of Chiefs of Police, Proceedings, 1900,* pp. 40–41; John L. Thompson, "National Identification Bureau's I.A.C.P. Pioneer's Legacy," *Police Chief* (January 1968), pp. 15, 17. The name of the national association was changed to International Association of Chiefs of Police in 1902.

50. Thompson, "National Identification Bureau's I.A.C.P.," pp. 16, 18–21.

51. Ibid., pp. 22–24. U.S., Congress, House Report 10068, *National Bureau of Criminal Identification,* 57th Cong. 1st sess. 1902.

52. C. Murphy to Robert A. Pinkerton, 11 December 1901, Binder 15, Vol. 3, Pinkerton Papers (Pinkerton's Archives).

53. Thompson "National Identification Bureau's I.A.C.P.," p. 28; *Detective* 20 (March 1905), p. 2.

54. *Chicago Sunday Record-Herald,* 29 October 1911, pt. 5; *Chicago Sunday Examiner,* 14 October 1917.

55. Berthold Laufer, "History of the Finger-Print System," *Annual Report of the Smithsonian Institution, 1912* (Washington: Smithsonian Institution, 1912), p. 631, Jurgen Thorwald, *Century of the Detective* (New York: Harcourt, Brace and World, [1965]), pp. 94, 98, 100–101.

7. PROFESSIONAL CRIMINALS AND CRIMINAL APPREHENSION

1. Alfred D. Chandler, Jr., *The Visible Hand: The Managerial Revolution in American Business* (Cambridge, Mass.: Harvard University Press, 1977), pp. 145–85, 381.

2. David R. Johnson, *Policing the Urban Underworld: The Impact of Crime on the Development of the American Police, 1800–1887* (Philadelphia: Temple University Press, 1979), pp. vii, 46–47, 137.

3. *Chicago Mail,* 5 April 1887; *Chicago Tribune,* 9 December 1900.

4. George H. Bangs to William A. Pinkerton, 12 December 1872, and George H. Bangs to Allan Pinkerton, 12 December 1872, Binder 1, Vol. 1, Pinkerton National Detective Agency Papers (Pinkerton's Incorporated Archives, New York).

5. Allan Pinkerton to Robert A. Pinkerton, 28 December 1874, 5 April 1875, 20 July 1878, ibid.; Allan Pinkerton to Robert A. Pinkerton, 31 August 1878, Pinkerton National Detective Agency Papers (Library of Congress, Washington).

6. [Charles H. Hermann.], *Recollections of Life and Doings in Chicago: From the Haymarket Riot to the End of World War I, by an Old Timer* (Chicago: Normandine House, 1945), pp. 22, 93–95, 126, 260–61; Hugh Bradley, *Such Was Saratoga* (New York: Doubleday, Doran and Co., 1940) pp. 292–93.

7. Herbert Asbury, *Gem of the Prairie* (New York: Alfred A. Knopf, 1940) pp. 205–06.

8. William A. Pinkerton to Allan Pinkerton II, 4 March 1910, Shinburn Loose Folder 11, Pinkerton Papers (Pinkerton's Archives).

9. Hermann, *Recollections of Life and Doings in Chicago,* pp. 26–61.

10. *Chicago Record-Herald,* 12 July 1912.

11. Robert A. Pinkerton to John Shore, 29 September 1891, Binder 2, Vol 1, Pinkerton Papers (Pinkerton's Archives). See also William Pinkerton, "The Professional Sneak Thief," *Proceedings of the International Association of Chiefs of Police, 1906,* pp. 31–32.

12. "Criminal History of Joseph Killoran, alias Joe Howard, John Knowles," Binder 2, Vol. 1, Pinkerton Papers (Pinkerton's Archives).

13. "Criminal History of Langdon Moore," Binder 28, ibid.; Langdon Moore, *Langdon Moore, His Own Story of His Eventful Life* (Boston: L. W. Moore, 1892), p. 634.

14. "Criminal History of George Miles White, alias George Bliss, etc., Bank Burglar," Binder 29, Pinkerton Papers (Pinkerton's Archives). See also George White, *From Boniface to Bank Burglar* (New York: Seaboard, 1907).

15. William A. Pinkerton to John A. Sterling, 16 July 1895, Binder 16, Pinkerton Papers (Pinkerton's Archives).

16. Robert A. Pinkerton to J. E. Woodward, 7 July 1899, Binder 5, ibid. Byrnes, *Professional Criminals,* pp. 252–56.

17. Allan Pinkerton, *Thirty Years a Detective* (New York: G. W. Dillingham, 1884), p. 341; Thomas Byrnes, *Professional Criminals* (New York: Chelsea House, 1969), p. 12; *New York Herald,* 4 April 1897.

18. "The Bank of England Forgeries and the Bidwell Brothers." Binder 26, Pinkerton Papers (Pinkerton's Archives); *Chicago Herald,* 26 January 1890; *New York News,* 26 January 1890; "Charles O. Brockway—Forger," Binder 39, Pinkerton Papers (Pinkerton's Archives); "Confession of Henry Wade Wilkes, alias George Wilkes, to the U.S. Consulate Representative, J. Schyler Corsby, December 25, 1880 in Milan, Italy," Binder 24, Vol. 1, ibid.; *New York Herald,* 4 April 1897.

19. *San Francisco Bulletin,* 28 September 1903; *New York World,* 18 September 1916; *Chicago Tribune,* 19 January 1919.

20. "A Partial List of Forgeries by Charles Becker," Binder 1, Vol. 1, Pinkerton Papers (Pinkerton's Archives); Charles Becker, "How I forged the $22,000 Draft," *San Francisco Examiner,* 25 December 1898.

21. Robert A. Pinkerton to R. J. Linden, 22 June 1891, Binder 93, Vol. 1, Pinkerton Papers (Pinkerton's Archives).

22. *Proceedings of the International Association of Chiefs of Police, 1897* pp. 46, 48; *New York Times* 24 July 1898.

23. Edwin H. Sutherland, ed., *The Professional Thief, by a Professional Thief* (Chicago: University of Chicago Press, 1967), pp. 123, 128.

24. "Report of Assistant Superintendent Seymour Beutler, March 27, 1901," Binder 2, Vol. 4, Pinkerton Papers (Pinkerton's Archives).

25. "Birdstone" to Chicago Office, 8 February 1904, Binder 67, ibid.

26. *Proceedings of the American Bankers' Association, 1910,* New York, p. 108.

27. Robert Pinkerton to William Pinkerton, 11 July 1907, Pinkerton Papers (Pinkerton's Archives).

28. *Chicago Sunday Record-Herald,* 5 November 1911.

29. *New York Times,* 3 August 1874.

30. William A. Pinkerton to George D. Bangs, 6 April 1912, Binder 6, Pinkerton Papers (Pinkerton's Archives).

31. *Chicago Herald,* 3 April 1887.

32. *Chicago Daily Inter-Ocean,* 18 September 1887.

33. William A. Pinkerton to Robert A. Pinkerton, 5 April 1899, Binder 1, Vol. 3, Pinkerton Papers (Pinkerton's Archives).

34. "Report of Seymour Beutler," 17 October 1901, ibid.; Patrick Flannigan to Seymour Beutler, 12 November 1901, Binder 2, Vol. 3, ibid.

35. Bill Boyce to William A. Pinkerton, 12 November 1911, Binder 33, Vol. 2, ibid.

36. William Pinkerton to Robert Pinkerton, 13 April 1899, Binder 2, Vol. 3, ibid.

37. "Report of Seymour Beutler," 8 May 1899, Binder 2, Vol. 2, ibid.

38. Seymour Beutler to Robert A. Pinkerton, 18 December 1900, Binder 2, Vol. 3, ibid.; Robert Pinkerton to Theodore Roosevelt, 24 December 1900, ibid.; Robert A. Pinkerton to W. F. Moore, 26 August 1901, ibid.

39. Robert A. Pinkerton to Governor Odell, 2 December 1902, ibid.

40. J. Maddox to William A. Pinkerton, 24 January 1906, ibid.

41. *New York World,* 30 June 1889; 23 February 1890; Robert A. Pinkerton to William Edson, 8 July 1889, Binder 5, Pinkerton Papers (Pinkerton's Archives).

42. *Boston Herald,* 3 July 1889; Robert A. Pinkerton to John Cornish, 19 November 1890, Binder 5, Pinkerton Papers (Pinkerton's Archives).

43. *New York World,* 30 December 1892; William A. Pinkerton to Robert A. Pinkerton, 29 December 1892, Binder 5, Pinkerton Papers (Pinkerton's Archives).

44. *New York World,* 13 January 1893.

45. Ibid., 15, 17, and 29 January 1893; Oscar Edwards to Robert A. Pinkerton, 13 January 1893, Binder 5, Pinkerton Papers (Pinkerton's Archives); William A. Pinkerton to George D. Bangs, 20 and 26 January 1893, ibid.

46. Robert A. Pinkerton to Oscar Edwards, 16 February, 10 May 1893, ibid.; Frank Murray to Robert A. Pinkerton, 1 March 1893, ibid.; Robert A. Pinkerton to James Dunlap, 10 May 1893, ibid.

47. William A. Pinkerton to Robert A. Pinkerton, 20 and 29 May 1893, 17 July 1893, ibid.; D. Robertson to William A. Pinkerton, 23 May 1893, ibid.; William A. Pinkerton to Robertson, 5 and 6 June 1893, ibid.

48. Robert A. Pinkerton to William Pinkerton, 17, 24 May 1898, Binder 64, ibid.

49. William A. Pinkerton to George B. Hankin, 27 October 1899, ibid. Seymour Beutler to William A. Pinkerton, 1 March 1900, ibid.

50. Robert A. Pinkerton to William A. Pinkerton, 30 January 1907, Binder 35, ibid.

51. William A. Pinkerton to D.C. Thornhill, 18 February 1913, Binder 2, Vol. 1, Pinkerton Papers (Pinkerton's Archives); D. C. Thornhill to William A. Pinkerton, 20 March 1913, ibid.

52. Robert A. Pinkerton to William A. Pinkerton, 2 May 1900, Binder 1, Vol. 1, ibid.

53. "Report of Assistant Superintendent Seymour Beutler," 9 December 1903, Binder 1, Vol. 1, ibid.; "Report of Robert A. Pinkerton," 14 December 1903, ibid.; William A. Pinkerton to John Cornish, 19 September 1904, Binder 1, Vol. 3, ibid.

54. William A. Pinkerton to Allan Pinkerton II, 4 March 1910, Max Shinburn Loose Folder 11, ibid.; Henry Moebus (Max Shinburn) to William A. Pinkerton, 15 March 1910, ibid.

55. Henry Moebus to Allan Pinkerton II, 11 January 1911, Max Shinburn Loose Folder 8, ibid.; William A. Pinkerton to Allan Pinkerton II, 23 April 1913, Max Shinburn Loose Folder 12, ibid.; William A. Pinkerton to George D. Bangs, 27 April 1913, ibid.

56. Robert A. Pinkerton to William A. Pinkerton, 11 July 1907, Binder 35, ibid.

57. Robert A. Pinkerton to William A. Pinkerton, 27 January 1901, Binder 73, Vol. 2, ibid.; William A. Pinkerton to E. S. Gaylor, 24 March 1902, ibid.; William A. Pinkerton to George D. Bangs, 29 September 1911, ibid.; William A. Pinkerton to James McParlan, 13 February 1912, ibid.

58. William Pinkerton to Allan Pinkerton II, 22 June 1908, Binder 67, ibid.

59. *New York World,* 16 February 1902; *Portland Oregonian,* 27 July 1902; *Birmingham* (Alabama) *News,* 13 May 1910.

60. [William A. Pinkerton], "Biography of Adam Worth," Binder 3, Vol. 1, Pinkerton Papers (Pinkerton's Archives) William A. Pinkerton to Robert A. Pinkerton, 12 February 1902, ibid.

61. William A. Pinkerton to Robert A. Pinkerton, 12 February 1902, ibid.

62. William A. Pinkerton to Robert A. Pinkerton, 2, 7, 9, and 12 February 1902, 21 May 1902, ibid.; Robert A. Pinkerton to William A. Pinkerton, 10 July, 19 August 1902, ibid; George H. Bangs to William and Robert Pinkerton, 23 September 1903, Vol. 2, ibid.

63. *Seattle Post,* 14 December 1902.

64. "Pinkertons by Birth" postcard, in possession of author.

65. *New York Times,* 29 May 1895.

66. For a Marxist interpretation, see Sidney L. Harring, "Class Conflict and the Suppression of Tramps in Buffalo, 1892–1894," *Law and Society Review* 11 (Summer 1977), pp. 873–911.

67. William Pinkerton, "Yeggman," *Proceedings of the International Association of Chiefs of Police, 1904,* p. 50.

68. *Kansas City Star,* 14 April 1903.

69. William Pinkerton, "The Difference Between the Burglars of Today

and of Twenty-five Years Ago," *Proceedings of the International Association of Chiefs of Police, 1900*, p. 19.

70. Pinkerton, "Yeggman," pp. 54–55. See also [C. T. Ludwig], *The Successful Detective* (Kansas City, Mo.: C. T. Ludwig Detective Training Correspondence School, 1913), pp. 47–48; Frank O'Sullivan, *Crime Detection* (Chicago: O'Sullivan Publishing House, 1928), pp. 485–95.

71. George S. Doughtery, *The Criminal As a Human Being* (New York: D. Appleton and Co., 1924), p. 233.

72. *Proceedings of the American Bankers' Association, 1907*, New York p. 20.

73. Josiah Flynt, "Policing the Railroads," *Munsey's Magazine* 22 (February 1900), pp. 658–64. Nels Anderson talks of the ongoing tension between hobos and private police. One of his hobos related a story of traveling in Indiana with a tramp named Sullivan or "Sully." As it turned out, Sully was an employee of the Pinkerton agency and was on the road to gather information on various hobos as agitators. See Nels Anderson, *The Hobo: The Sociology of the Homeless Man* (Chicago, University of Chicago Press, 1923), pp. 155–163.

74. Robert A. Pinkerton to William A. Pinkerton, 12 December 1905, Binder 65, Pinkerton Papers (Pinkerton's Archives); William A. Pinkerton to Robert A. Pinkerton, 15 December 1905, ibid.

75. Robert A. Pinkerton to William A. Pinkerton, 12 December 1902, ibid.

76. "Cipher Book," Pinkerton Papers (Pinkerton's Archives).

77. W. B. Laughlin to Asher Rossetter, 30 January 1909, Binder 123, ibid.

78. William A. Pinkerton to Robert A. Pinkerton, 15 December 1902, Binder 65, ibid.; Robert A. Pinkerton to William A. Pinkerton, 19 December 1902, ibid.

79. William A. Pinkerton to Fred Kohler, 28 June 1910, Binder 91, Vol. 3, ibid.

80. Birdstone to Beutler, 11 July 1902, ibid.; Birdstone was at this time the code name for John C. Arthur. Earlier it had been Brimstone.

81. Superintendent Irle to William A. Pinkerton, 19 December 1903, Binder 31, Vol. 3, ibid.

82. William A. Pinkerton to Fred Kohler, 28 June 1910, Binder 91, Vol. 3, ibid. See also Philip S. Van Cise, *Fighting the Underworld* (Boston: Houghton Mifflin Co., 1936), p. 97.

83. Robert Pinkerton to William Pinkerton, July 3, 1901, Vol. 2, Binder 3, Pinkerton Papers (Pinkerton Archives).

84. William A. Pinkerton to M. J. Conway, 21 September 1898, Binder 119, ibid.

85. L. O. Curan, *Chicago, Satan's Sanction* (Chicago: C. D. Phillips and Co., 1899), pp. 122–23.

86. Thomas Beet, "Methods of American Private Detectives Agencies," *Appleton's Magazine* 8 (July–December 1906), pp. 439–41.

87. *Detective* 23 (October 1906), p. 2.

8. PINKERTON OPERATIVES AND OPERATIONS

1. Robert M. Fogelson, *Big City Police* (Cambridge, Mass.: Harvard University Press, 1977), p. 97.

2. "Order No. 175—Operatives," December 4, 1905, Order Book, Pinkerton National Detective Agency Papers (Pinkerton's Incorporated Archives, New York).

3. Much of this and the subsequent administrative description of the Pinkerton office comes from Morris Friedman, *The Pinkerton Labor Spy* (New York: Wilshire Book Co., 1907), p. 4.

4. Ibid.

5. Ibid., pp. 5–7.

6. Ibid., p. 14.

7. Ibid., p. 191.

8. *Investigations of Labor Troubles at Homestead*, S. Rept. 1280, 52nd Cong., 2nd sess., 1893, p. 6.

9. For the pay scales of police officers, see *New York Times*, 22 October 1887.

10. *Investigations of Labor Troubles at Homestead*, p. 138.

11. Ibid., pp. 136–39.

12. Ibid., p. 71.

13. Ibid., p. 72.

14. U.S., Congress, House, *Employment of Pinkerton Detectives*, H. Rept. 2447, 52nd Cong., 2nd sess., 1893, pp. 135–37.

15. *New York Sun*, October 21, 1980.

16. [Robert Linden] to Robert A. Pinkerton, October 24, 1890, Binder 18, Pinkerton Papers (Pinkerton's Archives); *New Orleans Daily Picayune* March 15, 1891; Memorandum by F. P. Dimaio, December 2, 1938, Binder 18, Pinkerton Papers (Pinkerton's Archives).

17. Robert A. Pinkerton to Francis J. Bealsey, 1 July 1903 and F. P. Dimaio Report, September 17, 1941, Binder 72, Pinkerton Papers (Pinkerton's Archives).

18. "Charge off Book, 1879–1921," Pinkerton Papers (Pinkerton's Archives).

19. Morris Friedman, *The Pinkerton Spy* (New York: Wilshire Book Co., 1907), p. 15.

20. Dashiell Hammett, "From the Memoirs of a Private Detective," *Smart Set* LXX (March 1923), pp. 88–90.

21. Robert Pinkerton to Mr. Hitchcock, January 10, 1906, Binder 84, Pinkerton Papers (Pinkerton's Archives).

22. Charles A. Siringo, *Two Evil Isms: Pinkertonism and Anarchism* (Chicago: Charles A. Siringo, 1915), p. 46.

23. Tom Horn, *Life of Tom Horn: Government Scout and Interpreter, written by Himself* (Norman: University of Oklahoma Press, 1964), p. 222.

24. Friedman, *Pinkerton Labor Spy*, pp. 30–40, 51–64.

25. For a full treatment of this case, see David H. Grover's *Debator's and Dynamiters: The Story of the Haywood Trial* (Corvallis: Oregon State University Press, 1964).

26. Louis Filler, *Crusades for American Liberalism: The Story of the Muckrakers* (New York: Collier Books, 1961), pp. 214, 216–17.

27. Friedman, *Pinkerton Labor Spy*, pp. 2, 71–116, 120–45.

28. Siringo, *Two Evil Isms*, p. 3.

29. A. Kaufmann, *Historic Supplement of the Denver Police: A Review from Earliest Days to the Present Time* (Denver: Denver Police Mutual and Fund, 1890), pp. 627–29, 693.

30. Ibid.; Siringo, *Two Evil Isms*, pp. 10–11, 18.

31. Siringo, *Two Evil Isms,* p. 35.
32. Ibid., p. 21.
33. John Hays Hammond, *The Autobiography of John Hays Hammond,* 2 vols, (New York: Farrar and Rinehart, 1935), 1:195.
34. Siringo, *Two Evil Isms,* pp. 76, 83–87, 93.
35. Ibid., pp. 94–98.
36. *Pinkerton's National Detective Agency* vs. *Charles A. Siringo and W. B. Conley Company* (1910–11), Records, Supreme Court of Cook County (Chancey); Pinkerton's National Detective Agency vs. Charles A. Siringo (1914–15), ibid. For another critical treatment, see Robert Hunter, *Violence and the Labor Movement* (New York: Macmillan, 1914), p. 281–322.

9. "MUSHROOM AGENCIES" IN THE PROGRESSIVE ERA

1. Sarah Stage, *Female Complaints: Lydia Pinkham and the Business of Women's Medicine* (New York: W. W. Norton and Co., 1979), pp. 134–35.
2. *Chicago Tribune,* 9 December 1900.
3. "Employees Record Book From the Philadelphia Office, Dating Back to 1880," Pinkerton National Detective Agency Papers (Pinkerton's Incorporated Archives, New York).
4. Jurgen Thorwald, *The Century of the Detective* (New York: Harcourt, Brace and World, 1964), p. 91.
5. "Pinkerton National Detective Agency: Office and Managerial History," Pinkerton Papers (Pinkerton's Archives).
6. Charles Francis Bourke, "The Pinkertons," *Leslie's Monthly Magazine* 60 (May 1905), pp. 36–45, and ibid. (June 1905), pp. 205–14. See also Albert Sidney Gregg, "Pinkerton Tells How We Make It Easy for Swindlers," *American Magazine,* 88 (September 1919), pp. 28–29, 132.
7. *Philadelphia Times,* 19 April 1896. George Barton, *The True Stories of Celebrated Crimes: Adventures of the World's Greatest Detectives* (New York: McKinlay Stone and Mackenzie, 1909), p. 159; "Robert Linden," Binder 14, Vol. 1, Pinkerton Papers (Pinkerton's Archives).
8. George S. Dougherty, *The Criminal As a Human Being* (New York: D. Appleton and Co., 1924), pp. 3, 8–9, 14–15.
9. *Chicago Record-Herald,* 29 October, 5 and 12 November, 3 and 10 December 1911; *New York Times,* 14 December 1913.
10. "Gompers Speaks for Labor," *McClure's Magazine* 38 (February 1912), p. 372.
11. F. B. McQuiston, "The Strike Breakers," *Independent* 53 (17 October 1901), pp. 2456–58; John H. Craige, "The Professional Strike-Breaker," *Colliers Weekly* 46 (3 December 1910), p. 20.
12. Leroy Scott, "Strikebreaking as a New Occupation," *World's Work* 10 (May 1905), pp. 6194, 6200; William Brown Melony, "Strikebreaking as a Profession," *Public Opinion* 38 (25 March 1905), 440; Howard Barton Myers, "The Policing of Labor Disputes in Chicago: A Case Study" (Ph.D. dissertation, University of Chicago, 1929), pp. 400–401, 585.
13. Edward Levinson, *I Break Strikes! The Technique of Pearl L. Bergoff* (New York: Robert M. McBride and Co., 1935), pp. 37, 40, 121, 130; U.S., Congress, House, *Peonage in Western Pennsylvania,* H. Rept. 90, 62d Cong., 1st sess., 1911, pp. 8, 25–26, 79, 118.

14. Levinson, *I Break Strikes!* pp. 313–14; Jerold S. Auerbach, *Labor and Liberty: The LaFollette Committee and the New Deal* (New York: Bobbs-Merrill, 1966), pp. 97–107.

15. Morris Friedman, *The Pinkerton Labor Spy* (New York: Wilshire Book Co., 1907), p. 54. See also Robert Hunter, *Violence and the Labor Movement* (New York: Macmillan, 1914) and Joseph R. Buchanan, *The Story of a Labor Agitator* (New York: Outlook, 1903).

16. Report of J. McParlan to Frank Gooding and the Orchard Confession, 29 January 1906, Binder 15, Pinkerton Papers (Pinkerton's Archives); David H. Grover; *Debators and Dynamiters: The Story of the Haywood Trial* (Corvallis: Oregon State University Press, 1964); Melvyn Dubofsky, *We Shall Be All: A History of the Industrial Workers of the World,* (Chicago: Quadrangle Books, 1969), pp. 53, 98–105.

17. William Preston, *Aliens and Dissenters: Federal Suppression of Radicals, 1903–1933* (Cambridge, Mass.: Harvard University Press, 1963).

18. Jeremiah Patrick Shallow, *Private Police: With Special Reference to Pennsylvania* (Philadelphia: American Academy of Political and Social Science, 1933), pp. 57, 61–62, 85; U.S., Congress, Senate, Committee on Education and Labor, *Violations of Free Speech and Rights of Labor,* S. Rept. 6, pt. 2, 76th Cong., 1st sess., 1939, p. 6.

19. Robert Hunter, *Violence and the Labor Movement* (New York: Macmillan, 1914), pp. 278–80, 296; Friedman, *Pinkerton Labor Spy,* pp. v, 222.

20. *New York Times,* 8 August 1897, 21 November 1898, 14 and 23 March, 8, 10, 14, and 21 April 1899; 11 and 12 November, 9 December 1900.

21. Bruce Smith, *The State Police: Organization and Administration* (New York: Macmillan, 1925), p. 253.

22. The portion of time spent by Pennsylvania troopers on strike duty:

1906	24%	1914	12%
1907	9%	1915	9%
1908	8%	1916	55%
1909	12%	1917	0
1910	35%	1918	0
1911	34%	1919	11%
1912	23%	1920	1%
1913	16%	1921	0

Bruce Smith, *The State Police,* p. 55.

23. Victor A. Olander, *The State Constabulary Bill: A Statement by Victor A. Olander, Secretary-Treasurer of Illinois State Federation of Labor* ([Chicago]: Illinois State Federation of Labor, 1921), pp. 3–4, 6–12. See also "The Question of State Police," *New Republic* 6 (1 April 1916), p. 230.

24. Katherine Mayo, *Justice to All: The Story of the Pennsylvania State Police* (Boston: Houghton Mifflin, 1920), pp. xxxi, 65, 67–68, 78, 99, 116, 153; New York State, *Committee for State Police (Second Annual Report) 1918* (Albany, 1918), pp. 4, 14, 19.

25. Raymond B. Fosdick, *American Police System* (New York: Century, 1920), pp. 336, 338, 342.

26. George H. Gaston, "The History and Government of Chicago: The sixth paper. The Police in Chicago," *Educational Bimonthy,* (December 1914), p. 149.

27. *Observer* (14 November 1896); *Gopsill's Philadelphia Business Directory,* (Philadelphia: James Gopsill, 1900); *Boyd's Philadelphia City Business Directory* (Philadelphia: C. E. Howe, 1908); Arthur Train, *Courts, Criminals and the Camorra,* (New York: C. Sribrer's Sons, 1912), p. 112.

28. *New York Times,* 31 January 1904.

29. Leonard Felix Fuld, *Police Administration: A Critical Study of Police Organization in the United States and Abroad* (New York: G. P. Putnam's Son, 1910), p. 241.

30. George H. Bangs to Allan Pinkerton, 20 June 1870, Letterbook, Pinkerton National Detective Agency Papers (Library of Congress, Washington); *Detective,* 23 (August 1907), p. 2.

31. *International Association of Chiefs of Police, Proceedings, 1903,* pp. 62–66.

32. *Detective* 20 (January 1905), p. 3.

33. *San Francisco Call,* 25 October 1902; Robert A. Pinkerton to W. W. Willard, 3 November 1902, Binder 26, Pinkerton Papers (Pinkerton's Archives).

34. Allan Pinkerton II to William A. Pinkerton, 18, 23 November 1909, 2 December 1910, Shinburn Loose Folder 14, Pinkerton Papers (Pinkerton's Archives).

35. George Dougherty, *The Criminal as a Human Being* (New York: Appleton and Co., 1924), p. 9.

36. James Brooks to Robert Pinkerton, 11 December 1888, Binder 95, vol. 3, Pinkerton Papers (Pinkerton's Archives); Andrew L. Drummond, *True Detective Stories* (New York: G. W. Dillingham, 1908–09), preface.

37. *Detective,* 23 (December 1907), p. 2; ibid. 24 (July 1908), p. 2.

38. *New York Times,* 17 September 1926.

39. *Fingerprint Magazine,* 3 (September 1921), p. 1.

40. Train, *Courts, Criminals and the Camorra,* p. 93.

41. *New York Times,* 22 September 1921.

42. Train, *Courts, Criminals, and the Camorra,* p. 93.

43. Ibid., pp. 125–26.

44. *New York Times,* 23, 31 January 1904.

45. *Detective* 20 (March 1905), p. 2.

46. For the professionalization of urban police departments during the Progressive Era, see Samuel Walker, *A Critical History of Police Reform* (Lexington, Mass.: Lexington Books, 1977), pp. 53–79.

47. *Chicago Sunday Record-Herald,* 25 September 1905. *Proceedings of the International Association of Chiefs of Police, 1910,* pp. 64, 76–77.

48. *Chattanooga Daily News,* 2 March 1911.

49. *Observer,* 14 November 1896.

50. *Chicago Tribune,* 9 December 1900.

51. Gene Caesar, *Incredible Detective: The Biography of William J. Burns* (Englewood Cliffs, N.J.: Prentice-Hall, 1968), pp. 20, 24, 30–21, 56–73.

52. Lincoln Steffens, "The Taming of the West: Discovery of the Land Fraud System; a Detective Story," *American Magazine* 64 (May–October 1907), pp. 489–505, 585–602; Henry S. Brown, "Punishing the Land-Looters," *Outlook* 85 (23 February 1907), p. 427.

53. Calvin B. Brown, "San Francisco Regeneration," *American Review of Reviews* 36 (August 1907), pp. 195–201; William Ingles, "For the Kingdom of California," *Harpers Weekly* 52 (23 May 1908), pp. 10–12; ibid (30 May

1908), 10–12; ibid. (13 June 1908), pp. 10–12; Walton Bean, *Boss Ruef's San Francisco: The Story of the Union Labor Party, Big Business, and the Graft Prosecution* (Berkeley: University of California Press, 1952), pp. 70–71, 152–55, 198–211.

54. From 1894 the Pinkerton agency received approximately $450,000 from the American Bankers' Association. See *American Bankers' Association, Proceedings, 1910,* p. 108.

55. William Pinkerton to Richard Sylvester, 25 February, 5 March 1910, Binder 72, Pinkerton Papers (Pinkerton's Archives); William Pinkerton to George D. Bangs, 12 February 1910, ibid.; Robert Pinkerton to Bangs, 11 August 1906, ibid.; Frank Dimaio Report, 17 September 1941, ibid.

56. *American Bankers' Association, Proceedings, 1910,* pp. 105–6, 108, 118.

57. *New York Times,* 8 April 1914, 10 August 1915.

58. William Pinkerton to Richard Sylvester, 25 February, 5 March 1910, Binder 72, vol. 5, Pinkerton Papers (Pinkerton's Archives).

59. *American Bankers' Association, Proceedings, 1910,* p. 116.

60. *New York Times,* 4 December 1911; H. J. O'Higgins, "Dynamiters: A Great Case of Detective Burns," *McClure* 37 (August 1911), pp. 346–64; "How Burns Caught the Dynamiters," ibid. 38 (January 1912), pp. 325–29. Seventeen articles appeared in 1911–1912 extolling the exploits of William Burns in Los Angeles. Burns felt that the *Los Angeles Times'* case was so important to his career that he wrote a book on it. See William Burns, *The Masked War* (New York: George H. Doran Co., 1913).

61. Leonard Dinnerstein, *The Leo Frank Case* (New York: Columbia University Press, 1968), pp. 4, 31, 84, 139–41; "The Case of Leo M. Frank," *Outlook* 110 (26 May 1915), p. 166; *New York Times,* 2, 6, 9, 22, and 23 April 1914, 20 and 23 November 1915.

62. William A. Pinkerton to Sylvester, 4 August 1916, Binder, 91, Vol. 2, Pinkerton Papers (Pinkerton's Archives); *New York Times,* 12 April 1914.

63. *New York Times,* 1 April 1914.

64. William A. Pinkerton to C. C. Cook, 8 January 1913, Binder 167, Pinkerton Papers (Pinkerton's Archives); William A. Pinkerton to Asher Rossetter, 14 January 1913, ibid.

65. U.S., Congress, House, "Representative Smith speaking against the Treasury Department's Secret Service," 60th Cong., 2d sess., 25 February 1909, *Congressional Record,* 43:3126; Lincoln Steffens, "William J. Burns, Intriguer," *American Magazine* 65 (April 1908), p. 625.

66. William John Burns, *The Masked War* (New York: George H. Doran, 1913), p. 319.

67. Ramon F. Adams, comp., *Six-Guns and Saddle Leather: A Bibliography of Books and Pamphlets on Western Outlaws and Gunmen* (Norman: University of Oklahoma Press, 1954), pp. 322, 325.

68. "Burns—Star of the Secret Service," *Overland Monthly* 51 (January 1908), p. 58.

69. Gene Caesar, *The Incredible Detective: The Biography of William J. Burns* (Englewood Cliffs, N.J.: Prentice-Hall, 1968), p. 161.

70. Allan Pinkerton, *Professional Thieves and the Detectives* (New York: G. W. Carleton and Co., 1880), pp. 191–285; *New York Times,* 14, 15, 16, and 18 October 1883, 6 January 1892.

71. Samuel Dash, Richard Schwartz, and Robert E. Knowlton, *The*

Eavesdroppers (New Brunswick: Rutgers University Press, 1959), pp. 25, 208.

72. *New York Times,* 21 May 1916.

73. "Police Espionage in a Democracy," *Outlook* 113 (13 May 1916), pp. 235–36.

74. "Wire-Tapping Cases in New York," ibid., p. 234.

75. *New York Times,* 25 April, 14 June 1916.

76. Ibid., 22 April, 19 and 20 May, 14 June 1916, 14 March 1917, 6 August 1919, 3 March 1921.

77. U.S., Congress, Senate, *Devices for Preventing Spies From Tapping Telegraph and Telephone Wires; A letter from Acting Secretary of War in Response to S. Res. of March 19, 1918,* S. Rept. 207, 65th Cong., 2d sess., 1918, pp. 1–2.

78. Dash, Schwartz, and Knowlton, *Eavesdroppers,* pp. 27–28, 208–209, 213–15, 225–29.

79. *New York Times,* 6 August 1919.

80. *American Bankers' Association, Proceedings, 1910,* New York, p. 91–95.

81. *Proceedings of the International Association of Chiefs of Police, 1911,* p. 66.

82. *New York Times,* 29 May 1915.

83. Ibid., 30 August 1915.

84. "Lawrence M. Farrell, Check Swindler," Binder 27, vol. 1, Pinkerton Papers (Pinkerton's Archives); J. H. Schmacher to D. C. Thornhill, 19 April 1916, ibid.; Bangs to H. H. Linter, 22 February 1917, vol. 2, ibid; Report of Superintendent H. S. Mosher, 4 January 1917, ibid.

85. *New York Times,* 10 October 1917, 21 June 1918, 17 January 1921; *New York Herald,* 23 December 1918; William Pinkerton to Lintner, 28 December 1918, Binder 27, vol. 1, Pinkerton Papers (Pinkerton's Archives).

86. "Startling Evidences of Methods Employed by W. J. Burns and His Detective Agency," Binder 27, vol. 2, Pinkerton Papers (Pinkerton's Archives).

87. *Washington Star,* 21 April 1908; Homer Cummings and Carl McFarland, *Federal Justice: Chapters in the History of Justice and the Federal Executive* (New York: Macmillan, 1937), p. 373; Arthur Chester Millspaugh, *Crime Control by the National Government* (Washington: Brookings Institution, 1937), pp. 62, 67, 72–73.

88. Robert A. Pinkerton, "Detective Surveillance of Anarchists," *North American Review* 173 (November 1901), pp. 609, 613–14.

89. *Chicago Inter-Ocean,* 3 January 1904. See also U.S., Congress, House, "Evidence presented against the Treasury Department, Secret Service," 60th Cong., 2d sess., 4 January 1909, *Congressional Record,* 43:462–63.

90. *Washington Star,* 21 April 1908; U.S., Congress, House, "Representative Fitzgerald on the debate over the creation of a detective force in the Justice Department," 60th Cong., 2d sess., 8 January 1909, *Congressional Record,* 43:679.

91. *New York Times,* 8 June 1919.

92. Don Whitehead, *The F.B.I. Story: A Report to the People* (New York: Random House, 1956), pp. 18, 56.

93. Homer Cummings and Carl McFarland, *Federal Justice: Chapters in the History of Justice and the Federal Executive* (New York: Macmillan, 1937), p. 382.

94. *New York Times,* 23 April 1913.

95. LeRoy H. Wagar, *Confessions of a Spotter* (St. Louis: Wilson Printing, 1918), pp. 121–22.

96. *New York Times,* 29 April 1917; Ernest W. Mandeville, "Counterfeiting Uncle Sam's Agents," *Outlook* 144 (13 October 1926), p. 209; Ernest W. Mandeville, "Some Very Secret Service," ibid., (20 October 1926), p. 242.

97. Massachusetts (1879), Maine and Nebraska (1885), Colorado and Pennsylvania (1887), and Rhode Island (1892) had licensing laws before the period under discussion. *New York Times,* 12 May 1921; Daniel W. Sullivan, "Recent Legal Decisions Regulating the Business of Private Detectives," *American Federationalists* 32 (December 1925), 1189–92; "License Law for Private Detectives," *Monthly Labor Review* 21 (December 1925), p. 1344. In 1909 Ontario became the first province in Canada to regulate private policing by the enactment of the Private Detectives Act.

98. *New York Times,* 5 September 1915, pt. 2.

99. Frank Dalton O'Sullivan, *Crime Detection* (Chicago: O'Sullivan Publishing House, 1928), p. 547.

100. Stephen A. Doyle, *Startling Disclosures of the Private Detective Agency* (Rockford, Ill.: Labor News Printing, 1920), p. 8.

101. *New York Times,* 17 March 1921, 8 May 1923.

EPILOGUE

1. *Sinclair* v. *U.S.,* 279 U.S. Reports (1928), pp. 749, 765.

2. Allan Pinkerton II to D.C. Thornhill, 26 and 30 March 1908 and William A. Pinkerton to Allan Pinkerton II, 1 April 1908. Binder 67, Pinkerton National Detective Agency Papers (Pinkerton's Incorporated Archives, New York). See also *Proceedings of the International Association of Chiefs of Police, 1914,* p. 132.

3. Irving Bernstein, *The Lean Years: Workers in an Unbalanced Society* (Boston: Houghton Mifflin, 1960), pp. 84, 90, 149.

4. For a history of this committee, see Jerold S. Auerbach, *Labor and Liberty: The Lafollette Committee and the New Deal* (Indianapolis: Bobbs-Merrill, 1966), pp. 97–107.

5. U.S., Senate, Committee on Education and Labor, *Violations of Free Speech and Rights of Labor, Strikebreaking Services.* 76th Cong., 1st sess., Report No. 6, Part 1 (Washington: Government Printing Office, 1939), pp. 19, 20, 107.

6. Ibid, p. 23.

7. Ibid, pp. 21, 34.

8. Ibid, p. 25.

9. U.S., Senate, Committee on Education and Labor, *Violations of Free Speech and Rights of Labor, Industrial Espionage.* 75th Cong., 2nd sess., Report No. 46, Part 3, (Washington: Government Printing Office, 1938), pp. 17–21.

10. Ibid, pp. 17, 21, 24, 26, 28.

11. Ibid, pp. 9–10, 12–15, 53, 58–59, 61.

12. Ibid, pp. 121–22. For another work on labor espionage in the 1930s, see Leo Huberman, *The Labor Spy Racket* (New York: Modern Age Books, 1937). For a very good general study of private police, see Jeremiah Patrick Shalloo, *Private Police: With Special Reference to Pennsylvania* (Phila-

delphia: American Academy of Political and Social Science, 1933), pp. 135–200.

13. Urban police could get involved with the controversy of labor relations as well. See Donald G. Sofchalk, "The Chicago Memorial Day Incident: An Episode of Mass Action," *Labor History* 6 (Winter 1965), pp. 3–43.

14. For these developments, see Robert M. Fogelson, *Big City Police* (Cambridge, Mass.: Harvard University Press, 1977), pp. 93–116, 167, 192, and Samuel Walker *A Critical History of Police Reform* (Lexington, Mass.: Lexington Books, 1977), pp. 109–137. Bruce C. Johnson, "Taking Care of Labor: The Police in American Politics," *Theory and Society* 3 (1976), pp. 89–117.

15. Mark H. Haller, "Civic Reformers and Police Leadership, Chicago, 1905–1935," *Police in Urban Society,* ed. Harland Hahn (Beverly Hills, Calif.: Sage Publications, 1971), pp. 39–56.

16. Frank T. Morn, *Academic Disciplines and Debates: An Essay on Criminal Justice and Criminology as Professions in Higher Education* (Chicago: Joint Commission on Criminology and Criminal Justice Education and Standards, 1980), pp. 9–10.

17. August Vollmer, "Police Progress in the Past Twenty-five Years," *Journal of Criminal Law and Criminology* 24 (May 1933), pp. 161–75.

18. Nathan Douthit, "Police Professionalism and the War against Crime in the United States, 1920's–1930's," in George L. Mossee, ed., *Police Forces in History* (Beverly Hills, Calif.: Sage Publications, 1975), pp. 317–33.

19. John H. Wigmore, "State Cooperation for Crime-Repression," *Journal of Criminal Law and Criminology* 28 (1937–1938), pp. 327–34.

20. David Geeting Monroe, *State and Provincial Police* (Evanston, Ill.: International Association of Chiefs of Police and the Northwestern University Traffic Institute, 1941), pp. 5–6; Leo J. Coakley, *Jersey Troopers: A Fifty Year History of the New Jersey State Police* (New Brunswick, N.J.: Rutgers University Press, 1971), pp. 13, 18–20; Bruce Smith, *The State Police* (New York: Macmillan and Co., 1925); and California, *Bureau of Criminal Identification and Investigation, Report* (Sacramento, 1918), pp. 7–8.

21. J. Edgar Hoover, "The United States Bureau of Investigation in Relation to Law Enforcement," *Journal of Criminal Law, Criminology and Police Science* 23 (1932–33), p. 439. Volumes 23 and 24 are replete with Hoover's statements.

22. Murray Kempton, "Son of Pinkerton," *New York Review of Books,* 17 (20 May 1971), pp. 22–25.

Index